Ladies Errant

LADIES ERRANT

Wayward Women and Social Order

in Early Modern Italy

DEANNA SHEMEK

Duke University Press   *Durham & London*   1998

© 1998 Duke University Press

All rights reserved

Printed in the United States of America on acid-free paper ∞

Designed by Deborah Wong

Typeset in Monotype Bembo by Tseng Information Systems, Inc.

Library of Congress Cataloging-in-Publication Data appear on
the last printed page of this book.

   Chapter 1 was previously published in *Renaissance Quarterly* 48
(1995); chapter 2 previously appeared in *Annali d'Italianistica* 7
(1989). Both appear in this volume with permission.

For Tyrus,

che mi porta il girasole

Contents

Acknowledgments

This book bears the marks of my experiences at four institutions, each of which represents for me a stage of its development and a community of people with whom I delighted in learning. I began to think about Renaissance literature in relation to feminist questions during my doctoral studies at Johns Hopkins, ultimately writing a dissertation (1988) focused on Ariosto's treatment of gender, genre, and the *querelle des femmes*. To Eduardo Saccone I express my enduring gratitude for his meticulous eye and unfailing honesty as a reader, and for the generous good humor, intellectual intensity, and high standards he brought to our work together. The sudden death of Gregory Lucente in the summer of 1997, as this book goes to press, leaves me sadly unable to share it with him. I would have wanted to thank him once again for his unflagging friendship, his support for my feminist interests, his training in professional matters, and the literary-theoretical teaching he imparted to me. It was Kathy Ogren who first introduced me to rigorous feminist thinking in those Hopkins years. Her sharp and generous mind has provided sustenance both intellectual and personal over the long haul from Baltimore to California, and I take this opportunity to thank her warmly. While finishing my doctorate, I taught for two years at the University of Pennsylvania, where I profited from the collegiality and mentorship of Victoria Kirkham and Georgianna Ziegler, among many others. To them I express my heartfelt thanks.

I came in 1988 as an assistant professor to Yale, a university to which I returned by several twists of fate for the two years in which I completed this study. My colleagues in the Department of Italian during those two phases—Giuseppe Mazzotta, whose professional and intellectual sustenance in particular has been indispensable and is deeply appreciated; Paolo Valesio; Fiorenza Weinapple; Ernesto Livorni; Mary Ann McDonald Carolan; Stefano Velotti; and Olivia Holmes—provided a pool of expertise and interest in Italian literature unrivaled by that of any other U.S. institution. Just a few blocks away in Comparative Literature, David Quint generously read my entire manuscript in its nearly final stage, saving me from a number of errors and encouraging me to sharpen my readings in key places. Lynn Enterline, with whom I savored many a long conversation on matters feminist, chivalric, and psychoanalytic, commented to my great benefit on the Introduction and chapter 3. María Rosa Menocal, whose friendship predates our shared time at Yale, helped me in ways she never knew. At crucial moments she charmed me into believing that finishing a book was easy (and thus made it possible); and more important, she encouraged me by example to reshape this work, breaking it free from its earlier monographic form. To Reynolds Smith at Duke University Press, who initially spurred me in this direction (and whom I resisted at length), I now register my sincere gratitude. He and senior editorial assistant Sharon Parks have been communicative and enthusiastic throughout this process of publication. Pam Morrison, assistant managing editor, and copy editor Mindy Conner brought precision and care to the final stages of revision, for which I thank them here.

In my current institutional home at the University of California, Santa Cruz, I shuttle through the redwoods between the overlapping campus communities of Cowell College, the Literature Department, and the Pre- and Early Modern Studies group (PEMS). The ambitious interdisciplinary range, theoretical expertise, and serious playfulness that characterize work in this environment have taught me enormously, and their effects are visible everywhere throughout this book. Margaret Brose read it all at different stages with care and imagination. Many others improved parts of the manuscript with their criticisms and suggestions. Among these I must thank especially Harry Berger Jr., Karen Bassi, Carla Freccero, Margo Hendricks, Sarah Whittier, and Catherine Soussloff. Elizabeth Pittenger, a stone's throw further afield, proofread the book at an earlier stage and offered excellent criticisms.

I also owe numerous debts of gratitude to colleagues in Italian studies. Albert Ascoli has been my critic, champion, and friend since the day I tapped him on the shoulder in the Florentine Biblioteca Nazionale, interrupting his work to introduce myself. His support in many phases of the project's development has been invaluable. Valeria Finucci, my fellow *guerriera* in Ariosto, has been a frequent, implicit interlocutor and a generous colleague. Daniel Javitch, Elissa Weaver, Robert Rodini, Armando Petrucci, Franca Nardelli, Dennis Looney, Sergio Zatti, Pamela Benson, Julia Hairston, Margaret Rosenthal, John McLucas, Patricia Parker, Timothy Hampton, Stephanie Jed, James Ward, Ignacio Navarrete, and Naomi Yavneh have also given generously, both through their work and in their willingness to share information and ideas. With so many people improving its quality this book should be perfect, but alas, I know it is far from that. I alone am responsible for its weaknesses and flaws.

Difficult for me to express, because nearly boundless, is the degree to which I have treasured the friendship and teaching of those with whom I have spent my private time in Italy over these many years. Luisa De Vecchi and her family have given me a Triestine home away from home since my very first stay in Italy as an undergraduate. Over countless hours at their kitchen table I have savored not only the cuisines of the Veneto but the words, culture, and history of Italy. At a later stage I came to share living space with Valeria and Agnese Spadoni, and this arrangement too blossomed into lively friendships from which I continue to learn. These people have been my teachers, too, as they have turned a potentially detached academic inquiry into a life textured with laughter and tears; stories and recipes; etymologies, dialects, and baby talk; rustic wine and salty Mediterranean air. Surely I would not have worked, or lived, so happily without them.

The Fulbright Commission, the American Philosophical Society, the National Endowment for the Humanities, the University of California Regents, and the University of California Committee on Research provided generous and crucial financial support at different phases of this project. Especially in these years of dwindling funds, I thank them heartily for their confidence in this project. Chapter 1 has been minimally revised since its appearance in *Renaissance Quarterly* 48 (1995); and chapter 2 appeared in slightly different form in *Annali d'Italianistica* 7 (1989). I thank these journals for permission to reprint.

I take this occasion, finally, to thank my entire family. They have surely often wondered just how long a person can spend writing a single academic book—and why anyone would want to do so—but they have tactfully refrained from putting these questions to me and instead have supported me in countless ways throughout the process. I dedicate this book to one who knows its story from beginning to end, in all its digressions, dilations, interruptions, and generic permutations, and whose encouragement and editorial and critical suggestions have really made it possible: to Tyrus Miller, my incomparable partner in errancy and adventure alike.

Introduction

La donna è mobile.[1] In the strains of Verdi's best known aria, from the third act of *Rigoletto,* the spirited lover offers his memorable encapsulation of women's "fickle nature" while he chases a lithe young maid about the room. If the amusing irony for Verdi's audience lies in the evident fact that it is the Duke—and not his sweetheart, Gilda—who is "mobile," no matter.[2] The lilting refrain marks men's age-old dismay at their failure to "fix" woman in her place, to prevent her straying from the express wishes of fathers, husbands, brothers, and lovers. Mobility in this instance carries both the positive connotations of adaptability and free flow, and the negative overtones of inconstancy and error. Its double edge cuts both ways through the concerns of this book. *Errancy,* at least since the *Divina commedia*'s Christian pilgrim confronted Dante's dark wood, has named a wandering away—be it spiritual, moral, or geographical—from the straight path that is thought to be right and good. Errant spirits both diverge from the norm and stray from the course of truth, rectitude, or purpose. Everyday usage often recalls the second meaning recorded in the *Oxford English Dictionary* for *wayward:* "Capriciously wilful; conforming to no fixed rule or principle of conduct; erratic"; but my subtitle dwells equally on an additional sense of the word: "Disposed to go counter to the wishes or advice of others, or to what is reasonable; wrongheaded, intractable, self-willed; froward, perverse. Of children: disobedient, refractory."

Taking as its backdrop the vast literature devoted in the Italian Renaissance to the "proper" conduct and education of women,[3] this book presents the problem of wayward feminine behavior in five different cultural articulations of that period. Each text examined here presents "woman" as the site of potential disorder. Each entertains in a different way the possibility that woman might exceed whatever bounds society has set for her, might

I

deviate from the path authorized by a culture centered on male privilege, and might for this reason pose a danger to individual men or to the order of the community as a whole. My title is meant to evoke the explicit early modern fear that feminine initiatives, which almost by definition lapse from the rigid norms of decorum, could lead orderly society itself astray. At the same time, it celebrates the determined efforts of women (then as in other moments) to venture beyond the social and cultural bounds set for them by men: errancy, in this sense, must be seen as more than casual or unwitting "error"; it must be understood as an act of resistance.[4] To the present-day reader, as for interpreters of the sixteenth century, the female figures who populate my discussions may seem improbable, fantastic, strange. Prostitutes race about the streets of European cities; an Indian princess flees through magical forests, dodging and duping her none-too-chivalrous pursuers; lady knights rove a treacherous romance landscape; a woman poet infiltrates the stanzas of an earlier classic with her own rebel verses; and a courtesan runs afoul of the law, stalking away unrepentant after her grisly and spectacular punishment. Fictional representations and historical references blur together in these pages, making it difficult at first glance to discern which were the living participants in a collective life and which sprang from the literary conjurings of the poets. This blurring of the given (or the "natural") with the created, however, is precisely the process by which gender (the *social* understanding of what it means to be male or female) takes on its smudgy contours; and the juxtaposition of women real and imagined in this volume is intended to recognize the inextricability of associations between the two. Each of these figures, whether historical or imaginary, captures the sixteenth-century efforts to arrest the ever mobile, ever elusive meaning of the difference that men located in women as a way of defining themselves. Each, finally, points to a powerful cultural logic dictating that any woman who insists on her mobility—whether of mind or of body— invites on herself the suspicious denomination of "wayward" and "errant."[5]

As many have already attested, a considerable literature of the fifteenth and sixteenth centuries promulgates ideas about the education, social roles, and moral worth of women. Stemming from traditions as diverse as humanist learning, mercantile economics, Old and New Testament theology, and the Greek schools of medicine, writings on nearly every aspect of women's lives flourished to an unprecedented degree in early modern Italy. These works span an enormous generic range, from moral sermons to guides for household management, from tracts on feminine education to philosophical meditations on the soul, from catalogues of famous women to misogynist catechistic dialogues, from beauty manuals to handbooks on courtly manners. Also participating variously in the Renaissance *querelle des femmes* were the plays, romances, novellas, and lyric poetry of the period.[6] Early modern writers in all the modes mentioned above, moreover, regularly conjoined the "order" of sexual difference with broader social concerns, explicitly troubling themselves over the potential errancy of women in the social world. Whatever our interpretation of its individual works, the sheer volume of this literature establishes the matter of woman's place—and the implicit possibility that she might stray from it—as one of the period's most persistent cultural questions.

In the chapters that follow, I look beyond that openly prescriptive literature on womankind, toward a broader space of cultural representation within which ideas about sexual difference circulated, a space that both helped shape these advisory and didactic writings and in turn formed the arena in which their effects were felt. Specifically, I discuss the appearance of discourses about the feminine in examples from chronicle, law, festival, painting, fictional narrative, poetry, and literary theory, individually and in their interactions with one another. Implicit in the juxtaposition of these different media and genres is my interest in discerning points of contact between marginal and centralized, authorized and unauthorized scenes of signification. It is indeed the case that early modern thinking about women spanned contexts both privileged and lowly; if we wish to understand better the stylization of femininity in that epoch and its later ramifications, we must open our gaze to the very wide frame in which womanhood acquired its meanings. Apparent even in the writings of progressive humanists is the assumption that women of all classes share more with each other than with the men of their social group.[7] Given the authority and the general scope of this belief in the period I examine, I consider elite and popular culture as alternative but interconnected spheres. I thus focus especially on substantial exchanges between them, on ways in which the one at times seems implicated in the other.

Each instance I take up here in effect reveals the internal operation of something that lies "outside" its apparent frame: a contest among prostitutes discloses a crucial concern with female chastity; an idealized "foreign" woman turns out to be the (weak) hinge of European male personhood; a domesticated martial maid stands paradoxically poised to supplant the male epic hero; a female poet haunts and quarrels with the text of her "feminist" male predecessor; and a courtesan walks away, oddly heroic, from the scene of her public whipping. My aim in focusing on such relations is partly to take in a more varied, more differentiated vista of a historical moment that, when defined narrowly as a Renaissance, relegates to the background many of its most interesting figures. It is, in particular, to open up the cultural interstices where women's role in that moment has lain hidden, and to suggest, through concrete historical and literary critical investigations, methods by which certain kinds of unrecognized information embedded in textual forms may be brought to light. For though "Renaissance" texts themselves tell us only a part of women's story, they also reveal much more about gender relations than traditional criticism has generally assumed. By attending to the "double voicing" of cultural expressions such as those I take up here, by exploring the competing perspectives at work in the spectacles, painting, poetry, law, and storytelling of the fifteenth and sixteenth centuries, I aim to discern especially those traces that may teach us how Renaissance culture thought about women.[8]

A center for humanist thought and a cradle of mercantile capitalism, Italy occupied a unique cultural position in early modern Europe. Yet in contrast to its cultural and economic strength, the peninsula was by the sixteenth century politically feeble. Italians' dismay over their inability to resist foreign invasions of more centralized states such as France and Spain lent urgency to humanist concerns with identity, both national and individual. As Italians dedicated their energies to analytical and prescriptive works that codified language, literary theory, political leadership, and domestic economy, their creative efforts in painting, architecture, and literature also produced model texts for a Renaissance of continental scope. Italy's artistic and intellectual productivity, however, stood in stark contrast to its real vulnerability as a political entity. Indeed, the efforts of intellectuals and artists to experiment with new creative frameworks (visual, literary, architectural) often ran up against a contrary wish to solidify existing systems (linguistic, political, domestic) and halt the proliferation of potential meanings and practices. Of central interest to me is the way early modern notions of womanhood figured in both of these conflicting social processes. Representative works in virtually all of the genres named above celebrate an evolving place for women in Renaissance culture, but they also betray a consistent fear that unstable boundaries for feminine behavior might forbode more generalized social disorder.

My opening chapter, "Circular Definitions," spans the temporal range of the subsequent chapters as it examines not a written text but an enduring popular festival that evolved over several centuries in Ferrara. The Palio di San Giorgio, an annual celebration in honor of that city's patron saint, featured a footrace by local prostitutes as well as parallel contests for horses, mules, and men. A holiday sponsored by the ruling Este dukes, the *palio* was typical of early modern celebrations in European cities. Its primary purpose was to commemorate the power of the city's government and reinforce the orderly behavior of the populace. The spatial design of this event, as Francesco del Cossa's fresco illustrates from its place on a wall in Ferrara's Palazzo Schifanoia, contrived that Ferrara's proper women look down from their protective balconies on the violators of Christian feminine mores, who ran in exhibition through the city's streets. The married and marriageable women of the city thus served to illustrate—indeed to literalize in their height above these proceedings—the superiority of chastity over more transgressive feminine behaviors.

The *palio* remapped the city as a field of play. The city-as-gameboard functioned generally to demarcate the power relations between the dukes and their subjects, but it also reinforced differences among these subjects themselves. Contemporary chronicles and statutes indicate, in addition, that civic *palios* in Ferrara and elsewhere had direct ties to earlier races run by the prostitutes who accompanied armies in their assaults on rival cities. In the military races, the running women symbolized the dominance of even the least respected members of the aggressing populace over the doomed enemy city. In the later urban races, the women acted out their subjection to contemporary rules of gender that cast sexually active women as deviant. In both performances it is the prostitutes' wayward embodiment of feminine sexuality and their errancy from the approved path of female behaviors that assign meaning to their participation.

The Palio di San Giorgio illustrates the main concerns of this book because the women played a central and exemplary role in the race, which was clearly intended (at least in part) to stake out the boundaries of feminine behavior within the community of Estense Ferrara. The *palio* also reveals the ambivalence and reticence that surround gender construction in early modern Italy, even in what seem to be its most public displays. Official descriptions of the event resort to euphemism, generalities, and other evasive language to record the women's participation, eliding from view their profession and the rhetorical force of their performance. As a participatory event, however, the *palio* emphasizes the collective and consensual nature of gender construction, as each person present lends meaning and validity to the tableau. Like the writings discussed in succeeding chapters, the *palio* discloses its fullest meaning only when considered in a broader context that well exceeds its generic classification as entertainment.

Finally, in opening a book largely focused on literary texts with an exploration of a public event, I mean to signal my understanding of literature as embedded in multiple contexts and in many other discourses.[9] Artistic expression, it follows, may be appropriately studied within a set of interfaces, not only among genres and media but also between elite and popular cultures. This is not to argue away the different degrees of complexity or sophistication that mark works intended for different purposes and audiences; it is rather to disturb the notion of a neat separation between the contexts in which different kinds of works are created and in which they operate. For example, my early investigation of the fresco in which Cossa commemorates Ferrara's festival alerted me to the apparent suppression, in virtually every commentary I encountered, of any information that might relate this high-cultural artifact to the world of prostitutes, soldiers, hangmen, and the general populace of Ferrara—groups that seemed nonetheless to contribute extensively to its meaning. As evidence mounted in support of this connection, my *palio* research took its place beside an already developing—and similarly hybrid—interest in the relations between literary romance and popular oral narrative and song. I do not deny, in this regard, that Ariosto modeled his poem on those of Virgil and Boiardo, or that much of the *Orlando furioso*'s poetic richness arises from a set of literary relations too numerous to list here. I express only my further interest in his interactions with popular performers and audiences, and in responses by a number of sixteenth-century readers to this element of romance culture. The chapters in this volume approach different texts in varied ways.

Not all of them exhibit to the same degree the concerns I outline here, because the research and writing of each marked a different stage in my investigations. The contiguity of the chapters themselves, however, and the framing positions of two considerations treating apparent outsiders to elite culture (chapters 1 and 5) should convey my interest, strengthened in the course of my research, in the fluid boundaries between early modernity's different social and cultural spheres.

This movement from site to site—my own methodology of errancy—follows from the necessity of seeking women's cultural traces through detours from the more linear narratives of male-centered history. Such detours have sharpened my concern for historical specificity and detail, but they have also heightened my awareness of all discourse's capacity to say more than an author or speaker intended. My employment of the language and methods derived from psychoanalysis, anthropology, literary theories, and cultural history has been guided overall by Mikhail Bakhtin's cautionary remarks on three general ways in which we may interpret texts. If we seek to identify only meanings the author had in mind or that contemporaries may have recognized, notes Bakhtin, we "enclose" a work within its epoch and relinquish any grasp of its larger significance and its vibrant "life" in later times. We also radically reduce the potency of artistic expression to distinguish itself from other kinds of communication. If, on the other hand, we modernize works with no regard for their historical context, we turn them into mere markers of our own contemporary concerns and lose the opportunity to learn from them in any way that could be "true" to the works themselves. The first approach impoverishes the reader's potential; the second sacrifices that of the writer. When, however, we carefully view creative and expressive works as "noncoincident" with themselves, as inherently capable of plural significations, then we can interpret them so as to exploit potentials latent but not yet historically actualized by them. Bakhtin insists on the surplus of potential meanings that makes works, cultures, and even individuals "unfinalizable" in the most positive sense and allows them to continue speaking, even though interpreters in previous epochs may not have heard them in quite the same way.

For Bakhtin, the enduring appeal of particularly rich authors and texts resides in their successful articulation of more than they immediately understand to be their intention, argument, or task; and he sees this continued ability to articulate ideas as the evident aim of great works. The continued development of the potential meanings of such texts, moreover, is enhanced by the perspective of more than one culture. Thus the "outsidedness" of a given interpreter, the distinctness of his or her interpretive tools and context, are—combined with historical attentiveness—important resources in the process of "creative understanding." As Bakhtin puts it, "*Creative understanding* does not renounce itself, its own place in time, its own culture; and it forgets nothing."[10] In this sense, feminist theory and psychoanalysis appear as the most marked symptoms of my own outsidedness to the early modern sites I study here. My aim is not to enlist these authors in the service of postmodern projects—reducing Cossa, Ariosto, Terracina, or Bandello to verifications of current theoretical and political models—but to place these various ways of representing women and the world in dialogue with each other, and thereby to attempt their mutual illumination for readers today.

Drawing on evidence from popular and elite spheres, from literary and theoretical writings, from pictorial and festival culture, and from legal and outlaw behavior, the chapters of *Ladies Errant* at the same time circle around a single, yet seminal, literary phenomenon: the publication of Ariosto's *Orlando furioso*.[11] A diplomat and humanist intellectual employed by the Este lords of Ferrara, Ludovico Ariosto (1474–1533) wrote plays, satires, lyrics, and—most famously—a forty-six-canto poem in rhymed octaves entitled *L'Orlando furioso*. Ariosto's decision to take up the well-worn materials of Charlemagne's eighth-century wars against the Saracens and write "a little sequel" to Matteo Maria Boiardo's enormously popular *Orlando innamorato* (1495) appears at first blush to be a decadent move. Orlando was, after all, only the Italian reincarnation of the French Roland, nephew to Charlemagne; and he seemed to have reached the pinnacle of his literary development in Boiardo's poem a generation earlier, a poem that was itself the culmination of decades of experimentation by Italian poets with imported romance materials.[12] Boiardo had interlaced his Carolingian character's story with magical and erotic elements from the twelfth-century French Arthurian cycles. Thus among other striking innovations, the *Innamorato* treated its readers to the traditionally austere Orlando's unprecedented tumble into the throes of love for Angelica, princess of Cathay. Popular as Boiardo's poem still was, however, most writers of Ariosto's day saw it as part of an outmoded culture rapidly being supplanted by works with a humanist orientation not toward France and Spain (the lands of vernacular romance) but toward ancient Greece and Rome.

Ariosto foresaw further possibilities for Orlando and his gallant fellows, however, possibilities already signaled (though not developed) in Boiardo's unfinished poem. Grafting onto the romance's chivalric themes abundant allusions to the vernacular tradition of Dante, Petrarch, and Boccaccio, he also wove into it the overarching narrative of national foundation we find in Virgil's *Aeneid*. In so doing, Ariosto wrote the narrative poem of his century, a text that would come to stand as Italy's playful and serious contribution to the genre of Renaissance epic. Ironic and learned, musical and fast-paced, highly sophisticated and yet accessible to an audience with no learning at all, the *Orlando furioso* occupies a truly pivotal space: it gathers into its pages the dual heritage of vernacular and classical literatures, allying itself at the same time with a literary future when Spenser, Monteverdi, Cervantes, and eventually even Italo Calvino would integrate it into bold new artforms.[13] The *Furioso*'s fusion of modes makes way for a modern sensibility no longer compelled to separate out the threads of experience into comic, tragic, ironic, and lyric presentations. Its aggressive handling of narrative form, moreover—its employment of ambitious, multiplotted, and suspenseful interconnected sequences—stands as an early model not only for masters of the long novel but for specialists in those latter-day channelers of narrative desire, the genres of suspense and serial narrative.[14]

I place the *Furioso* at the material center of the present volume for several reasons. It was the most popular literary work of its century. This poem filled with women warriors, amorous adventures, and political parables was the first literary work, moreover, to enjoy wide appreciation by elite and popular readers alike. The *Furioso*'s success was due not only to its poetic distinction but also to a combination of other factors: a booming print industry, rising literacy rates, and the public's familiarity with the characters and scenarios the poem resumes from previous romances. Circulating in cheap, scrappy paged editions at the same time it was enjoyed in luxury presentation copies richly adorned with illuminations, it was also recited for the unlettered in the piazzas, inns, and farm fields of Italy. It became the basis for dozens of madrigals sung in the courts and towns of Italy and abroad; and it inspired numerous literary sequels, some of them by women. We have good reason to believe that girls of the sixteenth century, like their later counterparts who delighted in the novel, were especially attracted to the *Orlando furioso* and other romances, because contemporary writers on female education and morals railed with particular vehemence against the corrupting capacities of this fanciful and immoral genre. Even outside the bounds of the printed page, Ariosto's poem generated texts. Staged versions of episodes from the *Furioso* were sufficiently popular in the *commedia dell'arte* to constitute the basis of substantial careers for actresses and female playwrights in the latter Cinquecento, women whose beauty and professional travels evoked for their audiences all the charming errancy of the characters they played.[15] Other women took more literary inspiration from the *Furioso*'s female characters and its attention to injustices against them; encouraged by the Ferrarese poet's arguments, they cited his defense of their sex when they began to circulate new works representing women's perspectives. Both women's advocates and their critics, then, saw Ariosto's poem as more than literature; it represented, in addition, a provocative intervention into their fervent discussions of women's proper role in an evolving culture.

Ariosto clearly recognized his generation's concern with relations of power between the sexes, for he incorporated some of the best known arguments of the contemporary *querelle des femmes* directly into the text of the *Orlando furioso*. Yet he does far more than merely record the various positions espoused by ancient and contemporary writers. Rather than simply illustrate the opinions of his peers or take a position on one side or the other of the misogynist/philogynist exchanges among his poem's characters, the poet of the *Furioso* sets the two facets of this argument side by side and highlights the limitations of the terms employed by each.[16] By blurring seemingly clear dichotomies between Christian and Muslim, friend and enemy, even good and evil, Ariosto's poem unrelentingly exposes the difficulties of all interpretation in a world of contingency and moral dilemma. The *querelle des femmes* too appears in this flawed framework of dualistic categories: it functions as a recurring example of the analytical and ethical issues at the heart of the *Furioso*. Ariosto weaves the debates over women into major episodes of his poem and shows in each instance how arguments of this kind are inevitably related to the specific interests of their proponents. Carrying this focus on the subjective nature of the *querelle* one step further, he fashions a narrator who cannot make up his own mind about women. At the very foundation of the *Orlando furioso,* then, we encounter a narrator who is as "errant" as his perpetually fickle knights, at least where women are concerned. He turns his argument this way and that, races head-long into passionate praise or tirade, then pulls up short, as if forgetting his goal or falling ingloriously from his writing chair. It is in the exquisite distinction between this narrator and the author of the *Furioso* that the poem reveals its remarkably modern grasp of the *querelle des femmes*.

Though readers over the centuries have generally not considered the gender debates an important feature of Ariosto's text, they immediately intuited the allure of a character who, as Benedetto Croce later put it, "symbolizes Woman." The role of the supremely beautiful, exotic princess Angelica, who inspires the pursuit of so many of the knights in the poem and thus sets in motion Ariosto's centrifugally structured narrative, is the subject of chapter 2, "That Elusive Object of Desire." There, I follow the lead of that consistent response from readers and argue that Angelica may indeed function in the *Furioso*'s narrative as a sign for quintessential femininity. But such a sign, when seen in the context of Ariosto's questioning of the gender opposition, can only be a phantasm created by the desires of those who cast themselves as its opposite and perfect complement. Each of Ariosto's principal male knights makes his entrance into the poem by *seeing* Angelica and registering his desire for her. It is this entwinement of seeing with desire, seeking to encircle Angelica from without, that defines the Indian princess's primary role in the poem. In simplest terms, she is the (vastly overinvested) object of the desirous gazes of pursuing men. Yet this function in no way exhausts her character as unfolded by the poet, who accords her a will and desires of her own. If Woman's desires are antithetically related to the overheated fantasies of her pursuers in the *Orlando furioso*, herein may lie the poet's wisdom.

With remarkable consistency, Angelica acts on her own desires only when she recedes from the knights' gaze by fleeing their advances or when she becomes completely invisible through magic. Since each knight pursues Angelica oblivious to the gaze that constitutes *her* as subject, the revelation that she has desires of her own—that she has fallen in love not with a cavalier but with the lowliest of soldiers—triggers the madness of her most dedicated admirer, Orlando. What is more, Orlando's mental collapse in the absence of Angelica signals the figurative disintegration of the entire order of chivalry. It is not just one character among many, we are bound to recall, but the very embodiment of knighthood who sheds his armor and embarks on a campaign of terrorizing destruction in the countryside: Orlando jilted is effectively a code run amok. Orlando's madness reveals the pathological face of the chivalric dedication to a code of absolutes. Because Angelica emerges from precisely this code as ideal Woman, Ariosto's title episode points to fantasies regarding the feminine as a precarious foundation for masculine — or cultural — identity.

Even more than Angelica, however, another female figure captured the imaginations of sixteenth-century readers and quickly came to be regarded by many as the most positively portrayed character in the *Orlando furioso*: the female knight Bradamante. Chapter 3, "Gender, Duality, and the Sacrifices of History," presents this warrior heroine as the *Furioso*'s positive alternative to the idealized but illusory femininity that Angelica represents. While Angelica flees or suffers capture and transport by her pursuers, Bradamante roams the French countryside in service to her king and in search of her beloved, Ruggiero. By donning armor she conceals her sex and enjoys free movement as a martial champion. This guise allows Bradamante to appropriate both male and female roles for herself and to defer the traditional feminine functions (marriage and childbearing) that the poem reserves for her at its end. It also permits the poet to explore in an audacious way the foundations of custom and belief on which gender identity appears to rest.

The movements of these two female characters also trace competing narrative structures for the poem. Angelica's constant flights from danger typically lead her to unfamiliar perils among new contenders for her charms; she thus tends to open new, spiraling romance episodes in the *Furioso*. In contrast, Bradamante's commitment to the prophecy that destines her to marry Ruggiero and found the family of Ariosto's patrons (the Este of Ferrara) carries these spiraling plot lines toward a purported historical telos. Her journey toward "history," and thus toward mortality as well as fulfillment in love, runs parallel to Ariosto's shift of his poem out of romance's endlessly digressive structure into the closure of historical epic. This movement toward closure includes what many readers have rightly called Bradamante's domestication, for she abandons her role as a formidable warrior in order to assume a subordinate position as the wife of a monarch. As my discussion will show, however, the "taming" of Bradamante is not nearly so complete as feminist criticism has argued of late. In any case, Bradamante's undeclared gender allegiance and her wandering adventures through most of the poem are what inspired female readers of Ariosto's poem through-out the sixteenth century. The behavior of this warrior heroine—far from acceptable in the view of many contemporary readers—was also among the features of the *Furioso* that appeared most transgressive and undisciplined to the canon theorists of the latter sixteenth century.

The *Orlando furioso* enjoyed unprecedented popularity in Italy and beyond for several generations. Its numerous reprintings and translations, its public recitations and elaborations into music, its countless imitators, and even the willingness of Europeans to name their children after its characters made it in a real sense the outstanding literary work of its time. The wildly digressive narrative of Orlando's mad love for Angelica became a favorite of the illiterate populace and the educated courtly circles alike. But among poets and intellectuals in the generation immediately following the author's death, the text inspired hot debate. The diverse class composition of the *Furioso*'s audience brought critics face-to-face with issues of social distinction, hierarchy, and order. Ariosto's detractors clashed with his partisans over whether such a "popular" poem should be considered a part of the illustrious Italian literary tradition. At stake in the highly charged arguments over the *Furioso*'s generic innovations, fantastic elements, and nonlinear narrative was nothing less than the competitive strength of a specifically Italian literature against both classical and modern rivals. In this explicit way, the debaters' political commitments and sense of social proprieties informed their literary judgments. The debate on national literature was also strongly colored by the general problem concerning social order and hierarchy within which, as I have suggested, women were perceived as a perturbance if not an outright threat. The sense of women as a problem left its specific mark on the literary debates in questions about the propriety and decorum of female characters and their actions, and about the effects these characters might have as examples for readers, "lady" readers most of all.

Of especial importance for several of the romance's most prominent critics, for these reasons, was their understanding of Ariosto's portrayal of women such as Bradamante. For though much of their debate addressed questions of the *Furioso*'s conformity or innovation in relation to classical models, a recurring point of tension for critics on both sides was Ariosto's depiction of independent female warriors. Disturbingly for these readers, the "wayward" characters Bradamante and Marfisa outshone their male comrades not only in moral rectitude but also in martial prowess. Beneath these critics' apparently quaint concerns for the "verisimilar" and the "decorous" lie ancient questions about the powers of art and the media still pressing today: What is the relation between imagined events and experience or action in the real world? Can literature affect the behavior of its readers? If it can, must we dictate that only proper and desirable images circulate? Whatever our own responses to such questions may be, women readers of the *Orlando furioso* were clearly moved by the poem's representation of their sex and by its acknowledgment of the irrationality in prevailing notions of femininity. They tell us so in their own writings.

Chapter 4, "Getting a Word in Edgewise," explores one sixteenth-century female poet's response to Ariosto's poem. Living in Naples in the decades following Ariosto's death, Laura Terracina was one of his most avid readers. More important, she also took the repeated advice of the *Furioso*'s narrator, who urged women to counter the misogyny of history and literature by becoming writers themselves. Terracina published eight volumes of poems between 1548 and 1567, an extraordinary degree of activity and popularity among her contemporaries, which, however, has garnered her almost no recognition in literary histories of the period. Her most popular lyric sequence, the *Discorso sopra tutti i primi canti d' "Orlando furioso"* [Discourse on the beginnings of all the *Orlando furioso*'s cantos], appeared in more than eleven editions between 1549 and 1608. In this unusual work, Terracina strikes an intimate structural and thematic relation with the *Orlando furioso*: each of her forty-six cantos corresponds to the identically numbered canto in Ariosto's poem. The work's title reflects a specific pattern of citation, moreover, wherein Terracina breaks apart the opening octave of each *Furioso* canto, inserts seven of her own poetic lines between each of Ariosto's, and produces a new set of eight octaves, each of which ends with a line from the earlier, model poem. Notably, Terracina's *Furioso*-in-miniature dwells not on Ariosto's narrative plot, but on the ethical themes of his canto exordia, a number of which take up the *querelle des femmes*. This ingenious appropriation of a contemporary classic allowed Terracina to adopt the *Orlando furioso* as a highly visible platform for her own opinions, even when they differed markedly from those of her model poet. Her resourceful compositional strategy offers an intriguing illustration of women's efforts to find their way into the pages of published books and take their place among poets past and present. At the same time, the *Discorso*'s clear dependency on a previous, well-established text by a prominent male poet also stresses the extent of women writers' secondariness to a literary tradition that had overwhelmingly excluded them from its ranks.

My final chapter turns to a figure who exemplifies the kind of feminine error with which I opened the volume, newly complicated by the cultural and political developments of Tridentine Rome. A descendant of the military prostitutes who first performed in the early modern *palios,* Isabella de Luna served with the army of Charles V before establishing herself in Rome and building a career as one of the most successful courtesans of the Renaissance. She also came to be the protagonist of two novellas by the genre's most prominent writer in sixteenth-century Italy, Matteo Bandello. Bandello presents us with an Isabella who is part streetwise prostitute, part Bradamante, as he highlights both the rough edges and the astonishing bravery of his heroine in these two tales. But the dangers of waywardness for women like Isabella point to a future less entertained by such matters than was the age of Ariosto. In Bandello's first treatment of this character, the Spanish courtesan earns the approving laughter of her comrades by outsmarting a man who hoped to defame her before her friends. But her escapades in the second tale place her in the streets of Rome, outside the Colosseum, where she must finally submit to a public whipping for her impertinence before the law. Isabella's defiance of the law and her clash with legal authority are shadowed, moreover, by the ritual burning of another military prostitute, evoked by Bandello in the second tale's preface. These figures together intimate the danger accompanying women's transgressive behavior throughout early modernity, and they heighten the logic of ritualized humiliation so crucial to the Ferrarese *palio* I discuss in chapter 1. Bandello's tales, for their part, pose a powerful counterimage to idealized versions of the Renaissance woman.

If there is still some argument over the question Joan Kelly answered in the negative twenty years ago ("Did Women Have a Renaissance?"), this is no doubt because women experienced both gains and losses in liberty as a result of the social, economic, and cultural transformations of early modernity.[17] Female literacy and education under humanist influence suggested for the first time that (social) gender might be disjoined from notions of women's presumed (bodily) limitations as a sex; and women began to learn, write, and even speak for themselves in unprecedented numbers. At the same time, these numbers remained too small to be considered representative; and women paid dearly for their intellectual accomplishments, which were regarded by the majority with immense moral suspicion.[18] Postfeudal economies, historians suggest, may have depended more than earlier ones on the certainty of paternity, hence the strict surveillance of women's chastity to ensure proper inheritance. The consequence for many women was not an opening up of the world of ideas but their own enclosure in a shrinking domestic sphere.[19]

The chapters of this volume are united by their focus on early modernity's inability to "capture" the movement of gender, and on the sense held by many at the time that much was at stake in contemporary efforts to arrest—or set free—its transformations. Each of these discussions is intended as an individual reading of the texts it takes up; but together they aim to illustrate the cardinal function of a clear gender dichotomy in early modern conceptions of an orderly world. Italy's Renaissance is justly celebrated as an age of creative innovation; but it was also a moment of intense cultural normalization. The outpouring of manuals and theories of good government, proper speech, appropriate social behavior, efficient household management, effective education, clear morals, and other matters in the fifteenth and sixteenth centuries points, surely, to humanists' exhilaration at the prospect of their own self-edification. This activity also evinces, however, an urge to govern and limit meaning amid palpable social change. In the interstices of these conflicting factors I locate the feminine figures discussed in this book. Creatures of compromise and ambivalence as much as of headstrong rebellion, they trace the early modern notion of women "out of place," of wayward ladies dangerously errant.

1 Circular Definitions: Configuring Gender in Italian Renaissance Festival

I n a memorable passage on the philosophy of art, phenomenologist
Maurice Merleau-Ponty observes that the human subject's power to
act and to perceive as a separate being arises from a body at once
discrete unto itself yet continuous with the world around it: "The enigma
is that my body simultaneously sees and is seen. That which looks at all
things can also look at itself and recognize, in what it sees, the 'other side'
of its power of looking. . . . This initial paradox cannot but produce others.
Visible and mobile, my body is a thing among things; it is caught in the
fabric of the world, and its cohesion is that of a thing. But because it moves
itself and sees, it holds things in a circle around itself."[1]

The subject's paradoxical continuity with and difference from its surrounding world likewise became a recurring motif in the seminars of
French psychoanalyst Jacques Lacan. At various times in his career Lacan
attempted to theorize the intricate social relations between vision, corporeal experience, subjectivity, and gender identity, deriving several of his
formulations from his critical reading of Merleau-Ponty.[2] Subjectivity, or
the sense of self, Lacan argues, is constituted by the *gaze*. As Lacan defines
it, however, this gaze is not the look each of us directs out into the world,
but rather the presence of an exterior Other who looks back, corroborating
our existence as subjects resembling, but distinct from, that Other.

Such a view of human selfhood is likely bound by historic conditions;
but these conditions began to coalesce in the early modern thought of
humanists, merchants, and teachers who devoted their writings not only
to the powers of individual subjects to "make" themselves but also to the
importance of *performance* in the constitution of one's social, political, and
ethical persona. From Pico to Alberti to Machiavelli to Castiglione to Igna-
tius Loyola—to name only a few cardinal figures—we trace the rise of a

modern subject not only aware of its interiority (soul, character) but also engaged in the modeling and social display of that interiority for instrumental purposes.[3] In Lacanian terms, we might go so far as to say that what the Renaissance integrated was the power of the gaze. Nowhere is the political manipulation of this power more apparent than in the visual culture of early modernity, in which painting, theater, and public pageantry constructed both spectacle and audience in the service of state legitimacy and expressly masculine power.

Focusing on a public festival in Renaissance Ferrara, with particular interest in the communal dynamics of political ritual and gender construction, this chapter explores a circularity of gaze peculiar to the experience of the festival's female participants. The festival examined here offers a colorful illustration of Lacan's and Merleau-Ponty's conceptions of a subjectivity that comes from the outside, from the gazes of others. In this case a ritualized, judging male gaze reinforced not only traditional standards of female conduct but also hierarchical models of power for the family and the state. As any complex cultural phenomenon, particularly from the past, strains against the methods of a single academic field and necessitates interdisciplinary investigation, I shall employ a variety of historical, anthropological, and theoretical approaches in modulating between imagined performance, written documents, and political context. As my point of departure I take an object that would have especially appealed to both Merleau-Ponty and Lacan: a painting.

High on the crumbling, frescoed walls of Ferrara's Palazzo Schifanoia, visitors today discover a curious scene from Renaissance city life. Above the door in the east wall of its Sala dei mesi loom the arresting profiles of scantily clad women and men running within a cityscape, apparently chasing a group of mounted jockeys (fig. 1). Above these figures, in the same scene, placid onlookers gaze from courtly spaces on two higher planes: just over the group involved in the chase, city officials preside from a raised platform; still further above, noble ladies nod blankly toward the spectacle from high palace balconies, the expressions on their faces half erased by time.

These painted figures record a favorite feast in the civic calendar of Duke Borso d'Este (d. 1471), who commissioned the entire Sala dei mesi, or Salon of the Months, as a monumental tribute to his own rule over Ferrara. The scene of the Palio di San Giorgio described above forms an inset detail in the panel Francesco del Cossa painted for the month of April between 1467 and 1469 (fig. 2).[4] As a whole the composition depicts twelve months under Borso's good government in mythological, astrological, and political images, resulting in a remarkably intricate panorama of political power, myth, and community. I happily concede the full explication of this enormous ensemble to specialists in its medium.[5] My own interest lies rather in the enigmatic historical practice to which the city scene described above refers: the annual races held on the feast day of Saint George, Ferrara's patron saint. I return later in this chapter to Cossa's rendering of them in the Schifanoia fresco.

Like other celebrations of its kind in early modern European cities, Ferrara's *palio* was a public relations extravaganza organized by the local government.[6] Typically for such city-sponsored holidays, the program of amusements was orchestrated to impress the populace with the beneficence, wealth, and power of the ruling family.[7] Thus, though clearly intended to entertain, these feasts were more like official pageantry than the carnival events celebrated by Mikhail Bakhtin as "offered not by some exterior source but by the people to themselves."[8] The statutes pertaining to the *palio* that were introduced shortly after the inauguration of Estense rule tie its administration, if not necessarily its historical origin, to this regime.

In 1279, just twenty years after the Este came to governing power, city statutes specified the prizes for a horse race "in festo beati Georgi": to the first-place rider a piece of elegant cloth [*palio*], to the second a roast pig [*porchetta*], and to the third a cock [*gallo*].[9] Borso's reformed laws of 1456 indicate that by then the original horse race had expanded into a kind of festive theater: a race of *barbari* [Arabian horses] in the afternoon was to be followed by races of asses, men, and women in the early evening after vespers. The entire affair commenced with a morning Mass, itself the culmination of preparatory blessings of all participants (both human and equestrian) at sign-up on the eve of the races.

Nineteen years later, the chronicler Ugo Caleffini described in his *Diario* an essentially unchanged *palio*. For 24 April 1475 Caleffini records: "Festa di S. Giorgio. La mattina si corse il palio di panno d'oro. Nel pomeriggio corsero gli asini con fanti a cavallo, . . . gli uomini con premio di sette braccia di panno rosso e infine le donne con quello di sette braccia di panno verde." [In the morning the *palio* was run for the gold cloth. In the afternoon, the asses

Figure 1. Detail, Francesco del Cossa, *Aprile,* Sala dei mesi, Palazzo Schifanoia, Ferrara. Courtesy of the Fototeca, Palazzo Schifanoia.

ran with the mounted jockeys, . . . [then] the men for a prize of seven ells of red cloth, and finally the women for that of seven ells of green cloth.] [10] Another important Ferrarese chronicle mentions that for Saint George's Day a quarter century later, "Furno per barbari corso il palio de brocato d'oro. . . . Et dopoi desinare corseno li homini, femine, et aseni, *juxta solitum*." [The race for the *palio* of gold brocade was run, and after dinner ran the men, women, and asses, *as usual*.] [11] Such descriptions indicate the enduring solidity of the *palio* as an institution. They also reveal that Cossa's panel alludes not to a single race between all the figures pictured (as some have assumed), but rather conflates four contests occurring over a whole day of celebration.

Social anthropologists have argued that performances, exhibitions, and rituals primarily symbolize relations: relations among a community's members, and relations between rulers and their subjects. [12] Public ritual particularly serves this function, for its cyclic repetition and grand scale at once

Figure 2. Francesco del Cossa, *Aprile,* Sala dei mesi, Palazzo Schifanoia, Ferrara. Courtesy of the Fototeca, Palazzo Schifanoia.

evoke power relations within a community and *reproduce* those relations, binding them within an authorized, controlled frame of meaning. This frame is especially effective in rituals of hierarchy, which magnify invented authority by projecting it onto a cosmic stage where it attains the weight of nature and inevitability. Moreover, public ritual both embodies and enacts a regime of power through its enforced positioning of individual bodies in a superindividual spectacle.

Seen in this context of social construction, the first event in Ferrara's Palio di San Giorgio would seem to reaffirm the Este family's oligarchic rule over the city. The flamboyant race of prize military steeds displays the superior power, wealth, and elegance of the ducal family before a breathless populace, clearly exhibiting the dominance of an aristocratic, masculine state power. The race of the asses, which according to the statutes follows this martial display, might be read as a whimsical or even parodic repetition of the first contest. The majesty of the ducal steeds is nowhere more evident than in contrast with the sturdy but less graceful asses, who may serve here to figure the Court's disdain for any contenders for its powers.

The rhetorical force of the other contests, however, remains more obscure and complex. The men's and women's races within this festive frame raise intriguing questions about the relations being reinforced among groups *within* the populace. For while the first two contests display a general courtly power "at play," a power that basks in self-regard before its subjects, the latter two races have political and social connotations that remain ambiguous, at least to the modern viewer.

Who are the characters running in this display, and whom do they represent within the community? Identifying the *palio* players is in fact no simple task, because the chronicles and statutes refer to the contestants simply as women [*donne* or *femine*] and men [*huomini*].[13] Twentieth-century sources exhibit a similar decorum. Guido Angelo Facchini's 1939 history of the *palio,* for example (an otherwise valuable source), aims to reinstate the historic festivities in modern-day Ferrara: it thus depicts a thoroughly idealized event, expressly tailored to the grandiose patriotism of fascist Italy. But if Cossa's fifteenth-century fresco is even vaguely documentary, a number of questions arise. By all accounts of the social customs of early modern Italy, "respectable" women did not run through the streets, except perhaps in flight from danger.

Facchini himself offers some unintended assistance. Unable to resist a coy remark about some of the historic race's participants, he suggests an important detail in the rhetorical force of the early Palio di San Giorgio:

> È da ritenere per certo che nelle prime edizioni la corsa delle donne avesse uno spiccato carattere . . . boccaccesco poiché sappiamo che a tale competizione partecipavano, in vesti succinte, quelle donne che i Ferrarresi chiamavano «mingarde» e che appartenevano ad una classe piuttosto equivoca. (12–14)

> [We can be certain that in its earliest versions the women's race had a distinctly . . . "Boccaccesque" flavor, since we know that partici-

pating in that contest, in brief costumes, were those women whom the Ferraresi called "mingarde," and who belonged to a rather equivocal class.]

Traveling the road not taken by Facchini, I shall explore in the following pages the likelihood that the *palio*'s runners (at least for a time) were anything but respectable to the Ferraresi, and that the contestants' social station was not an incidental detail but rather a significant theme in the Palio di San Giorgio. A principal rhetorical aim of the races, I will argue, was to reaffirm a social hierarchy in Ferrara that encompassed the moral, political, and sexual spheres.[14]

Chronicles from other cities indicate that throughout Italy and other European territories, from the late thirteenth century to the mid-fifteenth, members of that "equivocal" female class—the local prostitutes—regularly performed in several types of public races. The prostitute's role in civic *palios,* as Richard Trexler's work has shown, followed on an earlier practice by the women who accompanied medieval Italian armies in their assaults on rival cities.[15] Attacking armies customarily staged elaborate theatrical exhibitions outside the gates of towns under siege. In these charades, the city walls marked a point of inversion. While the threatened citizens cowered inside their city, the attackers took liberties outside its borders. Customarily, they cut down the largest tree beyond the city walls and began minting victory coins near its stump. Such symbolic castration gestures aimed to humiliate and demoralize the besieged inhabitants: they taunted the desperate populace with the specter of a future day when, their great city toppled, coins would circulate to commemorate its capture.

At the same time, the mounted soldiers, looters, and prostitutes of the aggressor army took turns competing in races outside the embattled city's gates. This sport may have been a mocking mime play of the beleaguered opponents, now "on the run," who were thus forced to witness repeatedly a symbolic enactment of their own defeat. Akin to Freud's *fort/da* game played out on a grand scale, these games served to accustom the besieged populace to the idea of losing.[16] In addition, the spectators must have been acutely aware of the contrast between their own entrapment and immobility and their attackers' freedom to move and act.

On returning to its own city, the victorious army sometimes put the enemy's *palio,* or banner, in a prostitute's hands. She would carry the cloth upside down, signifying the sexual as well as military subjugation of the defeated enemy. The prostitutes' role in these ceremonies was, of course, an ambivalent one: they represented the very lowest rung in the social hierarchy, but their lack of respectability lent them a relative honor in this moment. Their abject position, in other words, made them the ideal means by which to humiliate the vanquished in a carnivalesque inversion. "Even the prostitutes of the victorious army," the ceremony clearly implies, "are superior to the warriors of the defeated one. The least of our citizens can run freely about the weak enemy's territory and mock its most cherished symbols."

Through most of the fourteenth century, Italian cities explicitly connected the civic races they held on feast days to such military insult displays.[17] A look at the Villani chronicles, for example, reveals that early races on the feast day of Florence's patron saint, San Giovanni, often took place not at home, inside Florence, as they do today, but outside the walls of her rival cities Pisa, Lucca, and Arezzo.[18] In October 1330, the Florentines ran races outside Lucca, "per vendetta di quelli che fece correre Castruccio a Firenze" [in revenge for those Castruccio had instigated at Florence]. As Villani describes this performance, the first race was run by horses for a prize of twenty-five gold florins, "e l'altro fu di panno sanguigno, che'l corsono i fanti a piè; e l'altro di baracane bambagino, che'l corsono le meretrici dell'oste" [and another (race) was for crimson cloth, which was run by the footsoldiers; and another was for sheepskin cloth, and was run by the whores of the army].[19] Later, in 1363, the Florentines ran their San Giovanni races outside Pisa in retaliation for feast day races held by the Pisans outside Florence in 1362.[20]

The form of these displays remained ritually consistent and hence recognizable by all witnesses. Giovanni Morelli recounts in his *Ricordi* for 1363 how Galeotto Malatesti, on the day of the Palio di San Vittorio, having performed all other possible insults in the traditional repertory, including the felling of the tree and the proleptic minting of coins outside Pisa, finally resorted to the "palio de' barattieri e pelle meretrici" [the race of the gamblers and the whores] as the ultimate derision against the enemy city.[21] For all its regularity, however, the pattern of offenses in these performances is intricate indeed: the overlays of insult and honor even include races performed by oppressing armies on the feast days of the *victim* cities. Like the minting of coins, these spectacles anticipate and symbolically enact the full incorporation of the threatened city's identity.[22]

Such accounts hint at a gap between official Ferrarese records of the *palio* as a civic celebration and the event's far less benevolent overtones as a traditional rehearsal of military power. In their textualization of an idealized image of Estense rule, the chronicles written under ducal supervision reinforced a "controlled frame of meaning" dictated by public statutes and government edicts. The Este dukes, we surmise, intuited what Machiavelli would later so frankly point out to his Prince: the political rewards of public ceremony depend on its successful manipulation. In the case of the Estense government, this manipulation included the decorous elision, from all official accounts, of the context of war and subjugation that formed the historical backdrop for the games on Saint George's Day. Integral to both this military past and the evolving demands of urban rule were the negative exemplars of community morality, who found themselves performing in exhibitional games on many public feast days.

Contemporaneous with the first races by infamous groups on Italian military fields were the earliest documented races run by prostitutes and other social marginals *inside* European cities. Although the military insult races disappear from documents around the mid-fourteenth century, the festive races that bear close affinities to them continued in many European cities for centuries.[23] Because the well-known Roman races instituted under Pope Paul II in 1467 featured a derisive race for Roman Jews, many have assumed that in Ferrara's *palio* and others the male runners were also Jews.

As both Jews and prostitutes were marginal members of the community, this attribution has a certain plausibility. Both were stigmatized in Ferrara and other cities by laws forbidding them to touch foodstuffs in public markets and requiring them to wear distinguishing signs on their clothing.[24] Like other racisms, moreover, anti-Semitism traditionally invests the object of its hatred with legendary sexual excesses that are both envied and despised; this type of association may represent one more tie between Jewish men and prostitutes in the imagination of early modern Christian Europe. But probably a more compelling link would have been the economic fact that both groups profited financially from their willingness to transgress Christian mores—the prostitutes by selling sex, the Jews (who were actively recruited to medieval cities to practice their banking trade) by loaning money. The source of profits for each was considered "endless," insofar as both prostitute and lender make their incomes (at least in theory) at a zero expenditure rate. Thus each group represented an alternative type of "productivity" that compounded the significations especially of urban festivals dedicated to fertility, or "reproductivity," and plenty.

Earlier sources recounting the military races, however, suggest that a different community furnished the male runners in many urban contests. Competing in many festive races, it appears, were men from another social group known as the *ribaldi*.[25] Ribalds were the lowest dregs of the army. Together with the prostitutes, they were responsible for collecting the spoils after assaults on enemy cities. One man selected from among these ranks held the title King of the Ribalds, which conferred the added responsibility of supervising the operations of the prostitutes and pimps in the army's employ. Once the practice of military *palios* died out, this governing role transferred within the city, where the King of the Ribalds often held the additional office of town executioner.[26]

If the men in Ferrara's *palio* were ribalds, then their sexual and financial violation of the general morality is clear enough, and their association with the prostitutes is one of direct management and cooperation. The ribald was defined by some Italian statutes as "one who undresses down to his underclothes while gambling"; and ribalds were apparently known for going into battle barely clad.[27] This evidence suggests that Cossa may have been signaling a social type as well as recording the attire worn by the men in Ferrara's *palio* when he painted the figures of his male runners. It may even be that Dante's reference to the Veronese *palio* at the pilgrim's encounter with the sodomites in *Inferno* 15 served as an obvious reference to contemporaries regarding the sexual transgressions of this same group.[28]

Many cities featured the ribalds in their festive races. A 1329 Ivrean statute regulates a race on May Day by that city's public women for the prize of a drinking bowl purchased by the King of the Ribalds out of his annual salary.[29] A Pavian chronicle of 1330 mentions that races by ribalds and prostitutes were run in conjunction with the horse races that annually honored the city's patron, San Siro.[30] These domestic contests may have followed directly from the tradition of the military field races run by the same groups; in this connection they seem to signify the cities' internalization of their wars against foreign enemies.

In fact, certain features of the races themselves disturb the surface glamour painted by the chronicles. The rewarding of prizes might suggest that prostitutes participated voluntarily in the games. But consent in the case of the prostitute tells us little about her experience of these events, conditioned as it must have been by need. The prostitute, after all, is a figure at once sought and despised by societies that place a high value on feminine chastity. Her role in the community is consequently susceptible to frequent and violent reversals. A grim example of this ambivalence comes to us from the military field races. On one occasion in 1390, when Bologna's army returned defeated rather than victorious, two of the prostitutes who under happier circumstances might have carried the enemy city's *palio* to the cheers of their welcoming town were instead "recast" as internal representatives of the foreign enemy. They were publicly stripped and flogged so violently that one of them later died.[31]

Such ambivalence thoroughly characterizes urban prostitution itself. Recent histories of medieval prostitution chart a common shift in the legal strictures regarding sexual trade in late thirteenth- and early fourteenth-century Italy and France.[32] These years witnessed the transfer of sexual trade from outside the city walls to inside. Accompanying this relocation were new laws that required prostitutes to wear distinguishing marks—typically yellow sleeve bands and bells—in an effort to sort out the "public women" for visual distinction from the rest of the female populace. These divisions were also embodied in a new organization of city space, as towns throughout Europe designated special districts in which they obliged prostitutes to live as well as work.[33] In exchange for their compliance with the law, however, the women received some legal protection against rape and permission to practice their trade within the city walls, which was generally considered safer.

Toward the end of the fourteenth century, many cities, including Ferrara, designated a single *postribulum* as the only legal house of prostitution in the municipality.[34] City governments regulated the public houses through taxes, inspection for diseases, and restrictions on allowable clientele. Increasingly repressive measures in later years, however, culminated in the closing of most municipal brothels by the early sixteenth century. At this point many governments took steps to expel prostitutes from the cities altogether.[35]

These long-term developments in urban prostitution indicate an initially pragmatic appreciation by early modern rulers for the advantages of administrated sexual commerce in urban areas. In the first phase, municipal leaders welcomed prostitutes and even actively recruited them from other cities, often on the stated assumption that the legal sex trade protected the community's marriageable women from assault. According to this logic, the brothels provided a necessary outlet for men who might, in the absence of such services, resort to sexual aggression against townswomen. Violence of this sort, legislators argued, would upset the marriage market, in which chastity was the only asset most women could claim. In effect the prostitutes functioned as surrogates for the local female community, circulating as the signs of a submerged male aggression, which, in official eyes at least, was manageable only through provision of *some* female object on which to vent itself.[36] The official preference for prostitutes from distant towns or even foreign countries also discouraged any association of sexual availability with women of the home community.

This period of relative tolerance was followed, however, by a growing recognition of both the ideological contradictions of such policies within a professedly Christian state and, more practically, the difficulties of controlling the sexual marketplace. Yet the government policies of the fourteenth and early fifteenth centuries, which sponsored limited sexual trade, and the later state gestures to banish prostitution may represent more a continuum than a reversal of policy. Trexler argues that the apparent permissiveness of the fifteenth-century transfer of prostitution inside the city walls of Florence, for example, resulted not from a relaxation of moral surveillance on the part of the government, but rather from instrumental, even repressive aims. The Ufficio dell'Onestà [Bureau of Decency], established in Florence in 1403 to regulate public morality, favored prostitution for two explicitly stated reasons: it discouraged homosexuality, which was perceived as a pervasive danger; and it "promoted" heterosexual activity, which helped increase the plague-depleted population.[37]

In Florence and in Ferrara as elsewhere throughout this period, the importance of maintaining the distinction between the "public" women and the rest of the (presumably "private") female populace became a recurring legal theme. Many statutes aimed to enforce dress codes among marriage-able women in order to keep them visually distinct from the women of the trade. Ercule d'Este complained that proper women, if their dress were not regulated and if they were not kept at a distance from immoral feminine examples, could be mistaken for prostitutes or even enflamed to lascivious corruption through unwitting contact with such negative models.[38] An un-expected disturbance of these visual and spatial boundaries arose in Florence when, to the dismay of city officials, prostitutes there began to dress like "respectable ladies." Similarly, the Florentine effort to promote male hetero-sexual activity through legal prostitution backfired when women in the brothel found that their business improved if they themselves dressed up *as men.*[39]

The express illegality of such cross-dressing indicates again the govern-ment's strenuous efforts to fix gender boundaries in early modern cities, as well as its concern to reinforce a single model of acceptable behavior for marriageable women.[40] For their part, by crossing class and gender lines "in disguise," the prostitutes employed an early version of the mimicry that Homi Bhabha identifies in colonial societies. The subalterns' imita-tion of the ruler is, for the dominant class that assigns them their "proper place," both resemblance and menace. Mimicry confuses stable identifica-tion through a resemblance that repeats with ironic literalness the outer signs of the original model. It thus allows an authorized version of other-ness (like licensed prostitution) to interrupt a discourse of power. Mimicry is the site of a potential reversal, Bhabha notes: "The look of surveillance re-turns as the displacing gaze of the disciplined, where the observer becomes the observed," and the identity of power suffers a momentary threat.[41]

Such moments of disturbance were brief, however. The legislators' frank observations connecting the marriage and prostitution markets in early modern cities testify to a systematic commodification of women coincid-ing with the rise of both mercantile capitalism and early modern state-hood. Feminist theorist Luce Irigaray's remarks on the capitalist economy of masculine sexuality illuminate the connection further. Irigaray observes that the prostitute is crucial in this economy: while the virginal woman functions between men as pure exchange value, and the mother must be excluded from exchange in order to maintain her worth, the prostitute's body is valuable precisely because it has already been used. "In the extreme case the more it has served, the more it is worth. Not because its natural assets have been put to use this way, but, on the contrary, because its nature has been 'used up,' and has become once again no more than a vehicle for relations among men."[42] It was precisely the difference between the prostitute's body as commodity for one kind of exchange among men and the virgin's body for exchange between fathers and husbands on the marriage market that early modern merchants and rulers sought to maintain.[43]

The proclamations on moral offenses issued by Borso and his successor, Ercule, provide a suggestive gauge of the growing anxiety regarding sexual activity and other behavioral trespasses in ducal Ferrara. Borso's 1462 document begins unceremoniously with the duke's commands; but Ercule's proclamation of 1496 opens with an inflated, moralizing preamble:

> Desiderando sopramodo el m. Ill. Sig. M. hercule ecc. che in questa cita et ducato de ferrara et in tuto el suo dominio se vive bene costumatamente et secondo la fede et religione cristiana . . . ha deliberato totalmente extirpare cusi del resto del suo dominio come de questa cita et ducato tuti li vitij.

> [The most illustrious Lord Ercule, desiring over all else that in this his city and duchy of Ferrara and in all of his dominion people live well and courteously and according to the Christian faith, . . . has deliberated to extirpate all vices totally from the rest of his domain as well as from this city and duchy.][44]

Ercule's rhetoric of moral absolutism coincides with a general increased surveillance of the bounds of all public behavior in Ferrara and other cities in these years. It also recalls the dukes' perennial efforts to "clean up" the *palio*. Useful as the civic insult races may have been to the Este in general as a message to both the mainstream community and the city's marginal underworld, the prostitutes' contest in particular inspired official ambivalence as early as Borso's reign. He reportedly sought to eliminate the women's race from the festival in 1456 but was unsuccessful.[45] Twenty years later, Ercule issued an edict calling on families to send their daughters under the age of twelve to run in the *palio* the next day. His solicitation of "pute honeste et da bene" [honest and proper young girls] registers its full, *reascriptive* force only if we bear in mind the traditional participants in earlier events, whom

Ercule was attempting to exclude from public view.[46] Isabella d'Este's still later edict is explicit in this regard: she informs the Mantuan populace that in 1495 during the feast of Saint Peter the *palio* will be run not by the usual prostitutes but by country maids. The *contadinelle* are invited to come forward as volunteers, with the marchesa's assurance that they will suffer neither insult nor injury for participating.[47]

We are left to wonder what forces compelled the continuance of this rehearsal of power and erotic display in the years spanning Borso's and Ercule's reigns, despite their documented attempts to eliminate or change it. As I observed earlier, the *palio* was generally not a carnivalesque event: controlled and orchestrated as it was by its institutional frame, it reinforced existing power relations without the topsy-turvy role reversals and transgressions described by Bakhtin and his revisers; it appears to have served most effectively as a mirror in which the Este could enjoy a moment of despotic self-regard. Its popular appeal as a holiday may nonetheless have posed the threat of community violence should the festivities be toned down. Reinforcing this conjecture are records of contemporary edicts regulating the wearing of masks during public celebrations, where disguises afforded anonymity to spectators tempted to engage in unlawful behavior.[48]

If the women's role in the Renaissance *palio* is somewhat unclear today, it is both because that role was being redefined and because it was a source of embarrassment within the moralizing decorum that characterized the project of early modern state building. The *palio* was, among other things, a locus of tension and doubt regarding the effects of foregrounding a "heterogeneous social element" within the city.[49] As Steven Mullaney observes, in early modern cities, "ceremonies of power were ceremonies of loss as well. . . . When it did not exile or execute them, early modern power licensed those things it could neither contain nor control"; and this licensing often took the form of public performance.[50]

In Italy's case, the 1494 invasion of the peninsula by Charles VIII of France commenced an unprecedented period of political anxiety over the lack of social order and control, confirming the vague dread that runs through earlier chronicles. Throughout the following century Italy suffered almost continuous invasion by Spanish and French forces and was often represented by prominent cultural spokesmen as "feminized" in its political helplessness.[51] At the same time, Reformation tendencies chipped away at

Italy's claim to centrality in a universal church: the Council of Trent (1545–63) and the reestablished Roman Inquisition are just two measures of Italy's new investment in the values of social surveillance and reform. In my view this same desire for order and renewed hierarchical value fueled the reappearance of the *querelle des femmes* in Renaissance writings of all genres: in what appears to be a displacement from the disordered sphere of public political relations, writers rehearsed and rehashed the proper relations of sexual and domestic order.[52]

But the *palio* was not so easily schematized. As the military connotations of festive contests faded, the public's possible interpretations of such events became perhaps too multifarious. The surplus meanings generated by the prostitutes' bodily presence, together with their possible agency in this irrepressibly salacious ritual display, threatened the dukes' capacity to limit the *palio*'s polysemy on the stage of hierarchic society. Prostitutes in some cities, for instance, took advantage of the spectacle to advertise themselves, thus enraging local citizens. Of course, the mixture of titillation with insult was potent in the race from its earliest days, however mystified by politics or religious ceremony. A seventeenth-century Perugian account, for example, recalls a race in 1335 in which "prostitutes raised their clothes up to the belt" as a sign of contempt before the enemy. This gesture (not surprisingly) "gave marvelous pleasure to all [the Perugian] soldiers," the historian continues, "since it is only natural for soldiers to be happy at the moment that vendettas are executed."[53]

Display of the genitals is a traditional warrior's gesture of contempt, but it acquires far more complex (and less controllable) meanings when practiced by women, in this case women whose trade relied on sexual intercourse. It not only recalls Caterina Sforza's infamous taunt, as she lifted her skirts, that if her children should be killed by her enemies, she could always make more.[54] It also resonates with mythological fertility legends like that of the old hag Baubo, who raised her skirt and made the mourning Demeter laugh, thus moving her to release the season of spring; and the Celtic goddess of fertility, Sheela-na-Gig, who typically smiles as she reaches down to open for display an enormous vagina.[55] This detail of exposure reappears unmistakably in Cossa's fresco (fig. 3), where the dress of one female runner flies well above her bare genitals.

The vicissitudes of women's participation in the Palio di San Giorgio,

Figure 3. Detail, Francesco del Cossa, *Aprile,* Sala dei mesi, Palazzo Schifanoia, Ferrara. Courtesy of the Fototeca, Palazzo Schifanoia.

I have argued above, were intricately tied to the process of Estense state building and the political fortunes of early modern Italy. They reflect not only the transformation of an unwieldy popular festival into a more dignified state display during the fifteenth and sixteenth centuries, but also the contemporaneous legal codification of boundaries for sexual behavior within early modern cities, and the sometimes incomprehensible resort to nearly empty public ceremony.[56] The social context for the *palio* shifted over several generations from a minimal frame of codification (represented by the reticent chronicles and statutes, which speak only of "women" and "men" running the traditional contests) to the heavy textualization of ducal edicts regulating not only prostitution but other sexual conduct as well.

The *Diario ferrarese,* for example, offers a panorama of the sexual violence and demoralization that characterized Ferrara in the year 1500. On 4 May, the author records the invasion of the home of a "good man" and the attempted gang rape of his daughter. When the rapists were unsuccessful, they beat the girl's parents with clubs. On 8 June, Ercule issued more laws against sodomy and the keeping of concubines. In October, there were frequent formal processions, "and no one could understand why, other than that the Duke was ordering them." Finally, in November, the demoralized diarist complains especially of the working class:

> Hogi dì in Ferrara et quasi da per tuto sono piu tristi li puti et pute che già non erano li vechi et vechie, et non è in Ferrara qui faciat bonum, et non se trova massare a stare cumaltri, et quelle che se trovano, se sono zovane, sono putane, et se sono vechie, sono rofiane, et potius le voleno andare apitochiare che a stare con altri.

> [Today in Ferrara and almost anywhere, boys and girls are more miserable than old men and women have ever been, and there's no one in Ferrara who does good things, and good serving girls are not to be found; and those one finds, if they're young, are whores; and if they're old, they're ruffians; and they'd rather go begging than work for others.] [57]

In April 1501, Ercule restricted the prostitutes to the neighborhood behind the church of Sant'Agnese. It was apparently in the earlier context of government tolerance of prostitution as a useful evil that the women's participation in public festivals such as Ferrara's Palio di San Giorgio became routine. One of the most common games, which combined support for the prostitutes with their surveillance, was the annual prostitutes' race held in various cities on the feast day of Saint Mary Magdalene, the patron saint of their profession.[58] The festivities often included a census of all the women practicing the trade and featured a perfunctory sermon by a priest urging their repentance. Less congruous, but just as frequent, were races for prostitutes on the feast of the Virgin's Assumption, on Pentecost, and on many other saints' days.[59]

This conspicuous alliance between the cultures of military despotism, Christianity, and carnal pleasure, complex as it is, does not yet complete the set of motifs operating in *palios* like the one pictured on the Schifanoia wall. The feast's namesake, Saint George, is immortalized in historical record and Christian legend dating back to the Crusades; but little more than his name appears to survive in the *palio* held yearly in Ferrara on his feast day.[60] Instead, like many festivals of early modern Europe (and today), the Palio di San Giorgio combined motifs from the Christian tradition with those of Roman antiquity. The feast's association with traditional Roman rites reinforces the sexual connotations implicit in the military and Christian practices I have discussed here.

The twenty-third of April was for the Romans a festival of wine origi-nally dedicated to Jupiter but later associated with Venus.[60] On that day, the goddess of love received offerings from the prostitutes of Republican Rome, who also took a holiday from work in her honor. Another goddess associated with fertility festivals was Flora, at whose celebration the prosti-tutes of Rome ritually displayed their vulvas.[62] In the Floralia, the women's running or racing in circles was believed to bring fertility to the soil; and this may be another source for the structuring of the later *palio* as a race.[63] At the same time, rabbits and goats were allowed to roam as examples of randiness and fertility. The placement of Venus in the upper third of Cossa's April fresco, where many rabbits are also hopping about among the young people who kiss and flirt with each other in the goddess's company, sug-gests the presence of these associations in Ferrarese culture as well.[64] Also supporting this reading is the young man in the group on the lower right, who increases the erotic tension in this portion of the detail by venturing his hand between the thighs of his lady companion while kissing her cheek and encircling her neck with his other hand (fig. 4).

Some *palio* commentators refer to spectators deriding or pelting the run-ners in Ferrara's race.[65] These accounts suggest a further connection between the *palio* and the Roman Lupercalia. That festival, held in February, featured young boys who ran naked on a course through the city, striking female bystanders with reeds. The precise connotations of the Lupercalia remain obscure, but these gestures almost certainly signified both purification and an awakening of fertility in the women.[66]

Yet the peltings and derision in Ferrara's *palio*, if they are not simply a conventional classical reference, may have had a more contemporary reso-nance. Any practice of striking the passing runners would have evoked an unmistakable association with the standard criminal punishment known as *la scopa*, or "running the town." That punishment, which was generally re-served for adulteresses and for prostitutes and procurers who broke the laws of their trade, required the offender to run through the streets naked or barely dressed, enduring blows from rotting vegetables and other objects thrown by spectators on the sidelines.

Figure 4.
Detail, Francesco
del Cossa, *Aprile,*
Sala dei mesi,
Palazzo Schifanoia,
Ferrara. Courtesy of
the Fototeca,
Palazzo Schifanoia.

Perhaps the result of early modern audiences' taste for cruelty, this display seems to have been a favorite event for courtly as well as popular urban
spectators. Thus Michele Catalano, in his celebrated biography of Ludovico
Ariosto, remarks of courtly entertainments in Ferrara:

> Fra gli spassi di corte spiace di dover annoverare anche i supplizi,
> che erano atroci e ributtanti. Molto comune il castigo della scopa.
> Nel 1496 fu scopata la moglie di un capo di birri, rea di illeciti
> amori. La disgraziata fu costretta a percorrere a piedi le principali
> vie della città con una mitra in capo, ov'erano dipinti alcuni dia-
> voli, e infine fu condotta dinanzi ai cortigiani, che coprirono di

pomi, di rape e di zucche marce la penitente, il boja e i fanti del
capitano di giustizia.

[Among the amusements at court we regretfully must also count
the corporal punishments, which were atrocious and repelling.
Very common was the punishment of *la scopa.* In 1496 the wife of
a police captain was *scopata* because she was guilty of illicit love
affairs. The wretched woman was forced to run through the main
streets of the city on foot, wearing on her head a mitre with devils
painted on it; and finally she was conducted before the courtiers,
who covered the penitent woman, as well as the executioner and
the justice captain's horsemen, with tomatoes, turnips, and rotten
squash.] [67]

Catalano appends to this anecdote an excerpt from a letter to Isabella d'Este
from her favorite correspondent at court, Bernardo Prosperi, who kept the
marchesa informed of all the Ferrarese news she missed while residing at the
Gonzaga court of Mantua. Prosperi remarks of this event, "La festa qua fue
grandissima, el romore grande cum la mostra de le carne della povera dona
et fortemente battuta dal boglia et bersagliata dai putti et etiam da multi
grandi." [The celebration here was most grand and there was a great noise
on the display of the flesh of the poor woman, who was both vigorously
beaten by the executioner and targeted for blows by little children and by
many adults.] [68] Whether or not Saint George's Day featured similar treat-
ments of its contestants, the festive spirit in which Prosperi describes this
punishment for sexual misconduct brings it very close, as a performance, to
the *palio* race, in which the "professional" violators of the Christian code of
feminine behavior ran through the same city's streets.

The complex play of associations in the Palio di San Giorgio—celebrations of civic pride, military domination, and fertility, combined quite
possibly with exhibitions of cruelty, punishment, and humiliation—mark
the festival's tremendous multivalency as a cultural event. As Trexler observes, if in the early military field races the prostitutes and ribalds allied
themselves with their cities in the vituperation of an external enemy, in
the domestic races they themselves, as outsiders to the official Christian
mores being celebrated, represented forces threatening the moral code of

the community from within. Moreover, these dangerously heterogeneous elements thematized within the social order could, in turn, be symbolically brought under control, temporarily licensed and homogenized with the reigning power structure through their objectification in civic festival. In the festive performances, prostitutes and other moral outcasts were compelled to exhibit their subjection to the values of the Christian community that served the political aims of the Estense court. By dramatizing that subjection, the *palio* inscribed—within the space of the city, the time of both the natural and religious calendars, and the collective memory of the populace—a dichotomy between its mainstream members and those who strayed beyond its accepted social bounds. The festival thus reaffirmed a set of social divisions already operating firmly within the city while at the same time it recorded deep official ambivalence regarding the relation between these licensed marginals and the ducal reign of power.

Significantly, women functioned not only as performers subject to the race's theatrical subjugation; they also played an important role as one group of the spectacle's addressees. As we see both in Cossa's image and in statutes of cities such as Brescia, which instituted the prostitutes' race "ad . . . bonarum mulierum exemplum" [as an example for good women], the feminine audience to this spectacle was of particular importance.[69] The "good" women of Ferrara played their part in the celebration by literally looking down on and standing in judgment over the women who strayed from a sovereign moral code. Kept at a noteworthy distance, they gazed from the protection of the domestic structures afforded *only* to women who complied with confinement within the Christian family, and ultimately, of course, only to women of a certain class. Their separation reaffirms a traditional, fundamental difference between obedient women and those who transgress their place, while the game, by its very nature as spectacle, posits a brief identification between all the town's women (or womanhood itself) and those running the race.

It is here that I would locate the circular definitions referred to in my chapter title. The two classic categories of womanhood represented in the *palio* are gathered into a single circle of female subjectivity as they define each other through opposition, but also through implied likeness. It is important that the male spectators of the *palio* stand outside such circular or binary schemes. For while humanist culture and capitalist economic developments offered men an ever-broadening spectrum of identities as individual actors, Renaissance reflections on women returned with a vengeance to the dualism of chastity and nonchastity as the only choices available to women. As Margaret King observes:

> While the bearers of ideas—preachers and theologians, philosophers and physicians, lawyers, humanists and poets—defined men in terms of their worldly activity, they defined women in terms of their sexual role. The male world could be schematized, using the feudal hierarchies of those who fought, prayed, and worked; or, as those traditional categories broke down on the threshold of the modern era, as judges, merchants, and lawyers, pilgrims and invalids, peasants and artisans, monks, friars, and prelates, noblemen and gentlemen. Women, with very few exceptions, were categorized in terms of their relations to the female ideal of virginity and the nightmare of sexuality.[70]

Alongside humanist writings on the dignities of "man" that exulted in the infinite possibilities for differentiation within the human race, there flourished a separate literature on women that revealed their exclusion from such infinitude. The *querelle des femmes'* discussions of women's worth and proper roles in society revolve emphatically around the issue of chastity, the cultural linchpin of capitalist inheritance patterns.[71] With remarkable efficacy, in the Palio di San Giorgio the traditional association of fertility with the circular course drew the reproductive themes of this race like a tight cord around the community of women as a whole, binding them ritually to the state-condoned procreative functions of the feminine body while threatening community expulsion for sexual transgression.

In his essay on the "mirror stage" as constitutive of the "I," Lacan describes how the infant forms a full corporeal image as the locus of selfhood in a process of self-alienation and reappropriation before a mirror. Yet this process requires not just the child and its reflection, but also another subject to perform the confirming function of the gaze—in Lacan's ideal narrative of origins, the one who holds up the child, points to its reflection in the mirror, and exclaims, "Yes that's you!"[72] Lacan argues elsewhere that woman, as a general category, functions in Western culture as the "absolute

Other," a necessary construction in contrast to which the male is able to define himself as rational, strong, productive, and authoritative. Women's historic problem in this male-oriented representation of the world, argues Lacan, is that there is no "Other of the Other": a woman has only the male culture's projections of her identity on which to build her own subjectivity, since the most forcefully organized category operating to define her is the category of the "not man."[73] For early modern women, this lack of a discourse defining them as anything but man's undesirable opposite bound together promiscuous and chaste women as different and yet the same in a sharing of essential gender limitations that did not impose itself in analogous ways on the male category.

Anthropologist Victor Turner also conceives of events such as the *palio* in terms of mirroring. For Turner, ritual and aesthetic forms "represent the reflexivity of the social process, wherein society becomes at once subject and object; it represents also its subjunctive mood, wherein suppositions, desires, hypotheses, and so forth all become legitimate."[74] While a growing chorus of guidebooks on marriage and family life repeatedly warned men that *all* women are susceptible to excessive sexual desire, and as dress codes strained to keep their differences visually clear, ritual contexts such as the *palio* and the punishment of the *scopa* brought the prostitute and the wife desirous of extramarital sex into close proximity in the social imaginary. "There but for the grace of social constraint," says the feminine voice of this festival's subjunctive mood, "go I."

The contestants in the *palio* footraces were clearly marginal, outcast members of their communities, at least until legal reforms sought to erase their presence from the festive imaginary. The remapping of the ducal city as a field of play functioned generally to carve out the relations of power between the dukes and their subjects, but this power consolidation also reinforced differences among the subjects themselves. By virtue of its regularity and the space in which it unfolded, the festival placed those social relations, along with the moral oppositions that supported them, within a ritual order that fused the ancient with the everyday, the mythological with the sacred, the serious with the burlesque.

The Palio di San Giorgio is richly significant not only because it draws on so many sources for its meanings, but also because in a strikingly concrete way it followed ritual's general path toward reification and amnesia. Just when the Palio di San Giorgio and public theater itself began to seem inappropriate as social exercises for the elite (a moment contemporaneous with the development of the more privatized genres of the Italian courtly theater), the event literally *became an object* under the painterly hand of Cossa. The progressive interiorization of the *palio* races—from the gates of enemy cities to the gates of home cities to the streets within domestic city walls—ended in the intimate chambers of the Estense pleasure palace. Borso's apparent attempts to reform the *palio* into a more wholesome civic event gave way, ironically, to its preservation as a visual text; but its message would now be directed expressly to Borso and to the members of his coterie: a final flourish of sovereign self-regard, Cossa's grand panorama of power, order, and sexual and social difference played continuously for *their* eyes only.

Twenty-four meters long and eleven meters wide, with ceilings seven and a half meters high, the Sala dei mesi presents upper walls almost entirely covered by the multiauthor fresco cycle from which it takes its name.[75] Common to all the panels is a tripartite subdivision. The upper section of each bears a scene depicting one of the Olympian gods riding in a triumphal chariot and flanked by figures practicing the arts he or she favors. These are complemented by figures recalling both the deities' classical attributes and the associations assigned to them by ancient authorities on magic. A center band features the zodiacal figure governing each month, along with additional figures which, according to sources of Hellenistic, Persian, and Arabic astrological origin, dictate the fortunes of those born in the first, second, and third decades of each month.[76] The bottom section of each panel, finally, constitutes Borso's political apotheosis.

A gesture toward modern politics, these lower sections display not the military exploits common to compositions of similar genre, but rather events that represent the duke's ability to govern and please his subjects. Different months picture Borso listening to petitions from the people, receiving ambassadors, hunting, riding, and participating in celebrations. The lower bands also feature scenes of local town life and images of the seasonal feasts and agricultural occupations particular to the various months. According to Aby Warburg, the design of the cycle reflects a spherical structure laid out in two dimensions. Hence the entire ensemble may be imagined as Borso's projection of global governance: a top section of the sphere depicts the idealized realm of mythological rulers; the middle girth refers to the order of the planets and stars; and in an earthly zone of civic management Borso projects his own powers as natural parallels to those of celestial deities and sciences.[77]

The April *palio* detail repeats this tripartite division in miniature by depicting a three-tiered hierarchy of urban society. In the light of the cultural associations I've described above, from military spectacles of dominance to the Christianization of fertility rituals, from the management of prostitution for the satisfaction of male sexual license to the official promotion of monogamous marriage for women, the *palio* detail also discloses its interest in a visible social order of sex and class. In the lower band appear the contestants in the April race: violators of Christian sexual custom; in the middle band the courtly guards and officials; and in the highest band the ladies of the nobility, who peer down from the proverbial pedestals (here, the balconies) to which courtly love, Christian rhetoric, and mercantile inheritance patterns traditionally relegated chaste females. Mediating the two poles of women looking and women running is thus a group of men (including Borso himself), who might be viewed as the institutional glue (or the outside, corroborating gaze) that binds such firm oppositions as that between good and bad sexual behavior for women (fig. 5).

In its evocation of an internally schismed and culturally dispossessed female subject, the Ferrarese *palio* builds both dynamics identified by Lacan together in a single ritual form. Without a cultural ground on which to distinguish herself more specifically, the female spectator is here cast only as Other to the male governing community located in the detail's center band. That community, in its official discourse, "holds up" the images of prostitute and wife as distant mirror inversions of each other ("Yes, that's you!") while reserving for itself a nonpolar and more differentiated range of symbolic positions.

Cossa gives particular weight to the middle group by enlarging its figures beyond common conventions of perspective.[78] The upper and lower bands nonetheless continue to draw the eye, as their interaction sets up a series of striking tensions. Contrasting with the full clothing and the shell-like balconies of the women above the spectacle is the skimpy dress and head-to-toe visibility of the female runners. The noblewomen stand immobile or tilt their heads slightly; the women below are represented in full body move-

Figure 5.
Detail, Francesco del Cossa,
Aprile, Sala dei mesi,
Palazzo Schifanoia, Ferrara.
Courtesy of the Fototeca,
Palazzo Schifanoia.

ment. One of these, the most physically exposed of the female figures, sets the entire *palio* tableau off balance by twisting around to look behind her as her arms flail forward: perhaps a gesture of alarm or reluctance to proceed on the race's path (see fig. 3). She is passing before a doorway: a visual trope on the genitals revealed by her uplifted dress. Less subtly, her bare legs offer a striking counterimage to the enclosure of the noble ladies' lower bodies. The latter are bound not just within balconies, but also behind the tapestries adorned with family coats of arms: a perfect image of Bakhtin's early modern "closed body."[79] The system of paternal inheritance thus not only hides (both disavowing and forbidding) the sexual "half" of the woman, substituting for her sexuality a public, patriarchal legacy; it also displaces her sexuality onto the public prostitute running the race below. The tottering turn of this prostitute may in effect be Cossa's figuration of her later expulsion from the spectacle, for who else could the taller, clothed, athletic male and female figures in the fresco be but the *puti onesti* who would replace the more salacious runners in later editions of the race? Cossa's conflation of both the different rounds in the race and its several historical versions here anticipates a civic narrative in which Estense propriety was, at least officially, victorious.

The women's roles constitute only one of many facets in the intricate cultural artifact the Palio di San Giorgio and its surrounding discourses represent. This embeddedness of gender politics within other (sometimes more explicit) discourses and activities is typical; for the shifting roles of women in Renaissance culture intersected inevitably with broader developments in Europe. Among its other functions, then, Ferrara's springtime celebration of fertility contrasts two kinds of sexual activity: the state-condoned, family-oriented, contained sexuality of lawful society and the punishable transgressions of open and ignoble sexual commerce. In addition, the Schifanoia fresco reinstitutionalizes the exemplary relations it records, placing us as viewers in the position of spectators, more and less consenting, to its ultimate historical authority. At once participatory *and* monolithic, the early modern Palio di San Giorgio drew spectators forcefully into its logic. Cossa's version of this logic now exerts a less violent, yet enduring power as monumental art: a thing among things, caught with us in the fabric of our world.

2 That Elusive Object of Desire: Angelica in the *Orlando Furioso*

In this chapter and the following one I turn to the two most famous female characters of Ariosto's *Orlando furioso*. The poem casts these two women in contrasting roles, roles that appear to offer two very different models for feminine character and conduct. Through each, however, Ariosto manages both to expose and to reinforce the order of patriarchy while at the same time granting each character some leverage against the circumstances women share in this order.

Mischievously darting through the first half of the *Orlando furioso* is the alluring figure of the exotic Indian princess, Angelica.[1] Inexplicably blonde and supremely beautiful,[2] she inspires movement and thus sets off the narrative mechanisms of errancy that structure Ariosto's poem.[3] Angelica's repeated escapes from knights who dream of possessing her interrupt the linear progress of specific narrative threads and propel the *Furioso*'s centrifugal, straying story lines outward into the busy tapestry the poem becomes. Her role as the object of the affections of so many knights, including those of the love-mad Orlando of the poem's title, has led many readers to assign Angelica a nearly allegorical status as the symbol of all vain desires. Other commentators, from Ariosto's day to our own, equate Angelica instead with womanhood itself, as does Benedetto Croce when he characterizes her as "la donna che simboleggia la Donna" [the woman who symbolizes Woman], or Antonio Baldini, who claims that "non c'è donna più donna che lei" [there is no woman more woman than she].[4] Still largely unexplored, however, are the relations between the notions of womanhood and desire in the poem, and the ties between these two conceptions and Ariosto's presentations of selfhood and difference. Angelica's function in the *Orlando furioso* thus escapes readers nearly as efficiently as she herself eludes her relentless pursuers.[5]

Whether or not Ariosto intended Angelica as a figure for womanhood, the matter of gender difference and of the roles men and women ought to assume in Italian society was an explicit question among his contemporaries. The sixteenth century, according to a standard view, was a moment of unprecedented social freedom for women. To substantiate their point, proponents of this characterization of the age point to the humanist liberalization of female education, the activity of a number of women poets, and the prominence of the Gonzaga and Este women in Italy's courtly society. The courtly and middle classes of the fifteenth and sixteenth centuries, however, also institutionalized a role for women that relegated all of their newly granted skills to a subsidiary sphere. Early modern women, like those of later centuries for whom they provided a general and explicit model, were expected to learn for the essentially auxiliary purpose of reflecting, appreciating, and enhancing the superior skills of men.[6] This logic of feminine reflexivity in relation to a standard male subject took form in a large body of writings on women's education, household duties, beauty, and spiritual status vis-à-vis men. Taken as a group, the most polemical examples in this tradition constitute Italy's *querelle des femmes.*[7]

Ariosto directly imports several of these discourses into the text of the *Orlando furioso,* thus signaling his own interest in the contemporary debates that sought to codify male and female behavior. As I argue elsewhere, his treatment of the *querelle des femmes* in the poem indicates a profound skepticism regarding the rigid logical structure of these debates.[8] Ariosto responds to the opposed terms of the *querelle* by consistently blurring their boundaries. In the *Orlando furioso,* Rinaldo's advocacy of free love (canto IV) appears extreme by the medieval and Renaissance standards of the characters he addresses, and they choose marital fidelity; Rodomonte's diatribe against women (canto XXVIII) is turned against him by his own display of inconstancy (canto XXIX); and Marfisa shows that women are not necessarily more just than men when she institutes the merciless subjugation of males in Marganorre's formerly misogynist state (canto XXXVII). Most explicitly (as I shall discuss more fully in chapter 3), Bradamante's speech refusing competition in a beauty contest after she has already proven her valor as a knight exposes the inadequacy of a simple gender opposition to define complex human personalities (canto XXXII).

Most of the treatises and dialogues of Italy's *querelle des femmes* rest on a logical structure of polar oppositions derived from Pythagoras, Aristotle,

and Plato.[9] The *Orlando furioso* dismantles the validity of these oppositions not only with regard to the masculine/feminine dichotomy but also
when confronting other simple dualisms (friend/enemy, sane/insane, Chris-
tian/pagan) that purport to structure the poem's fictional chivalric world.
Angelica, I will argue, constitutes another type of response to the polarized terms of the *querelle*. Her early appearances in the poem cast her as a
signifier of pure, and thus impossible, sexual alterity. Moreover, Orlando's
case suggests that belief in this pure otherness is the most destructive force
within the narrative logic of the poem. For most of the *Furioso,* Angelica
functions less as a real character than as an abstract value, an endpoint for
the desirous gazes of the poem's male knights.[10] This simulacrum of a character disappears from the *Furioso* when, breaking Orlando's circular, self-
seeking gaze, she acts as an autonomous, desiring subject. Having perfectly
embodied up to this point the binary opposite to man posited in *querelle*
writings, Angelica exposes the *querelle*'s version of Woman as an illusory
reference point for male desire and self-definition. What is more, when she
reveals herself to be, *like* the knights who pursue her, a desiring subject—but
distinct from them in what she desires—the absolute oppositions that sustain
her existence as an ideal can no longer hold, and she falls out of the narrative.

The opening canto of the *Orlando furioso* establishes Angelica as a major,
controlling figure in the narrative of the poem. So marked is her presence
in octave after octave of this first canto that Attilio Momigliano referred
to it as "Angelica's canto."[11] Her name is introduced in octave 5, where we
learn (if we do not already know it from her appearances in Boiardo's earlier
poem, *Orlando innamorato*) that she is the object of Orlando's love. The narrator observes that Orlando "per lei / in India, in Media, in Tartaria lasciato /
avea infiniti et immortal trofei" (I.5.2–4) [for her sake had left behind infinite and immortal monuments in India, Media, and Tartary]. Angelica's role
is thus both conventional within the romance genre and ideal according to
elaborate Renaissance standards like those of Castiglione's Cesare Gonzaga:
she inspires the great, unforgettable (*immortal*) deeds of a man.[12] Orlando
has left these distant lands and his exotic quest for personal glory, however,
and has returned to France to serve his king, Carlo Magno, in a Christian
war against the "pagan" kings Marsilio and Agramante. Apparently as his
captive, Angelica accompanies Orlando back to the west. Her appearance at
the Christian camp arouses immediate disorder:

Nata pochi dì inanzi era una gara
tra il conte Orlando e il suo cugin Rinaldo;
che ambi avean per la bellezza rara
d'amoroso disio l'animo caldo. (I.8.1–4)

[A few days before, a contest had been born
between Count Orlando and his cousin Rinaldo;
for both their spirits were warm
with amorous desire for the rare beauty.]

Since he requires the full attention of his knights for the impending battle, Carlo removes Angelica from the two rivals and promises her as prize to the one who performs best in the day's military clashes. But Angelica, silent and elusive, escapes from captivity and embarks on a pattern of action that comes to identify her in the poem: withdrawal in flight.[13] So central to her character is Angelica's habitual flight from danger that it is repeated three times in this first, symptomatic canto.

Just as important, her successive appearances in different locations, as she flees from one danger to another, occasion the introductions of the male knights who appear in canto I. Each makes his actual entrance and thus comes into being in the *Furioso* by confronting Angelica and registering his desire for her. Before the end of the octave that narrates her escape from Namo's pavilion, where Carlo had ensconced her for safekeeping, the fleeing Angelica happens on another knight: "entrò in un bosco, e ne la stretta via / rincontrò un cavallier ch'a piè venia" (I.10.7–8). [She entered a wood, and on the narrow path encountered a knight who was approaching on foot.] Angelica sizes up the figure running toward her and verifies his knightly identity in a rapid indexing of the accoutrements of his social station: *corazza, elmo, spada, scudo.* Her instantaneous reaction is described as a move of instinctive self-preservation:

timida pastorella mai sì presta
non volse piede inanzi a serpe crudo,
come Angelica tosto il freno torse,
che del guerrier, ch'a pié venia, s'accorse. (I.11.4–8)

[A timid shepherdess never turned her foot so fast,
upon encountering a cruel snake,

> as Angelica pulled back the reins
> when she noticed the warrior who was approaching on foot.]

The narrator identifies the knight (whom readers recognize as Rinaldo) and explains his haste. He is the son of Amone, the lord of Montalbano. His horse, Baiardo, has escaped him only moments before.

The gesture that finally brings Rinaldo into focus before the narrative leaves him behind and follows the retreating Angelica is the fixing of his gaze on the princess:

> Come alla donna egli drizzò lo sguardo,
> riconobbe, quantunque di lontano,
> l'angelico sembiante e quel bel volto
> ch'all'amorose reti il tenea involto. (I.12.4–8)

> [As soon as he directed his gaze toward the woman,
> he recognized, even from afar,
> the angelic countenance and that beautiful face,
> which kept him tangled in the nets of love.]

Such moments of recognition are a topos of chivalric romance: the raising of a visor, the siting of a familiar coat of arms, the receipt of a particular lady's scarf all characterize the romance world as one where signs are assumed by characters to correspond reliably with meanings, and where, because of this supposed clarity, actions are performed and deciphered in accordance with certain—often binary—values.[14] The *Furioso*, true to the conventions of the genre, regularly disturbs this secure pattern of signification and foregrounds instead the blindness and desire that make true recognition nearly impossible: things are rarely what they seem in the labyrinthine world of romance. Where Angelica is concerned, gazes play a specific role in the narrative of deception: they activate desire and allow the gazer to posit himself as her opposite and as the missing masculine complement to her femininity. Ariosto leaves Rinaldo with his eyes raised to Angelica's face and, following Angelica, continues his narrative.

A mere eight lines later, Angelica stumbles on another knight, identified as Ferraù. Ferraù is tired from the recent battle and, moved by a great desire for drink and rest, has stopped at a river (I.14). Still frightened from her last encounter, Angelica charges on this peaceful scene of repose, screaming as loudly as she can. Ferraù is at the moment intently searching for his helmet, which has fallen into the river, but Angelica's cries bring him rapidly back to shore. Once again, the gaze surfaces in Ariosto's lines: "A quella voce salta in su la riva / il Saracino, e nel viso la guata" (I.15.3–4). [The Saracen jumps to shore at that voice, and he peers at her face.] Ferraù recognizes Angelica, despite her exceptional state of alarm, and rushes to her aid. This he does, the narrator intimates, *both* because he is *cortese* [courteous] and because "n'avea forse / non men dei dui cugini il petto caldo" (I.16.1–2) [perhaps his heart burned no less for her than those of the two cousins].

The duel that ensues between Rinaldo and Ferraù marks, in Eugenio Donato's view, the efficacy in the poem of a triangular structure of desire, which first appeared in the rivalry between Orlando and Rinaldo in octave 8.[15] Put simply, each contender for Angelica—or any other object of desire, be it a sword, a helmet, or a woman—wants what he wants *because* it is desired by someone else. An object for which there are no competitors loses its appeal and is desired by no one, for desire must be mediated through others. The paradigm of mimetic desire, however, has substantial limitations for interpretation of the *Furioso*. It is evidently gender bound, for it functions only with the male characters. It does not account for Bradamante's love for Ruggiero, even though she becomes jealous of Marfisa for a time. Nor does it find verification in the passions of Ginevra, Dalinda, Alcina, Olimpia, Isabella, Doralice, or Angelica herself.[16]

Angelica's position in the crisscrossing fields of male desire in the *Orlando furioso* depends in a substantial way on the mediation Donato describes. A more nuanced picture of her special role as prize emerges, however, when we also consider a dynamic of desire that is not triangular but rather circular and specular. French psychoanalyst Jacques Lacan posits just such a pattern in the process of human self-differentiation that gives rise to individual subjectivity and gender identity.[17] I invoked Lacan's theoretical fable of the "mirror stage" in chapter 1 to illustrate a ritual reinforcement of rules for feminine conduct in a culture predicated on female chastity and tolerant of male license. By positing polarized views of chaste and unchaste women, I argued, the *palio* symbolically locked women into one of only two possible moral positions, projecting and reinforcing these two positions on the stage of public spectacle. At the same time, the festival illustrated—

even dramatized—for men a more differentiated range of subject positions as the judges, recipients, and reinforcers of women's social and sexual behavior. Of interest to me in chapter 1 was the function of the gaze as an external corroboration of individual identity, the inescapable fact that we are defined not by ourselves but by constant interaction between the self each of us projects and the selves projected for us by others who, in turn, are engaged in their own projections of identity and desire.

In this chapter, I shall return in more detail to Lacan's model of the subject's entry into desire and human relations. Here my interest will be in his exploration of the *failed* articulations between subjects that may result from reductive and impoverished assumptions of gendered positions in desire. Lacan offers a highly schematic notion of traditional male desire that fits Ariosto's characters extremely well: no great surprise, given that this structure of desire derives from medieval models of "courtly" or "romantic" love, the broad outlines of which are current even today.[18] By acknowledging the presumed absence of feminine desire on which such models are predicated, however, Lacan's insights prompt us to question gender's foundation in social practices rather than in nature. These questions in turn may inform our study of all assertions about the feminine "essence," including the extravagant claims we find in the sixteenth-century *querelle de femmes*.

In her refusal to be captured in the flattened projections of womanhood offered by the knights who desire her, Angelica joins Bradamante in enacting more complex versions of human—and particularly feminine—character and desire. Since these versions remain largely elided by the binary schemes evident in courtly love, we are compelled to see these female characters' roles as questioning, even breaking down, those schemes themselves. In Angelica's movement through the poem, furthermore, we see how Ariosto intertwines two related but distinct forms of errancy: her diegetic "spatial" errancy, as she races in panicked flight through the woods or walks in circles around her would-be captors; and her generic "textual" errancy, which makes her an exemplary character within the proliferating story-system of romance.

I am less concerned here with the intricacies of Lacan's theories than with a rather straightforward staging of his models as heuristic devices for approaching the thematics of desire and frustration we find in romance texts. I begin with a short outline of Lacan's "mirror stage" narrative, to which I referred briefly in chapter 1. The remainder of this chapter traces in quite linear fashion the movements of Angelica through the *Furioso* as she appears and disappears to haunt the fantasies of the poem's male knights: as she flees, cries, speaks, nurses, loves, and flees again. My aim, in choosing this simple approach to the most elusive character of Ariosto's narrative, is precisely to track her errancy as any reader does in a beginning-to-end encounter with the *Furioso*'s interlaced structure, and to reassemble Angelica's many interrupted appearances for consideration of her role in the poem as a whole.

According to Lacan, the subject's entry into the Symbolic order (the realm of language, rules, and social interaction) carries with it, by definition, a sense of privation. Lacan argues that the infant in its first human relationship perceives its mother as a continuation of itself and thus enjoys an illusion of self-sufficiency and plenitude. This dyadic relationship, however, is interrupted when the child experiences the mother's absence as the bidding of a superior third party (Lacan's "phallic signifier" or "paternal metaphor"). The persistence of the dyad as an ideal to which the subject desires to return constitutes the undergirding psychic structure that Lacan calls the Imaginary. At the same time, the child enters into what Lacan terms the "mirror stage." This name refers to the moment of self-recognition in, and differentiation from, the image the child sees in the mirror. At once the child gains a coherent image of its own body *and* experiences that image as something outside of and different from its body. In Lacan's ideal, hypothetical narrative, these two simultaneous moments of the mirror experience ground a fundamental split in the subject. The same process that allows the subject to recognize and "appropriate" itself as a unified whole also requires that this unified self be possessed only *as an image,* a sign of the self.

The rupture intensifies when language becomes the necessary tool for communicating the child's needs and desires. In language acquisition the child enters a matrix of signs (an agreement about what words and behavior mean) that exists prior to any individual subject. This entry into sign use deepens the split between the dyadic, specular, idealized image of the self and the fragmented, overdetermined, contradictory self as defined by the discourse of others. These three events (the interruption of the perceived plenitude of the mother-child dyad, the splitting of the subject's self-image, and the entrance into the sign system of language) mark the subject's entry into the Symbolic and establish the dyadic constructions of the Imaginary *within* the Symbolic as sets of coded oppositions.

In Lacan's view (as in Freud's), human beings are forever wanting; they constantly seek to restore the lost illusion of plenitude once enjoyed in the infant-mother relationship. This striving for some object that will restore plenitude necessarily includes a sense that human fulfillment may lie beyond the realm of the speakable: in God, the sublime, or romantic love. In a Symbolic order in which history and discourse have been officially male spheres, woman is defined from a male perspective: as a universal symbol for lost plenitude and thus for the promise of renewed completeness. Woman, the ideal, is constructed in language (and thus in our historical world) as an absolute category: in her resemblance to that first, other being (usually the mother), she comes to symbolize the Other who may restore imagined completeness of being. But this return to a prelapsarian state prior to alienation in the community of other speaking beings is impossible. So too, then, is the "promise" of woman. "Woman" as sign is ultimately the sign of the impossibility of full recuperation of alienated being. An irreconcilable opposition in itself, the traditional conception of "womanhood" is thus a thoroughly ambivalent one.[19]

Within this scheme, the gaze, the act of looking on a desired object and feeling oneself projected in another's theater of vision, is a *space* in which a specular relation allows the subject to constitute its sense of "being there." The gazing subject enters a dialectic in which it annihilates the otherness of an other and absorbs the other into itself, positing the hoped-for "return" of plenitude.[20] This plenitude, however, is also predicated on the subject's perception of itself within the field of another's vision: the sense of being seen. Angelica functions for each of her would-be seducers in the *Orlando furioso* as a figure of womanliness in relation to which each reaffirms his own being as a desiring subject.[21] Like that other feminine Renaissance ideal, Baldessare Castiglione's palace lady, Angelica functions as the vehicle through which images of the male self, as her missing complement, are reflected back for self-recognition and gratification.[22] Moreover, the image returned to each desirous knight in this specular exchange posits the gazer's imagined possession of Angelica. At the same time her alterity is recognized, possession of her is established as an attribute of the gazing subject.[23] Each knight desires a connection with and an appropriation of his complementary term in an ideal human dyad.

While Rinaldo and Ferraù engage in a "crudel battaglia" over who will win her, Angelica again retreats from the scene of their competitive desires:

> Or, mentre l'un con l'altro si travaglia,
> bisogna al palafren che 'l passo studi;
> che quanto può menar de le calcagna,
> colei lo caccia al bosco e alla campagna. (I.17.5–8)

> [Now, while the one labors with the other,
> the palfrey must quicken its step,
> for the lady chases with him to the woods and the country
> as fast as her heels can make him go.]

Integral to Lacan's structural scheme as well as Ariosto's are the elements of escape and repetition. As the object of total mystification, woman always remains beyond comprehension, beyond the grasp. The movement toward appropriation of the feminine is therefore doomed to continuous repetition.

On noticing Angelica's absence, the two knights agree to a truce that prompts the narrator's ironic exclamation on their improbable courtesy, "Oh gran bontà de' cavallieri antiqui!" (I.22.1) [Oh great goodness of the knights of yore!] They join forces to track their lost prize until they reach a crossroads and their paths (and Ariosto's narrative design) part for separate adventures. At octave 32 Ariosto leaves off telling of Rinaldo and Ferraù and picks up the narrative thread of Angelica, who is still in flight. The next nineteen lines evoke the terror of Angelica's directionless escape:

> ma seguitiamo Angelica che fugge.
> Fugge tra selve spaventose e scure
> per lochi inabitati, ermi e selvaggi.
> Il mover de le frondi e di verzure,
> che di cerri sentia, d'olmi e di faggi,
> fatto le avea con subite paure
> trovar di qua di là strani viaggi,

ch'ad ogni ombra veduta o in monte o in valle
temea Rinaldo aver sempre alle spalle.

Qual pargoletta o damma o capriuola,
che tra le fronde del natio boschetto
alla madre veduta abbia la gola
stringer dal pardo, o aprirle 'l fianco o 'l petto
di selva in selva dal crudel s'invola,
e di paura triema e di sospetto;
ad ogni sterpo che passando tocca,
esser si crede all'empia fera in bocca.

Quel dì e la notte e mezzo l'altro giorno
s'andò aggirando, e non sapeva dove. (I.32.8–35.2)

[But let us follow Angelica, who flees.
She flees through frightful and dark woods,
through deserted, desolate, and wild places.
The stirring of the fronds and of the greenery
of elms, beeches, and rowans that she hears
makes her take strange paths here and there in sudden terror;
for with every shadow seen in hill or valley,
she feared she had Rinaldo at her heels.

Just as the baby fawn or the roe deer
who, among the fronds of its native woods,
has seen its mother's throat crushed by
the leopard or seen her sides or chest torn open,
takes flight from one wood to another away from the wicked one,
and trembles in fright and distrust
at every twig it touches passing,
and believes it has landed in the mouth of the pitiless beast.

That day and night and half of the next day,
she kept circling, and she knew not whither.]

With this assumption of Angelica's perspective as she runs, frightened, through unmarked forest, Ariosto darkens the tone and changes the stakes in an otherwise mischievous series of evasions.[24] The imagery of octave 34, as distinct from that of the preceding lines, is not playful but archetypally terrifying; its evocation of violence and paranoia dispels the smiles evoked by cardboard knights clashing over missing paper-doll spoils.

The *locus amoenus* where Angelica finally stops to rest is, as Peter De Sa Wiggins notes, void of light, and it therefore shields Angelica from not only the eye of the sun but all eyes.[25] Here she falls asleep in peaceful darkness. Soon, though, she is awakened by the heavy footsteps of yet another knight in armor. From her sanctuary in the darkness, Angelica is now able to look on her possible enemy while remaining herself unseen. This perspective, which she will assume again later in the poem, allows her the privilege of viewing herself through the projected gazes of those who, desiring her, efface her desire and thus her own perspective and gaze.

The knight, Sacripante, sits down by a stream and begins to lament that by now Angelica must have been claimed by someone else:

> Che debbo far, poi ch'io son giunto tardi,
> e ch'altri a corre il frutto è andato prima?
> a pena avuto io n'ho parole e sguardi,
> et altri n'ha tutta la spoglia opima. (I.41.3–6)

> [What am I to do, since I've arrived late
> and someone else has gone and culled the fruit before me?
> I barely got words and glances,
> and someone else got all the royal spoils.]

Sacripante's rendition of Catullus's metaphor (LXII.39–47: "Ut flos in saeptis secretus") compares the virgin maiden to a rose, which loses all its beauty and value once it is plucked from the stem (I.42–43). These octaves are often glossed for their harmony or for the psychological depth of Ariosto's recognition that beauty and love are vulnerable to the violence of passion.[26] Such readings deserve to be shaken back to attention, however, by a polite cough from Angelica, hiding in the thicket. Ariosto has expressly set Sacripante's figure and monologue within the frame of Angelica's peering eyes. It is from an ironic, feminine perspective that the scene is cast. Angelica's presence on this scene, after the terror of her two-day flight from characters just like Sacripante, provides a viewpoint from which not only the incongruity of comparisons (however lyrical) between female bodies and perishable goods, but also the cruel self-absorption of the knights' chase games becomes immediately evident.

Angelica, nonetheless, understands her role in the drama of courtly love, and she recites it with ease. The narrator remarks, perhaps with disappointment, that Angelica has no pity for this knight; she has heard his cries before (in the *Orlando innamorato,* I.xi). But she must get back home somehow, and her recent attempts to foil the desires of so many knights have proven the impracticality of taking off on her own again. The narrator describes Angelica's disinterest in Sacripante's charms as "sdegno" [disdain] and her creation of a strategic plan as "finzione" and "inganno" [fiction and deceit]. His own identification with frustrated lovers, however, may account for this sudden lack of sympathy for a character he described only sixteen octaves before as a helpless victim.[27]

With a full awareness that her appearance is a feast for the eyes of the love-smitten knight, Angelica steps out of the thicket and into her role as coveted prize:

> E fuor di quel cespuglio oscuro e cieco
> fa di sé bella et improvvisa mostra,
> come di selva o fuor d'ombroso speco
> Diana in scena o Citerea si mostra. (I.52.1–4)

> [And out from that dark, blind bush
> she made a beautiful and sudden show of herself,
> as Diana or Venus do when they come out
> on stage from a wood or cave.]

Angelica here dons a conventionalized mask and enters in a theatrical fashion made explicit by the terms *scena* [stage] and *mostra* [show, exhibit].[28] Moreover, in this conscious moment of self-presentation, the poet compares her to two extreme and opposite examples of female sexuality: the goddesses of chastity and love. This feminine role-playing is not wasted on Sacripante; the entire next octave develops this imagery of blindness and vision, likening the knight's gaze on Angelica to that of a mother finding alive a soldier son she had mourned as dead.[29]

The seeming plenitude of the mother-child reciprocal gaze is in fact central to the characterization of Angelica's function for the knights who strive to possess her. In her they intuit the promise of a satisfaction that continuously escapes them, depriving them of a completeness that Orlando will later say could have "placed [him] among the gods" (VIII.77).[30] As each knight looks on her, he seems to recognize not only Angelica as his complementary opposite, but also himself as a being who derives his psychic and social identity from his connection with her.

The close of canto I brings back Rinaldo. Sacripante has just been knocked from his horse by Bradamante and is receiving Angelica's consolation when Baiardo, Rinaldo's horse, wanders onto the scene and recognizes the princess from Cathay.[31] Rinaldo enters the thicket where Sacripante is being comforted, looks on Angelica, and ignites with desire: "come vide il cavallo e conobbe esso, / e riconobbe l'angelica faccia / che l'amoroso incendio in cor gli ha messo" (I.81.4–6). [When he saw the horse and recognized it, he also recognized the angelic face that put an amorous fire in his heart.]

For the rest of her existence in the poem, Angelica remains the cipher of a femininity that resides in the eye of male desire. Her moments of autonomous action occur only when she recedes from the gaze in flight, or becomes completely invisible by virtue of magic. When Orlando discovers that she has acted from autonomous desire, outside the circle of his self-defining gaze, the result will not be the sublime speechlessness of the gazes in canto I, but the disintegration of Orlando as subject, his regression from language, and his descent into madness. As for Angelica, her desire remains nearly as unrepresentable after her declaration of love for Medoro as before she met him. Having no place for this unforeseen subjectivity of Woman, the poem will relegate the narration of Angelica's life after love to other texts, in poems to be written by others (XXX.16–17).[32]

While Rinaldo and Sacripante exchange verbal injuries, Angelica's first action in canto II again repeats her movement in canto I. She flees from the litigious rivals but immediately encounters a new contender for her beauty. The hermit she meets at first appears a devout fellow, "di coscienza scrupolosa e schiva" (II.13.4) [of scrupulous and retreating spirit]. While his gaze appears to register a charity that distinguishes him from the knights, however, his conscience exerts a different force. As Emilio Bigi notes in his gloss of these lines, Ariosto here plays on the double sense of *coscienza,* which in Renaissance parlance functioned for both moral and obscene references:[33]

> parea, più ch'alcun fosse mai stato
> di coscienza scrupolosa e schiva.
> Come egli vide il viso delicato
> de la donzella che sopra gli arriva,
> debil quantunque e mal gagliarda fosse,
> tutta per carità se gli commosse. (II.13.5–8)

> [he seemed more scrupulous and retreating in conscience
> than anyone has ever been.
> As soon as he saw the delicate face
> of the damsel who was coming upon him,
> weak and timid as that organ was,
> it stirred him to compassion.]

The hermit avails Angelica by using a magic book to conjure a spirit, which he commands to set Rinaldo and Sacripante off the track with false information regarding Angelica's whereabouts. At this point, the poem follows the two knights' stories and narrates other adventures for several cantos. When, in canto VIII, Angelica's plot line reemerges, the patient hermit's real motives in helping Angelica also come to the fore:

> ma l'eremita a bada la tenea
> perché di star con lei piacere avea.
>
> Quella rara bellezza il cor gli accese,
> e gli scaldò le frigide medolle. (VIII.30.7–31.2)

> [but the hermit delayed her course
> because he took pleasure in being with her.
>
> That rare beauty ignited his heart
> and warmed his frigid marrow.]

His heart inflamed by the sight of Angelica, the hermit resorts to magic once again. He first injures her horse and then enchants it, rendering her departure impossible. No matter where she tries to go, the hermit's own desire holds sway and leads her to his chosen destination. When Angelica's horse ambles into the ocean despite her attempts to keep it ashore, a "lascivious little wind" is on hand to lift the skirt and loosened hair of the distressed maiden (VIII.35–36).

At octave 40 begins Angelica's thirty-eight-line complaint to Fortune on the difficulties of preserving a virtuous feminine reputation in an aggressive world. The water and the ridiculous posture in which Angelica is poised are perhaps responsible for the implicit tone of comic irony in many glosses on her monologue.[34] The sophistication of the lines resides, however, in the subtle mixture Ariosto manages to strike between authentic comedy and resigned pathos. If Angelica is Ariosto's figure for pure femininity in the poem, then it is significant that these are virtually the only words she utters in all forty-six cantos of the *Furioso*:[35]

> Dicea:—Fortuna, che più a far ti resta
> acciò di me ti sazii e ti disfami
> che dar ti posso omai più, se non questa
> misera vita? ma tu non la brami;
> ch'ora a trarla del mar sei stata presta,
> quando potea finir suoi giorni grami:
> perché ti parve di voler più ancora
> vedermi tormentar prima ch'io muora.
>
> Ma che mi possi nuocere non veggio,
> più di quel che sin qui nociuto m'hai.
> Per te cacciata son del real seggio,
> dove più ritornar non spero mai:
> ho perduto l'onor, ch'è stato peggio;
> che, se ben con effetto io non peccai,
> io do però materia ch'ognun dica
> ch'essendo vagabonda sia impudica.
>
> Ch'aver può donna al mondo più di buono,
> a cui la castità levata sia?
> Mi nuoce, ahimè! ch'io son giovane, e sono
> tenuta bella, o sia vero o bugia.

Già non ringrazio il ciel di questo dono;
che di qui nasce ogni ruina mia. (VIII.40–42.6)

[She said—Fortune, what more must you do with me
before you tire of torturing me?
What more can I give you, if not my
wretched life? But you don't want it;
just now you were quick to pull it from the sea,
when it could have ended its painful days;
you felt it more opportune to see me
suffer yet some more before I die.

But I can't see how you might hurt me
more than you already have.
On your account I've lost my royal throne
to which I have no hope of return:
I've lost my honor, which is even worse,
for though in effect I have not sinned
I give cause for everyone to say
I'm shameless for being a vagabond.

What further good could the world hold for a woman
who had lost her chastity?
It harms me, alas! that I am young and am
considered beautiful, be it true or false.
I give heaven no thanks for this gift;
for from it arises my every ruin.]

Angelica's lament, which has its roots in the threnodies of many a beautiful heroine of Greek romance, suggests that appreciation of the feminine ideal is a function of experience and perspective.[36] Though she remains an innocent maiden, her constant, necessary errancy has caused people to question her virtue; the beauty for which others regard her as fortunate is also a source of distress. Having lost her public honor, home, and family, she imitates her Greek counterparts and pleads now only for death.

Instead there reappears the hermit who led Angelica into this trap. When his advances are rejected, the hermit sprays a potion into her eyes that causes her to sleep. Angelica falls into a slumber that figuratively stresses her lack of autonomy by closing off her viewing faculties entirely: she is left invisible not to others but to herself. Ariosto's rascal hermit would be content to possess the simulacrum of the woman before him; but his attempt to rape Angelica as she sleeps fails in impotence. He falls asleep, unfulfilled, beside the object of his desire (VIII.49–50).

Angelica's survival is next threatened by a brutal custom initiated by the earlier rape of another woman. She and the hermit awake only to be captured by scouts from the Ebudans, a people who have instituted the custom of feeding virgin maidens to the sea orc. Long ago, the god Proteus molested the beautiful daughter of the Ebudan king and left her with child. The girl's father killed his daughter out of anger and shame, refusing to distinguish the girl's will from that of the god who took forceful possession of her. In vengeful response, Proteus launched a campaign of violence toward the village. The virgin sacrifices were instituted, on the advice of an oracle, to placate the enraged Proteus. Only the most beautiful maidens are acceptable feed for the monster, however, and Angelica's attractiveness to male eyes again places her in particular danger.

The narrator wryly echoes Angelica's earlier monologue with a bland understatement regarding this new melodrama: "Ben ch'esser donna sia in tutte le bande / danno e sciagura, quivi era pur grande" (VIII.58.7–8) ["Though being a woman is a misfortune and a disadvantage in every land, here it was especially severe]. Finally Angelica's beauty in the eyes of others is not only of no use to her but may, as she predicted, bring about her ruin through a literal, and not an amorous, devourment. Three times the narrator notes anaphorically the irony of Angelica's powerlessness despite her beauty, which exerts such force on her admirers:

> La gran beltà che fu da Sacripante
> posta inanzi al suo onore e al suo bel regno;
> la gran beltà ch'al gran signor d'Anglante
> macchiò la chiara fama e l'alto ingegno;
> la gran beltà che fe' tutto Levante
> sottosopra voltarsi e stare al segno
> ora non ha (così è rimasa sola)
> chi le dia aiuto pur d'una parola. (VIII.63)

[The great beauty that was placed by Sacripante
above his honor and his lovely kingdom;
the great beauty that stained the bright fame
and brilliant mind of the lord of Anglante;
the great beauty that turned all the West
upside down at her command
now is left so alone that she has no one
to offer her even a word of help.]

For a time, her loveliness wins the forebearance of the Ebudans (who *also*
enjoy looking at her), and Angelica is spared until the supply of other maidens runs out. Ariosto's narrator claims he is unable to endure the pain of
recounting what happens after Angelica is led in chains to the monster, so
he interrupts the story at this point.

Orlando, meanwhile, tosses in his bed, unable to sleep for thoughts of
Angelica. Fantasies of his missed opportunity to possess her plague him and
bring him to curse his loyalty to his king as the cause of losing her. It is for
Orlando that Angelica most fully functions as Lacan's *objet petit a,* the lost
object that generates the fantasy of an absolute fulfillment:[37]

Dove, speranza mia dove ora sei?
vai tu soletta forse ancor errando?
o pur t'hanno trovata i lupi rei
senza la guardia del tuo fido Orlando?
e il fior ch'in ciel potea pormi fra i dei
il fior ch'intatto io mi venia serbando
per non turbarti, ohimè! l'animo casto,
ohimè! per forza avranno colto e guasto. (VIII.77, emphasis mine)

[Where, my hope, where are you now?
Do you perhaps wander all alone?
Or have the wicked wolves found you,
without the guard of your loyal Orlando?
And the flower that could have placed me among the gods,
the flower that I kept saving for myself,
not to upset, ah, me! your chaste soul, ah, me!
of course they will have gathered it and spoiled it.]

Orlando's attribution to Angelica of the capacity to place him "among the gods" reiterates her function as the imagined promise of a plenitude that surpasses available human experience.[38] The fabricated, fantastic nature of this courtly feminine function has already been indicated, in part, by Angelica's monologue in octaves 40–44, which provided a less glamorous view of the erotic quest from her perspective. For Orlando, caught in the specular dynamic of the search for self-completion, Angelica's perspective (and thus her desire and personhood) are largely elided from view. Nonetheless, until now he has preserved at least some ties to the order of social rules and practices that prevented him from "upsetting" Angelica by ignoring her will completely and dedicating himself fully to his own pleasure.

After a dream in which he seeks, unsuccessfully, the image of her face and eyes, and in which a voice foretells that he shall never enjoy Angelica again on earth, Orlando wakes up, disguises himself as an Arab, and sets out to search for her again (VIII.80–83). Orlando's disguise, like his later abandonment of the search for Mandricardo, indicates his rejection of the Symbolic order of chivalric rules and his submission to an ideal of the Imaginary. His impersonation of another binary opposite to him within that order (the Arab) begins to signal as well the crumbling of the values such dichotomies support.

Angelica, in the meantime, has been tied, nude, to a rock by the Ebudans and awaits consumption by the monster. Ruggiero, who has recently become the master of the winged hippogriff, spots Angelica from his superior vantage point in the sky and descends to get a better look. But for her tears, which Ruggiero recognizes as real, she resembles an alabaster statue. As these rivulets run down her cheeks and breasts and as her hair moves in the wind, Ruggiero fixes his eyes on hers:

> E come ne' begli occhi gli occhi affisse,
> de la sua Bradamante gli sovenne.
> Pietade e amore a un tempo lo trafisse,
> e di piangere a pena si ritenne. (X.97.1–4)

> [And as in her beautiful eyes he fixed his own,
> he remembered his Bradamante.
> Pity and love transfixed him at once,
> and he could barely hold back his tears.]

Ruggiero's first response on seeing Angelica also elides the presence of her gaze as subject, but in a different way from the other knights met thus far. Her body resembles an alabaster statue and thus becomes a kind of impersonal or blank screen onto which Ruggiero projects an introjected image of his own beloved, Bradamante. Angelica again represents womanliness in general and not a specific, desiring subject. Ruggiero takes pity on her and expresses his rage over the Ebudans' mistreatment of her beauty. Angelica's reply of shame for her nudity, however, like her monologue earlier in the canto, goes unheard. The sound of her voice is smothered by the emergence of the sea monster, which Ruggiero begins to battle. In octave 111 Angelica resumes her pleas for Ruggiero to untie her rather than leave her bound in the midst of this watery battle, and he, "commosso dunque al giusto grido" [moved then by her just cry], unties Angelica and carries her away on the hippogriff.

Like the hermit in canto VIII, once Ruggiero gets Angelica to himself, he discards the mask of chivalric service and ignores her refusals. They ride through the sky on the hippogriff's back, and "Ruggier si va volgendo, e mille baci / figge nel petto e negli occhi vivaci" (X.112.7–8) [Ruggiero keeps turning around, and he plants a thousand kisses in her breast and her lively eyes]. He looks for an attractive place to land and brings down the hippogriff in a secluded meadow. Before he can escape from his cumbersome armor and free himself for proper enjoyment of Angelica, however, she places in her mouth the magic ring he had given her to hold, and uses its power to make herself vanish.[39]

Armed with this new weapon, Angelica in subsequent episodes will enjoy a privilege similar to the one she exercised in canto I, where she viewed Sacripante without being seen herself. For his part, Ruggiero is unable to acknowledge a desire that does not originate in his own. He calls Angelica "ingrata" (perhaps referring to the payment he expected for saving her life) and wanders through the thicket embracing the empty air of his objectless, blinded gaze:

> lo scudo e il destrier snello
> e me ti dono, e come vuoi mi spendi;
> sol che 'l bel viso tuo non mi nascondi.
> Io so, crudel, che m'odi, e non rispondi—

Così dicendo, intorno alla fontana
brancolando n'andava come cieco.
Oh quante volte abbracciò l'aria vana,
sperando la donzella abbracciar seco! (XI.8.5–9.4)

[my shield and my sleek steed
and myself I'll give you, and you can spend me as you like;
only do not hide your lovely face from me.
I know you hear me, cruel one, and you don't answer—

Speaking thus, he went around the fountain
groping like a blind man.
Oh, how many times he embraced the empty air,
hoping to draw the woman in his arms!]

Angelica again recedes in flight. Through the device of the ring, however, Ariosto effects a division of Angelica herself from the image the knights hold of her. This peeling away of the mask of Woman-as-Other gives her full control over her movements and enables Angelica's most autonomous actions in the poem. She stops at a shepherd's cave and dwells there, unseen, for a day. Then she dons the rags of a shepherd girl and sets out armed with both a disguise and the magic device of the ring (XI.11).

In canto XII she is still pondering how to get an escort home to India when she encounters not only all three of her pursuers from canto I, but also the simulacrum of herself. Angelica enters the castle where the wizard Atlante has imprisoned many of the knights met thus far in the poem. Each knight roams the halls of this enchanted place with a vision of his love object constantly before his eyes and sees nothing else. Angelica is invisible to the knights in her real person. She watches, however, as Orlando, Sacripante, and Ferraù pursue the imago Atlante has fabricated of her. Removed as they are from the worldly concerns Lacan locates in the psychic order of the Symbolic, the knights exist only in the regressive realm of primary narcissism. Each pursues Angelica oblivious to the gaze that constitutes her as subject; each orients instead to the nonseeing simulacrum that, in the space of the gaze, merely returns his own reflection. Ariosto has placed Angelica in the midst of a pattern of elisions, in contiguous relation to the Woman who is and is not she. He thus obtains a perfect illustration of the splitting away of woman's subjective gaze in the social construction of a feminine, ideal opposite and complement to male desire.

Thus freed from the projected, ideal simulacrum of herself, Angelica is able, as she was in canto I with Sacripante, to incorporate her own use of that image in the design of her own desire. As she observes them, she considers which of the knights would be the least troublesome guide for her voyage home. Orlando, she reflects, would be a better protector, but he would demand that she give herself to him in payment at the end of their journey. Sacripante, on the other hand, might be more easily discarded. Angelica removes the magic ring from her mouth to come into view as Sacripante passes. In doing so, however, she renders herself visible to Ferraù and all the knights. In addition, the ring, which performs as a truth charm if held in the hand, dissolves the entire spell that holds Atlante's castle in enchantment. In what Lacan might describe as an intrusion of the Real, all of the knights' projected images of Angelica fall away in the presence of the momentarily "unmediated" Angelica.[40] She immediately returns, however, to her status as ideal and universal complement to the knights' desires. Denied the ability both to be visible *and* to have her own desire recognized, she flees once again.

As if to reverse the pattern for emphasis, Ariosto presents Angelica remembering the ring's disguising properties as she runs away. She places the ring back in her mouth and vanishes before the eyes of her pursuers:

> Volgon pel bosco or quinci or quindi in fretta
> quelli scherniti la stupida faccia;
> come il cane talor, se gli è intercetta
> o lepre o volpe a cui dava la caccia,
> che d'improviso in qualche tana stretta
> o in folta macchia o in fosso si caccia.
> Di lor si ride Angelica proterva,
> che non è vista, e i lor progressi osserva. (XII.36)

> [They turn their shocked faces now here,
> now there in haste throughout the wood;
> like a dog when the hare or wolf it chases
> suddenly ducks into some narrow den
> or throws itself into a thicket or ravine.

The pitiless Angelica laughs at them,
unseen, and observes their progress.]

The hunting metaphor that always appears in Angelica's escapes heightens
the impersonal character of the chase. In this instance, moreover, it re-
duces the knights to the status of dogs working at an instinctive game.
Angelica's retraction from the field of their gazes, however, again furnishes
her autonomy, and she laughs from a superior vantage point at her hunters'
inability to find her (XII.36.7–8). So disoriented are they that as they move
forward to seek her on the only road in view, Angelica calmly proceeds
behind them, "con minor fretta" (XII.37.8) [in less haste].

A fight breaks out between Orlando and Sacripante and then another
between Orlando and Ferraù over Orlando's helmet. They hang the object of dispute on a tree and begin a duel while Sacripante sets out to
look for Angelica. Angelica herself has not left the scene, however; she
watches Orlando and Ferraù for a while and then, in a mischievous attempt
to stop their fighting, steals the helmet from its place and runs away with
it (XII.52–53). The two opponents attribute the deed to Sacripante and
commence a new chase for him. Meanwhile, Angelica stops to drink at a
stream and hangs the helmet on a nearby branch (XII.57). In order to drink
from the brook, Angelica evidently has removed the ring from her mouth.
Ferraù spots her just as she disappears again, having replaced the ring and
mounted her horse to ride away, invisible. Angelica eludes his gaze, but the
long desired helmet substitutes for her, at least momentarily:

> Armossene il pagano il capo e il collo;
> che non lasciò, pel duol ch'avea, di torlo;
> pel duol ch'avea di quella che gli sparve,
> come sparir soglion notturne larve. (XII.60.4–8)

> [The pagan armed his head and neck with it;
> despite the pain he felt he did not neglect to take it.
> The pain he felt for that one who disappeared before him
> like nocturnal ghosts are known to do.]

Though the world of combat and partisanship is an obvious source of satisfaction for the knights in the poem, it is also a world of strict rules and

self-discipline. In canto I the contiguous, and perhaps ambivalent, relation between military and erotic attractions for Ferraù was evident as he left off searching for his helmet in order to join the competition for Angelica. In canto XII, the helmet is revealed as only a partial fulfillment of the knight's desired self-image. As he dons this headwear, he turns his thoughts to the task of gaining full gratification:

> Poi ch'allacciato s'ha il buon elmo in testa,
> aviso gli è, che a *contentarsi a pieno,*
> sol ritrovare Angelica gli resta,
> che gli appar e dispar come baleno. (XII.61.1–4, emphasis mine)

> [Then once he has the good helmet strapped on his head,
> he realizes that to *satisfy himself fully*
> he only has to find Angelica,
> who appears and disappears before him like lightning.]

Angelica functions explicitly as the apparent promise of plenitude, the missing object that advances and recedes from a desirous gaze that seeks to complete the self. If canto I brought each knight into being in the poem through his visual contemplation of Angelica and initiated his love quest within the space of Ariosto's narrative, then canto XII turns inside out the same design to show that the direction of these gazes depends on the submersion of Angelica's own. Angelica thus exists, in the *Furioso,* as two irreconcilable halves. As a desiring subject she cannot be comprehended within the gazes of others, and thus resides outside the sphere of the visible; and when acknowledged by others she is denied the terrain of desire as a subject, absorbed instead in the self-projecting gazes of men. As her ring makes abundantly clear, Angelica's materialization (as object) paradoxically triggers her eclipse (as subject).

The one relationship that fuses these two halves of Angelica as feminine Other will also carry her beyond representation for Ariosto's narrator, who will assign to later poems the task of finishing Angelica's story (XXX.16–17). The poem returns to Angelica in canto XIX. In canto XII the narrative had broken off from Angelica's story just as she had come upon a youth lying wounded in the woods between two dead companions. Since, in a typical twist of Ariosto's technique of *entrelacement,* the events that brought the youth to his present state have not yet been recounted, the story must double back at this point to bring the other threads of the narrative into the design. Thus Angelica remains poised, significantly, *looking* on this youth for six cantos.

Canto XIX loops back the narrative to dilate on and relate in detail this moment of encounter. Angelica has most recently been reflecting on her relations with the rival knights and, with great disdain, registers particular regret for her past love of Rinaldo. Love himself hears her haughtiness and in response takes aim with his arrow just as Angelica looks on Medoro. The arrow finds its target and takes immediate effect:

> insolita pietade in mezzo al petto
> si sentì entrar per disuse porte
> che le fe' il duro cor tenero e molle,
> e più, quando il suo caso egli narrolle. (XIX.20.4–8)

> [an uncustomary pity enters the center of her breast
> through unfamiliar doors;
> it made her hard heart tender and soft,
> all the more when he told her his story.]

The youth, Medoro, recounts the story found in cantos XVIII and XIX, in which Medoro and his friend Cloridano seek unsuccessfully to give their magnificent king, Dardinello, a proper burial after his death in battle. Eduardo Saccone has argued persuasively that far from being a generic, common soldier—a nobody whom Angelica loves by pure chance—Medoro functions in the poem as an exemplar of the highest virtue attainable by characters in Ariosto's projected world: loyalty.[41] Refusing to abandon his king's body even when threatened by enemy soldiers, he has suffered their attack and now lies wounded from the skirmish, a violence that left Cloridano dead beside him.

This unique instance of being told a story has an extraordinary effect on Angelica, and in her growing attachment to the youth she uses her knowledge of medicine to tend Medoro's wounds. She finds a shepherd to assist in the burial of Dardinello and Cloridano; then Angelica and Medoro stay some days with the shepherd while Medoro convalesces. As Medoro's wounds heal, those left in Angelica's heart by Love's arrow only deepen and grow more painful. In a variation on the medieval and Renaissance lyric traditions of love, Angelica's passage from the object to the subject position in desire takes place through her reception of Medoro's gaze:

> Assai più larga piaga e più profonda
> nel cor sentì da non veduto strale,
> che da' begli occhi e da la testa bionda
> di Medoro aventò l'Arcier c'ha l'ale. (XIX.28.1–4)

> [She felt a much broader and deeper wound in
> her heart from the unseen arrow, which the
> winged Archer launched from the beautiful eyes
> and the blond head of Medoro.]

The play of words, wounds, and gazes between the two lovers (in which Medoro even comes physically to resemble and thus mirror Angelica) suggests a reciprocal, back-and-forth exchange of the subject and object positions in desire. Lacan refers to the eyes of another person as the only place that disallows the self-reflection of the gazer; they paradoxically cut the circular space that allows the subject to posit its sense of "being seen" and complemented.[42] The totality of the self is *wounded,* but through this wound comes the possibility of exchange with the world. Angelica, as a woman, is marked by her anatomy as a being who is "cut." Medoro's wound, however, becomes the displaced mark of her desire. It is this wound that occasions her falling in love with him, in a free exchange of glances and words. Angelica soon appropriates the discourse of love and declares her desire to Medoro, amidst the narrator's cries of regret for all the men who have idealized her in the past. Angelica's declaration of love brings her down from the pedestal on which, if we may believe her monologue of canto VIII, she never wished to stand. Though her new, more fully human status in desire brings pain, it also grants her pleasure when Medoro returns her love. Not overly concerned with social protocol, they consummate their love and marry afterward, "per onestar la cosa" [to make the thing respectable]. Angelica's gaze is now the active look of an intensely desiring subject:

Più lunge non vedea del giovinetto
la donna, né di lui potea saziarsi;
né per mai sempre pendergli dal collo,
il suo desir sentia di lui satollo. (XIX.34.4–8)

[The woman could not see beyond the youth,
nor could she have enough of him;
nor for all her hanging on his neck in embrace
was her desire ever quenched.]

The cutting motif returns in an insistence of the letter as the couple inscribes their names together on trees and on the walls of their bedroom, asserting visible signs of their union wherever they go:

Fra piacer tanti, ovunque un arbor dritto
vedesse ombrare o fonte o rivo puro,
v'avea spillo o coltel subito fitto;
così, se v'era alcun sasso men duro:
et era fuori in mille luoghi scritto,
e così in casa in altritanti il muro,
Angelica e Medoro, in varii modi
legati insieme di diversi nodi. (XIX.36)

[Among their many pleasures, wherever a straight tree
could be seen giving shade to a fount or a pure stream,
a pin or knife was immediately fixed.
The same if there was some stone that was not hard.
And outside was written in a thousand places,
and in as many in the house, on the wall,
"Angelica and Medoro" in various ways
tied together by different knots.]

Before leaving the shepherd who has so hospitably shared his dwelling with them, the couple presents him with a bracelet belonging to Angelica as a token of their gratitude. They then begin to make their way back to India, following the coast. Before they arrive in Spain, where they hope to find passage on a ship, they encounter a madman.

This madman is, of course, Orlando. Canto XXIII, the center canto of the *Furioso,* relates the events that have brought him to this state. While searching for Angelica, the weary Orlando stops to rest in a wood. As he looks about, he notices handwriting on the surrounding trees; he feels certain the texts are inscribed in Angelica's hand:

> Angelica e Medor con cento nodi
> legati insieme, e in cento lochi vede.
> Quante lettere son, tanti son chiodi
> coi quali Amore il cor gli punge e fiede.
> Va col pensier cercando in mille modi
> non creder quel ch'al suo dispetto crede:
> ch'altra Angelica sia creder si sforza,
> ch'abbia scritto il suo nome in quella scorza. (XXIII.103)

> [He sees Angelica and Medoro tied together
> in a hundred knots and in a hundred places.
> The letters are as many nails,
> with which Love pierces and wounds his heart.
> His thoughts race, looking for a thousand ways
> not to believe what he believes in spite of himself:
> He strains to think that it must be another Angelica
> who has written her name on that bark.]

The letters carved into the trees now cut into Orlando's circular gaze. His confrontation with the inscriptions is an encounter with the Symbolic realm of language, but also with Angelica's wayward desire.[43] Their encounter functions thus as an interruption of the constant motion of desire and absence that has fueled his specular pursuit of the exotic princess from the beginning. It bears recalling that Orlando, as the most respected, wise, and illustrious of knights, exemplified, before his love for Angelica, a kind of mastery of the Symbolic. By abandoning Carlo and even dressing in the garb of the enemy, Orlando had forsaken the responsibilities of that order, escaped from its interdictions and his own relation to them, and sought exclusively the satisfactions of what Lacan calls the Imaginary. To be sure, the dyadic ideals of the Imaginary exist *within* the Symbolic order, but their dialectic relation with the rules and social constraints of the Symbolic (Freud's pleasure and reality principles) guarantees the tension that constitutes the perpetuation of human desire. Orlando's abandonment of his responsibilities in order to pursue Angelica may thus be seen as a regression from the dialectic of identity and difference in the specular relation of the gaze and a fall back into the Imaginary's exclusively dyadic terms.

Orlando leaves his duties behind to seek satisfaction in Angelica's image. Thus he "possesses" Angelica only in the Imaginary's dyadic terms. His encounter with the writing on the trees is an intrusion of the Symbolic order he has left behind inasmuch as the writing testifies to Angelica's alterity *and* to her desire. It also forces him to acknowledge the intrusion of Medoro as a third variable to interrupt the dyadic fantasy of fulfillment. Orlando's several attempts to misread the signs Angelica has left thus constitute a nearly hallucinatory work of the Imaginary to deny her difference in desire. These attempts to ignore the letter's breakage of the specular circle include the convictions that the name and the handwriting belong to a *different* Angelica and not his own (XXIII.103), that Medoro could be another name for Orlando himself (XXIII.104), and that someone is seeking to defame Angelica by misrepresenting her (XXIII.114).⁴⁴

When he takes up lodging with the same shepherd who hosted Angelica and Medoro on their honeymoon, Orlando hears the story of their love in the shepherd's words as well. The host produces the bracelet Angelica left with him, and Orlando recognizes it as one he himself had given Angelica as a gift. Orlando finally acknowledges that he has lost Angelica and, once in his bedroom, begins to cry.

> Poi ch'allargare il freno al dolor puote
> (che resta solo e senza altrui rispetto)
> giù dagli occhi rigando per le gote
> sparge un fiume di lacrime sul petto:
> sospira e geme, e va con spesse ruote
> di qua di là tutto cercando il letto;
> e più duro ch'un sasso, e più pungente
> che se fosse d'urtica, se lo sente. (XXIII.122)

> [Then when he could loosen the hold on his pain
> (as he was left alone and needed not mind the others)
> down from his eyes and trailing from his cheeks

there spread a river of tears across his chest:
He sighs and moans, and moves on heavy foot
here and there, looking for his bed.
And harder than a rock it feels to him,
and more prickly than if it were made of nettles.]

The shepherd's story appears in ironic symmetry to the story told by Medoro to Angelica. Each storyteller wounds his listener, but with opposite results: in one case the construction of desire; in the other, its unwinding. Even in bed Orlando cannot escape the newfound truth. The bed the shepherd gives him is the same one Angelica and Medoro shared, and Orlando painfully discovers their inscriptions of love on the walls beside it, despite the darkness. Orlando's cries present an ironic mirror of the *jouissance* he desired from Woman, which instead became the sexual pleasure of a very human Angelica in this same room. In desperation he leaves the house to roam the countryside.

Orlando's initial reaction to the realization of his loss is cast as mourning: he first cries and shouts in anger: "Di pianger mai, mai di gridar non resta" (XXIII.125) [He never leaves off crying or shouting]; and then in a kind of withdrawal of libido he lies silent and motionless for three days in a green meadow, staring up at the sky. The *successful* work of mourning, however, eventually strives to achieve a new contract of signs that allows the reconstruction of the self and a return to the Symbolic order.[45] Orlando's inability to mourn his loss in this way is testified by his complete refutation of the Symbolic order. He furthers his regression by taking revenge on that which precipitated his loss, language (and more specifically the mystifications of lyric poetry), by tearing up the trees in the forest in order to destroy the lovers' words. Moreover, Orlando's rejection of language is preceded by a refutation of himself as sign, and thus of all signs:

Non son, non sono io quel che paio in viso:
quel ch'era Orlando è morto et è sotterra;
la sua donna ingratissima l'ha ucciso:
sì, mancando di fè, gli ha fatto guerra. (XXIII.128.1–4)

[I am not, I am not the one I appear in face to be.
That one who was Orlando is dead and underground;

his ungrateful lady killed him:

thus, failing in faith, she made war on him.]

He takes the further path of shedding his armor, emblem of the elaborate social system of chivalry. Eventually he abandons even his clothing.[46] It is this figure whom Angelica and Medoro encounter on the beach. No longer recognizable as a human being, Orlando appears as a beast. The divine intervention necessary to bring him back to his senses and to his former eloquence in language will require that he be harnessed, chained, tied, and fought by several paladins, in an image of the necessary binding of energy that entry into the Symbolic involves.

The story of Orlando's madness is a tale of dedication to the realm of absolutes.[47] Since it is in the order of such absolutes that Angelica exists as ideal, as Woman, Ariosto's exposure of the unreality of such categories appears as a rejection of absolute gender opposites that is consistent with his undermining of other dualistic notions in the poem. Angelica's love for Medoro verifies her own subjecthood and desire; but for Orlando, who has constructed himself in an exclusive specular opposition to her, the price of Angelica's humanity is his own. Orlando's fate thus suggests that absolute oppositions are based on a fragile illusion, the sudden shattering of which results in no mythical plenitude, but a pouring out of the subject into madness. Angelica, in her restless errancy, haunts the *Orlando furioso* as a dream of plenitude that continues to slip through the grasp of all who would have her as Woman.

3 Gender, Duality, and the Sacrifices of History: Bradamante in the *Orlando Furioso*

"*Pro bono malum,*" declares the lapidary maxim at the end of the *Orlando furioso*'s first edition: "Bad things for the good."[1] Read with the warrior-heroine Bradamante in mind, the motto provides suggestive keys for interpreting her location in the poem's political underpinnings. Bradamante's privileged place in the *Furioso* results from her destiny, in the fictive historical dimension of the poem, to found along with the young knight Ruggiero the family line of the poet's patron, Ippolito d'Este. This genealogical function, which extends her character's efficacy into a determinate historical present, distinguishes her from all the other women in the poem, whose actions are contained by the text's romance narrative structure, with its tireless proliferation of new adventures and plot twists.[2] Bradamante is, of course, woven into the poem by means of the same interlace technique that anchors Ariosto's other characters. But in distinction from their wandering and serpentine paths, her movements carry the poem toward its resolution rather than continuing the multiplication of narratives typical of romance. This same curtailing movement aims to shift the *Furioso*'s mode, for through Bradamante's eventual union with Ruggiero the poem jettisons its romance baggage and claims its epic link with the narrative of Italian history. Unlike Ruggiero, moreover, Bradamante learns her historical destiny early in the poem and seldom wavers from her mission to fulfill it. While Ruggiero dallies in Alcina's garden, she works with a rescue team to free him from enchantment; while he employs the hippogriff to liberate Angelica from the sea orc and then tries to seduce the exotic princess, she intensifies her efforts to free him. In short, Bradamante, more than any other character, keeps track of the latent epic "thread" in Ariosto's romance tapestry.

The poem's movement toward a connection with sixteenth-century Italy poses the problem of its articulation with contemporary models of the family and the state. In this context, Bradamante as a character must illustrate a division of labor that requires her to relinquish her activities as both warrior and public figure, for private life will be the sphere of most women in the projected future of the Italian courts, women's public skills notwithstanding. More important still for Ariosto's epic resolution of the poem is that Bradamante finally takes up this subordinate role in the realm of the *family,* for this finale brings together the generic and social issues she embodies in the poem: the lady knight-errant, along with the genre in which she flourished, must be given over to the epic's structures and its social interests. It bears recalling that the poem's resolution comes about in part through other family circumstances: Ruggiero need not betray a Muslim heritage to marry Bradamante because it is discovered that he already comes from a Christian family. The Saracen female warrior Marfisa is in the end not a threat to the dynastic couple's union because she turns out to be Ruggiero's twin sister. And finally, Bradamante's elder brother Rinaldo intervenes on her behalf with their father, Amone, to resolve the dilemma of Amone's having selected another groom for his daughter. The family thus functions as a hidden truth within which all the mysteries of romance may be resolved and explained.

Ariosto's linking of the family structure with the entrance of Bradamante into the heritage of Estense statehood echoes important parallels between Renaissance theorizations of the family and those of the early modern state. Bradamante's exceptional status as both wife and queen allows her to embody the analogy employed in Alberti's *Libri della famiglia* and used time and again by later humanists.[3] For example, Giacomo Lanteri, in a typical treatise on family economy, advises his wife: "Fa stima che questa nostra casa ad ambidui noi e alla nostra famiglia commune, sia una piccola Città . . . della quale io sia il capo che abbia suprema autorità. . . . Et che tu sia . . . il Castellano, ò sia Luogotenente" [Consider this house, shared by both of us and by our family, as a little city . . . of which I am the governor who has supreme authority, . . . and you are the Keeper of the manor, or rather my deputy].[4] If Bradamante's role at the end of the *Furioso* resembles that of this new courtly/bourgeoise wife, her excellence as warrior, rhetor, and lover earlier in the poem provide ample measure of all she has relinquished to enter the narrative of epic history. Given the contrasts between her two roles, relating Bradamante's early exploits to her place in the *Furioso*'s final cantos (and both of these to the future the text projects for her) must constitute a principal part of our task as readers of the poem's social and sexual politics.

Recent readers have regarded Bradamante's abandonment of her chivalric exploits and her marriage to Ruggiero as the poem's definitive endorsement of patriarchal power and masculine rule. Such readings implicitly harbor a conception of narrative resolution akin to that of Fredric Jameson, a conception that in my view is severely limited by its determinism. Narrative resolution—the "end" of any story—appears, in Jameson's treatment, to render all other narrative and poetic elements "unrealized" and significant only as symptoms of what the text seeks to control or master.[5] Thus in remarkably authoritarian fashion, closure emerges as the ultimate key to meaning. This theorization, as will become more apparent in my discussion of Bradamante's narrative in later sections of this chapter, appears to me quite antithetical to literature's aims and to its powers of figuration. To view the fate of Bradamante and Ruggiero as somehow exempt from the ambivalence that surrounds the *Furioso*'s resolutions of other moral and political issues would rob the poem's closure-resistant ending of its full participation in the epic genre.[6] On the contrary, as Susanne Wofford has argued, heroic poetry is open-ended by definition, even in the face of its asserted ideological closure.[7]

The *Orlando Furioso* explicitly foregrounds the conflicts between desire, morality, politics, and poetry that color all of the heroic epic tradition. The playful register of the popular romance octave, indeed, afforded the Ferrarese poet substantial latitude to register his criticisms, tucking them in as he could between melodic rhymes and swiftly moving multiple plots. Among Ariosto's most frequent targets for criticism are the brutalities of war, the patron-poet relationship, the fickleness of human commitments, and—not least among these—the oppression of women by men. As Albert Ascoli has noted, the *Furioso*'s rendering of poetic and political ambivalence characteristically resides in an ironic juxtaposition and *mutual* undercutting of critical and poetic claims, a relation that results in what Ascoli aptly terms "cotextual irony."[8] Most of these cotexts still resonate at the *Furioso*'s end, where a number of narrative threads left dangling prohibit a final neat sewing up of the poem's ideology—and in particular its gender arrangements.

Ruggiero's looming death and Bradamante's abrupt marginalization (he jousts on their wedding day while she watches from the sidelines) and her prophesied future as his violent avenger all restrict our ability to view this moment of formal closure as a harmonious "resolution" of the poem's narrative. On the contrary, I find here what Wofford identifies in other poems as "the uncomfortable poetic and ideological work" of bringing literary form to cohere with a programmatic heroic politics.[9] In the case of Bradamante, we are left with a woman warrior domesticated to cohere, at least in appearance, with the reigning views of progressive humanists who sought to formalize a properly benign role for educated and capable women in a male-governed society.[10] This particular feminine figure is nonetheless deeply implicated by her military past as an agent in the political violence on the horizon of Ferrara's future. Which of Bradamante's social spaces is preferable (the martial world or the domestic sphere) is a question the poem does not address; she appears, if anything, to draw those spheres into a single orbit. From her marginal position at the end of the *Furioso,* Bradamante looms among Ariosto's most provocative poetic creations—at least the earliest readers of this poem thought so.

Shortly after its publication in the final edition (1532) Ariosto's poem became the object of a protracted debate over its "canonicity."[11] Initially, the *Orlando furioso* seems to have irritated only its most fastidious readers. The author's choice of title (too confusing), his occasional use of non-Tuscan vocabulary (substandard), and his appropriation of materials from Boiardo's poem (unacknowledged and therefore suspect) all constituted violations of a new program of standardization well under way in the early Cinquecento.[12] Seizing on the rediscovery and translation of the *Poetics* into Latin in 1536, several important voices registered dismay at Ariosto's neglect of what they took to be Aristotle's prescriptions for poetic unity. After Tasso published his *Gerusalemme liberata* in 1581, these complaints mounted to a full-scale debate that often pitted Ariosto's and Tasso's texts against each other as contrasting models for heroic poetry in the Italian vernacular.[13] From the beginning, arguments over the genre of the *Orlando furioso* were linked with contemporary sensibilities regarding such broader questions as the "national" Italian identity, the proper interpretation of history, and the preferred distribution of power between the sexes.[14] Literature's ability to stage persuasive social discourse fed the convictions of critics determined to conserve or reject well-established models for characters and linear conceptions of narrative (both fictional and historical).

A great problem was that Ariosto's poem adopts *both* a more extreme centrifugal narrative structure than the interlace of earlier romances *and* a historicizing, epic argument, a double-voiced generic structure in which, I will argue, Bradamante plays a crucial role. The poem thus frustrated readers in search of epic narrative's purposeful development of plot while at the same time openly displaying that genre's claims for historical orientation. The result, ultimately, was a disquieting reflection on history and its ability to be represented coherently: history, the text seemed to imply, is not an orderly narrative but a swirl of escaping and interrupted episodes.[15] More bothersome still to some readers, the *Furioso* presents a wide array of characters male and female, humble and noble, Muslim and Christian, who do not conform with the conventional boundaries of their social stations. Both of these features—the poem's complication of linear narrative and its variety of characterization—severely inhibit formulaic interpretation. As an argument, on the contrary, the *Furioso* asserts the world's disheartening complexity, its irreducibility to any single, clearly presentable story or perspective.

The debates over the *Furioso* and its classification as epic or romance parallel other cultural controversies of the century in their open concern for social order. As they unfolded over the Cinquecento, in fact, the discussions of heroic poetry intersected with a number of other cultural controversies, including the contemporary *querelle des femmes*. These concerns are perhaps best illuminated by Mikhail Bakhtin's description of genres as not merely established forms but as environments or mediatory devices that allow meaning to emerge and permit readers particular "ways of perceiving."[16] Genres, he observes, are also by definition adaptable and capable of resuming —thus redefining—their past usage, much as Ariosto's text allows us to see differently the epic, romance, and lyric precedents it incorporates. In their encounter with both Ariosto's hybrid genre and his errant female warrior, conservative readers found themselves disoriented in a new textual environment, fearful of what meanings might be actualized as they moved through its passages. Of particular concern seem to have been the possible responses of female readers. The voice of Juan Luis Vives, for example, rings with alarm at the thought of women's imaginative wanderings through the suggestive fictional realm of romance. Vives disapproves of romance reading by any-one, male or female. Nevertheless, in the Cinquecento's most widely pub-lished humanist tract on women's education, Vives cautions against women's particular predilection for the genre, remarking of chivalric romances:

> And verily they be but foolish husbands and mad, that suffer their
> wives to wax more ungraciously subtle by reading of such books.
> . . . Therefore a woman should beware of all these books, like as of
> serpents or snakes. And if there be any woman that hath such de-
> light in these books, that she will not leave them out of her hands,
> she should not only be kept from them, but also, if she read good
> books with an ill will and loath thereto, her father and her friends
> should provide that she may be kept from all reading, and so by
> disuse, forget learning, if it can be done.[17]

Vives was not the only humanist who implicitly longed for the days when women had not yet gained access to literacy. Giovanni Michele Bruto's popular *Institutione di una fanciulla nata nobilmente* (1555) observes that it would be better to prevent girls' learning to read at all; but given that a daughter might acquire this skill on her own, the next best recourse was to limit strictly her access to literary texts. Romances, along with Boccaccio's tales, were in Bruto's opinion to be especially shunned.[18]

Sixteenth-century critics who argued over the status of the *Orlando furioso* were following a long tradition of sorting both literature and its audience into higher and lower ranks.[19] Just as Plato identified musical and literary genres he thought would cultivate civic virtues among the elite, so humanist educators recommended different types of literature for the nobility and for the middle class.[20] These they arranged into categories suited to rulers and subjects, children and adults, men and women. Alessandro de' Pazzi's translation in 1536 of Aristotle's *Poetics* provided these systematizers with a more schematized framework for emulating the classics in the higher realms of literary production.[21] Italy's political weakness and disarray were such, moreover, that cultural discussions of such matters as the character of a "national" literary culture carried inevitable symbolic weight.

Giraldi Cinzio's 1554 *Discorso intorno al comporre de i romanzi* features long passages arguing that Italian romances *parallel* but do not derive from the

Greco-Latin tradition: Giraldi wishes to legitimate a separate, independent, and equally prestigious history of vernacular romance literatures.[22] At the same time, he takes pains to erase any traces of *popular* origins for the romance, differentiating this genre from the "cantar di questi plebei, che con le loro cianze tendono le reti alle borse di chi gli ascolta" (7) [singing of these plebeians, whose idle chatter casts out a net to the purses of whoever listens to them]. He notes with evident dismay that the adventures of Orlando and Rinaldo are now so common that even the cobblers are given to recounting them ("già divenute sì volgari, che si danno a descriverle infino i Zabatai" [14]). And he warns his contemporaries to be careful when borrowing material from the ancients, so as not to offend the sensibilities of their modern readers. Casting his argument in terms of verisimilitude (or plausibility), he specifies, for example, that Homer's account of Princess Nausica going with her serving maids to wash clothes in the river could be offensive to a modern Italian audience because "al nostro tempo sarebbe disdicevole non dirò a figlia di signore, o di gentil'huomo, ma di semplice artigiano" (31) [in our time this would be improper, not only for the daughter of a lord, or of a gentleman, but of a simple tradesman].[23] If Giraldi's main concerns of decorum regard class and religious identifications,[24] several other theorists and critics paused to consider whether the romance offended modern sensibilities in its representation of women such as Bradamante and Marfisa.

Giraldi's pupil, Giovambattista Pigna, focuses at length in *I romanzi* (also published in 1554) on romance's claim to ties with documented historical narratives.[25] Evidently responding to criticisms of the genre, he explains how it is that romances can feature martial women among their characters without violating either ancient or modern rules of decorum. Conflating Aristotle's discussion of character portrayal in *Poetics* 1454a with passages in Horace's *Ars poetica* (cf. 119), Pigna submits that the romance remains in keeping with ancient standards of decorum, plausibility, and consistency of character. He illustrates his point with Aristotle's observation that "the character before us may be, say, manly; but it is not appropriate for a female character to be manly or clever."[26] Pigna amplifies at some length on Aristotle's example. Events represented in romance, he notes, must indeed observe several types of decorum, including those of *nature* and of *relation*. Things must appear believable:

[Per *natura*], come, che le donne pratiche non sieno del mondo.
Per *relatione;* come, che esse donne poco pratiche sieno à rispetto
dell'huomo: & à lato à un fanciullo assai esperte . . . percioche
porre coraggiose le donne indifferentemente da gli huomini è fuori
del relativo convenevole & del [convenevole] naturale; in quanto
che elle di complessione e di corpo fredde si trovano, & d'animo
pauroso. . . . essendo commune sentenza delli scrittori che alle
mogliere s'appartenga il governo delle cose di casa; & delle cose
di fuori à i mariti: e che l'armarsi & con soldati tramettersi ad esse
leverebbe la pudicitia, che è la loro principal virtù: & che quando
non la levasse, sospetto ne darebbe; che è quasi il medesimo. (33–
35, emphasis added)

[(By *nature*), for example, women are not adept at worldly skills;
and *in relative terms,* for example, these women should be less adept
than men, and in respect to a child they may be quite expert. . . .
Thus, depicting women as courageous with no differentiation from
men is outside the boundaries of the relative and the natural, inasmuch as women are of cold body and complexion, and fearful
of heart. For it is the common judgment of writers that women's
realm is the government of the house, and to men pertain the
things of the outside world; and that arming themselves and mix-
ing in with soldiers would deprive women of their modesty, which
is their primary virtue; and that if it did not do so, it would in any
case make their modesty suspect, which is almost the same thing.]

Pigna's aim, as subsequent passages reveal, is to establish a kind of historical plausibility for the appearance of female warriors such as Bradamante
in the romance. The force of his discussion, however, is also to assure that
such figures pose no threat to current cultural practices, precisely because
of their historical remoteness.

Drawing on the established tradition of scholastic writings about
women,[27] in the passage above Pigna allies Galenic medical theory with the
general authority of men to assure his readers that in most cases, representations of strong, martial women would be unrealistic and even perhaps
dangerous. These observations, a sort of *captatio benevolentiae* for readers who

may have objections to such characters, allow Pigna to present romance's women warriors as figures who are not generalizable representatives of their sex. Instead, he implies, they refer to specific, distant cultures and times; their presence in the romance in fact indicates that genre's historical verisimilitude. Pigna goes on in some detail to explain the derivation of these characters from precise historical models and to remind his readers that romance also features other types of women:

> Non tutte le donne fan gagliarde, ne à tutte dan carico di cavalleria, ma à quelle sole che ò per fama ò per autorità di libri esser armigere ritrovano. Da prima elle nelle battaglie traposte non erano: ma poi che nelle guerre di Spagna, che ottocento anni durarono, gli Arabi d'Africa le consorti & meretrici loro trassero, & lor diero il potere alla libera guerreggiare, molte molto honoratamente riuscendo mostraro, che le donne nelle cose ch'a far si pongono, non son niente da meno de gli huomini. & à poco à poco questo uso di far che le nobili signore tali fossero, chente hora nella Fiandra la Regina Maria[28] d'Austria veggiamo, nelle spagnuole infanti s'introdusse, & indi in Francia trapassò . . . à questo modo, per quanto ne paia, il primo & il secondo genere [the categories of decorum mentioned above: nature and relation] non si sono tralasciati. percioche ogni femina non è forte, ma le famose guerriere solamente. (35)

> [Not all women (in romances) are valiant, nor are all of them assigned knightly roles, but only those who either according to fame or according to the authority of books are known as warriors. In the beginning, women were not placed amidst battles. But once the Arabs of Africa brought their consorts and their prostitutes into the Spanish wars, which lasted eight hundred years, and gave them the power to combat freely, many women succeeded in showing most honorably that women are not at all inferior to men in whatever things they set out to do. And little by little this custom of assuring that noble ladies were such as we see in Flanders in Queen Maria of Austria was introduced also to Spanish royal children, whence the custom passed into France. . . . Hence as far as I

can see, romance does not neglect the first and second categories (of decorum). Because every female (in romance) is not strong, but only the famous warriors.]

The establishment of decorous norms for literary representation, in this and in the other examples, develops as an explicitly contemporary social question. A major concern for Pigna is the decorous literary mimesis of a. current social order. Within that order, women's place appears to be fixed by nature and at the same time governed by culture and historical contingency. Conflicts between faithful "historical" mimesis and the demands of decorum regarding the current social strictures on women's activity appear also in several later treatises on romance. Evident in all of these texts is the sometimes uneasy fit between a desire for cultural autonomy, renewal, and liberation, on the one hand, and a weighty sense of the need for coherence and hierarchical order, on the other. If woman's function in this logic is to mark the persistence of understandable categories, Bradamante, as I will show in the later sections of this chapter, erases that mark.

It was not only Ariosto's supporters who associated violations of generic decorum with the order of gender. Filippo Sassetti, in his *Discorso contro l'Ariosto,* has much to say regarding the verisimilitude and propriety of Ariosto's poetic fictions. His list of complaints includes observations that the battle scenes in the *Furioso* are implausible, as are the topography of the moon and the objects Astolfo finds there.[29] In any case, Rodomonte could never have burned Paris singlehandedly; and furthermore,

> cosa conveniente non pare che quelle donzelle andassono così in truppa ver viaggio con cavalieri senza pericolo d'acquistarsi cattivo nome, pero che dove huomini si trovano e belle donne el lume si spegne, pare che di necessità nascano gli effetti d'Amore; ma io so che a ciò mi sarebbe risposto che quel tempo portava un tal costume. (108 [37])[30]

> [it hardly seems proper that those damsels went traveling about as they did in troupes with knights, without danger of acquiring a bad name. For where men and beautiful women are found together, and the lights go out, it seems a matter of course that the

effects of Love must be born. Still, I know people will answer me that such was the custom of that time.]

If historical perspective prevails in the case of moral behavior described above, it cannot quell Sassetti's irritation at Ariosto's rendering of Bradamante's personal qualities in comparison with Ruggiero's because, claims Sassetti, "since one must have regard for the differences among people, it is not right that a woman be imagined very prudent and the man inconsiderate" (dovendosi haver riguardo alla differenza delle persone non istà bene che una donna sia finta molto prudente e l'huomo inconsiderato [109 (38)]). For Sassetti even more than for Pigna (who allows some exceptions), women's actions must always be understood in relation to the behavior of their male peers. If not presented properly, they may constitute a violation of the entire system of "differences among people."

When Torquato Tasso finds fault with Ariosto's presentation of the poem's principal lovers, Bradamante and Ruggiero, he too casts some of his objections in terms of proper and improper gender representation.[31] Their love is indecorous, in Tasso's view, because Bradamante pursues Ruggiero rather than be pursued by him. This activity is unfitting "because the excellence of women consists in beauty, which moves to love, just as that of men consists in valor, which is demonstrated in actions performed for the sake of love" (perché l'eccellenza delle donne consiste nella bellezza, la qual muove ad amare, sì come quella degli huomini, è nel valore, che si dimostra nelle operationi fatte per l'amore [132]). In fact, Tasso observes, this flaw weakens the poem's verisimilitude: having spent too much time with the sorceress Alcina in her garden, Ruggiero does not seem to love Bradamante enough for their marriage to be a plausible event at the end of the *Furioso*. Tasso's overriding concern here is to devise a conceptual framework for a poetry that will be entertaining but also moral and thus will not lead readers into potentially corrupting fantasies of impossible actions. His task was a difficult one, however, as he sought to package his conservative thinking on women and the family for the same audience that took such pleasure in the exploits of characters such as Bradamante and the sorceress Alcina.[32] If his solution in the narrative of the *Gerusalemme liberata* is both brilliant and compromised in this regard, Tasso's response to the *Furioso*'s warrior heroine is also symptomatic of the dilemma poets faced as they sought to recast genres with long and popular histories for the consumption of Italian Christian audiences.[33]

Renaissance theorizing of the romance and epic genres was inseparable from the questions of literature's relation to contemporary social standards and historical narration. The recurrent arguments over gender in the *Orlando furioso* within these discussions of literary genre suggest the ways in which literature, then as now, implies its own relation to history and society. Important for the concerns of this study, the treatise writers' gender-bound conceptions of acceptable (decorous) representation indicate also the profoundly ideological functions inherent in canon formation—and even, more generally, in aesthetic judgment and representation as such. In these exchanges genre, in its extended sense, mediates several concerns: the matter of woman's place in society and in the text, questions of Italy's historical fate, and the cultural role of Ariosto's poem and other romances. These Renaissance debates and commentaries themselves indicate that the connections I draw here are not the projection backward of twentieth-century critical interests; nor are their implications strictly literary. Indeed, associations between the *Orlando furioso,* the unhinging of traditional roles for women and men, and a more general political disorder in Italy persisted beyond the Cinquecento.

Just after the turn of the century, Tommaso Campanella wrote his utopia, *La città del sole* (1602), from the prison confines of Castel Nuovo. The last remarks of the Genoese sea captain who has recounted his impressions of the marvelous City of the Sun begin:

> Essi dicono che la femina apporta fecondità di cose in cielo, e virtù manco gagliarda rispetto a noi aver dominio. Onde si vede che in questo secolo regnaro le donne, come le Amazoni tra la Nubbia e 'l Menopotapa, e tra gli Europei la Rossa in Turchia, la Bona in Polonia, Maria in Ongheria, Elisabetta in Inghilterra, Caterina in Francia, Margherita in Fiandra. La Bianca in Toscana, Maria in Scozia, Camilla in Roma e Isabella in Spagna, inventrice del mondo nuovo. *E 'l poeta del nostro secolo incominciò dalle donne dicendo:* "Le donne, i cavalier, l'armi e l'amori." E tutti son maledici li poeti d'oggi per Marte; e per Venere e per la Luna parlano di bardas-

cismo e puttanesmo. E gli huomini si effeminano e si chiamano "vosignoria." (Emphasis added.) [34]

[They say that woman in the heavens brings fecundity and that a power less vigorous than ours will have dominion. Whence we may see that in this century women have reigned — like the Amazons between Nubia and Menopotapa — and among the Europeans the Red One in Turkey, Bona in Poland, Maria in Hungary, Elizabeth in England, Catherine in France, Margaret in Flanders, Bianca in Tuscany, Mary in Scotland, Camilla in Rome, and Isabella in Spain: the inventress of the New World. *And the poet of our century began with women, saying, "Of ladies, knights, arms, and love."* And all the poets of our day are critics of Mars; and under the influence of Venus and the Moon they talk of pederasty and prostitution. Men turn effeminate and call each other, "Your Lordship."]

Campanella's survey of recent decades discovers not a collective experience of renascence but a sixteenth century emasculated and weakened by its skewing of traditional values. Linking the vast shifts of political power in contemporary Europe with a conception of women's alarming, cosmically ordained new authority, he alludes with contempt to the courtiers whose "effeminate" refinements have corrupted *their* gender and turned men against the warrior arts of Mars. And finally, he cites Ariosto's hybrid, transgressive poem as illustrative and even complicitous with women's prominence in contemporary politics. Campanella here ties together the errancy of women and their representation in romance as contiguous facets of a larger problem: the political and social disarray of Italian life.

The *querelle des femmes* is not the "main" focus of the *Orlando furioso* (which rejects outright such notions of unity); but for sixteenth-century readers the poem's representations of women were among its most distinguishing features. For some contemporaries, these representations constituted the poem's greatest transgressions against stable social relations. The abundance of Cinquecento treatises on various aspects of women's lives as described and dictated by men indicates the importance of the gender question to contemporary writers; and it compels our recognition of the *querelle des femmes* as a privileged medium for the *Orlando furioso*'s reflections on politics and social life. In the light of this context of controversy, it is no small matter that Ariosto chose to cast a woman as the most capable and controversial character in his poem.

The poet's revelation—and rejection—of Angelica as an object of projected desire makes way for his fuller concentration on Bradamante as a character ill fitted to preconceived notions of womanhood. Bradamante's eventual domestication, in my view, is conditioned heavily by the "uncomfortable poetic and ideological work" that ending the poem entailed for a sixteenth-century court dependent; and it diminishes only partly the extraordinary stature she maintains through the rest of the *Furioso.* In literary theoretical terms as well as in historical context, more noteworthy than her formulaic marriage is the fact that Bradamante commits herself to a prophecy that allows her to negotiate a leap from the sealed world of romance into the open space of "history." Her resituation in the "historical" narrative space of Estensi rule figuratively responds to the narrator's injunctions in the poem for women to correct misogynist myth by writing themselves into history, while at the same time it achieves the generic transformation of romance into heroic epic.

This role begins for her as early as canto II. Bradamante is already seeking Ruggiero when a series of treacheries leads her to fall into an underground cave (II.72–76). There she hears the voice of the ancient magician Merlino and meets his sorceress pupil, Melissa. Merlino reveals that fate has decreed Bradamante to mother a great race along with her destined partner, Ruggiero (II.17–19). Amidst Melissa's incantations Bradamante then witnesses a review of all her male descendants, beginning with the ghost of her still unconceived son, Ruggierino, and ending with Ariosto's contemporary patrons among the Estensi of Ferrara.[35] From this point on, all of Bradamante's actions have a dual aspect: on the one hand, her chivalric loyalty to King Carlo Magno, within a romance quest for Ruggiero; on the other, her epic future as the mother of Ferrara's Este dynasty. Her victories against enemy knights always carry this compound significance, at once adding episodes to the romance interlace and at the same time representing stages in the epic plot that will fulfill her foretold destiny. Her feminine identity, on which this epic resolution depends and through which the poem will substantially engage the *querelle des femmes,* also intensifies the marvel and renown of all her chivalric achievements.

Along her way to fulfilling Merlin's prophecy, Bradamante must surmount several obstacles. Notably, her future husband, Ruggiero, is unaware of the divine plan for their union and remains unimpressed by the need to leave off old loyalties and youthful pleasures. His foster father, the wizard Atlante, actively connives to support Ruggiero's carefree ways, plotting continuously to prevent the young hero from fulfilling his historical destiny. Together, these two factors combine in a classic romance of education, setting obstacle upon obstacle in the way of the young warrior's journey to adulthood, building deferral upon deferral into his story. In addition, Bradamante's own responsibilities, torn as she is between her commitments to Ruggiero, to King Carlo Magno, and to her family, periodically threaten to halt her progress. Finally, the gendered nature of her destiny as matriarch requires that Bradamante transform herself from androgynous warrior to wife and mother in order for the poem to achieve its anticipated closure, a task, we shall see, that represents a tremendous sacrifice of her character's scope.

A number of recent readers have viewed Bradamante's "domestication" as a return to stereotypical gender roles or as the *Furioso*'s principled defeat of femininity itself, arguing in different ways that reassertion of masculine power is an underlying telos of the poem's movement.[36] In my own view, Ariosto's frequent recourse to the issues of the *querelle des femmes,* his generous development of Bradamante as a character before the poem's final cantos, and his projection of a future for her beyond the bounds of the *Furioso*'s narrative all tend to qualify readings that would cast this woman warrior as thoroughly domesticated at the end of the poem. In addition, although Bradamante clearly undergoes a marked "feminization" or taming as a feature of the *Furioso*'s closure, a number of other questions persist when one reads from a slightly different perspective.

Why, for instance, should it be necessary that the female ancestor of the Este dynasty be a military champion rather than a woman from the ranks of more conventionally feminine heroines like Ginevra, Isabella, and Fiordiligi? *What kind* of "masculine" power is it that the poem appears to valorize in its epic resolution, and does this value remain unquestioned within the poem? If not, how do we interpret this tension between the body of the poem and its ending? What, if any, is the relation between the *Furioso*'s embrace of poetic closure and its commentary on the question of gender? Finally, given that Ariosto succeeds in ending with an epic resolution the romance Boiardo began, how do these two modes of the poem relate with regard to the gender questions I have discussed in earlier chapters?

If, as I argued in chapter 2, Angelica functions as a kind of pure sexual alterity and radical femininity in Renaissance terms, then Bradamante, in my view, resides not at the absolute feminine end of a gender spectrum but in a realm of extreme ambiguity. Unlike the other female knight in the poem, Marfisa, who refuses all identification with womanhood, Bradamante dwells at the masculine/feminine gender border.[37] Choosing behaviors from both traditional gender codes to suit her needs, Bradamante suspends difference within herself. By "adding" her consummate femininity to a masculine martial identity normally considered complete in itself, she exposes the myth of maleness as a standard of full being. This "excess" of being, which Bradamante sustains through much of the poem, gives her the capacity to substitute herself with overwhelming effectiveness in traditionally masculine roles.[38] She thus becomes a figure of supplementarity, herself a deferral of fixed gender meaning. Seen in contrast with precisely this competence, versatility, and fullness, Bradamante's marginalization in the poem's narrative resolution appears to reaffirm the *Furioso*'s sustained questioning of the epic heroic values it also praises.

Bradamante first appears in canto I. Arriving suddenly on the scene of Angelica's meeting with Sacripante, she further complicates the criss-crossings of real and supposed meanings already operating in this episode. Angelica has found Sacripante sobbing over his lost chance to pluck the flower of her virtue. In need, nonetheless, of an escort home, she wagers herself as sexual commodity and assures the king of Circassia that her virginity is still intact: she remains an unspoiled prize. The narrator, however, casts doubt on this claim as one that merely serves Angelica's need for protection:

> Forse era ver, ma non però credibile
> a chi del senso suo fosse signore,
> ma parve facilmente a lui possibile,
> ch'era perduto in via più grave errore. (I.56.1–4)

[Perhaps this was true, but hardly plausible
to a person in command of his senses;
to him, however, it seemed easily possible,
for he was lost in more serious error.]

Sacripante pretends to be Angelica's protector while scheming to force her chastity from her, confident in the assumption that all women want the very thing they most refuse. At the same time, Angelica feigns interest in the knight's affections when all she really wants from him is the service of protection. Into this scene of confusions and duplicities arrives an unidentified knight, revealed only later as Bradamante: "Ecco pel bosco un cavallier venire / il cui sembiante è d'uom gagliardo e fiero" (I.60.1–2) [Through the woods now comes a knight / whose bearing is that of a valiant and fierce man].

Both the withholding of the knight's identity in this moment of encounter and the emphasis on the figure's outward semblance are conventional *topoi* of the chivalric romance. Bradamante's investment in the game of concealed identity, however, is not an occasional manipulative ploy, as it is with the unspoken motives of Angelica and Sacripante, but rather an essential feature of her successful activities as a paladin. The emphasis in line 2 of octave 60 thus falls on the nouns (*sembiante* and *uom*, "semblance" and "man"), and not on the adjectives (*gagliardo* and *fiero*, "valiant" and "fierce"): Bradamante's *semblance* is that of a *man*. Other knights may also disguise themselves under special circumstances (Ariodante, IV.13; Orlando, VIII.80–83; Ruggiero XLIV.77–XLVI), but Bradamante, effectively, is always in disguise. It is important that her self-concealment dissimulates not her partisanship or her knightly identity, as is usually the case, but her sex.

In several episodes the *Furioso* focuses specifically on the contrast between Bradamante's experiences as woman and as knight. These narrative segments foreground the gap between the crude simplicity of standard gender characterizations and the more nuanced issues of identity, desire, allegiance, and ethics the poem explores. If Angelica uses magic to separate herself from a thoroughly conventionalized image of womanhood, Bradamante achieves a similar and superior autonomy by cloaking her feminine identity in armor. Whereas Angelica's ring—a circular and archetypally feminine symbol—renders her invisible and disintegrates the materiality of her female body, Bradamante dons a hard, exterior shell to enclose that body within an ostentatious but deceptive surface; and she arms herself with the ring's virile counterpart, a piercing lance. Shielding herself from the "blows" normally directed at women, she employs her martial persona to mediate between her body and her personal and historical identities.[39] When the narrator reintroduces her in canto II, he remarks that Brada-mante travels "così sicura senza compagnia, / come avesse in sua guardia mille squadre" (II.33.3–4) [as secure unaccompanied as if she had a / thousand squadrons on her guard]. From the outset, this autonomy contrasts with the desperate flights of Angelica. In canto I she swiftly unhorses Sacri-pante and gallops out of sight while Angelica remains safer for the moment, but still dependent on Sacripante's aid. The juxtaposition suggests a distinction not only between the powerful and the helpless versions of femininity the two women exemplify, but also between the real assistance Bradamante brings Angelica—not lingering even long enough to be thanked—and Sac-ripante's self-interested "chivalry" toward a damsel in distress.

The narrator consistently presents Bradamante as equal in valor and repu-tation to her brother Rinaldo (II.30). Nonetheless, Bradamante's revelation that she is a woman never fails to provoke a shift in her opponent's regard for her—and for himself. Sacripante's discovery of his victor's sex leaves him speechless with shame and wonder, indicated four times in a single stanza:

> il Saracin lasciò poco giocondo,
> che non sa che si dica o che si faccia,
> tutto avvampato di vergogna in faccia.
>
> Poi che gran pezzo al caso intervenuto
> ebbe pensato invano, e finalmente
> si trovò da una femina abbattuto,
> che pensandovi più, più dolor sente;
> montò l'altro destrier, *tacito* e *muto:*
> e *senza far parole,*[40] *chetamente*
> tolse Angelica in groppa e differilla
> a più lieto uso, a stanza più tranquilla. (I.70.6–71, emphasis added)

[The messenger left the Saracen so undelighted that he knew not
    what to do or say, and blushed crimson with shame.

Then when he had thought long in vain about
this chance happening and still found himself beaten by
a woman, which caused him more pain the more he thought
of it, he mounted the remaining horse, *mute* and *silent.*
And *without saying a word,* he *quietly*
took Angelica up into the saddle and deferred her
to a happier use in more tranquil settings.]

As subsequent episodes will reveal, Sacripante's response to his defeat is not
at all unusual. His counterparts later in the poem will repeat exactly his
loss of verbal faculties, as each of them falls from the rules of the Symbolic
(with its assumption of male privilege in the spheres of speech and action)
that I discussed in regard to Angelica in chapter 2. Though time and again
the poem reaffirms Bradamante's ability to compete among the best of the
knights, the principles motivating her battles remain distinct from those of
her male comrades. Bradamante's conflicts nearly always relate to her feminine identity as a knight and to her gendered historical destiny. Not by
chance is it she who arrives to save Angelica from Sacripante's aggressions
in canto I, for she becomes a forceful advocate of women in the poem.

Her most celebrated episode, which appears only in the 1532 edition of
the poem and takes place at the Rocca di Tristano [Tristan's Castle], features
another instance of this advocacy. In canto XXXII we find her en route
to Paris, where she intends both to aid Carlo in his war and to challenge
Marfisa, who she believes is her rival for Ruggiero's love. When she stops
to ask a shepherd for directions, she learns that her only prospect for lodging is the nearby Rocca di Tristano. In order to gain a bed for the night
there, however, a knight must first defeat and supplant the resident who
arrived before him. If a woman should seek shelter, she must be judged
more beautiful than the last female to arrive before her and, similarly, oust
a rival from her dwelling (XXXII.65–68).[41]

Nearing the castle, Bradamante learns from a guard that the previously
victorious group of men and women is just awaiting dinner. The guard's
message that the group includes both sexes reminds the reader that Bradamante has her choice of two modes of admission, the women's beauty

contest or the men's competition in arms. Bradamante, however, takes no note of the first option. She remains dressed in armor and issues a challenge to the knights in the castle. Only after defeating three opponents and gaining entrance to the castle does she disclose her gender.

In a revelatory gesture favored by martial women at least since Virgil's Camilla, Bradamante removes her helmet and lets down her long hair:

> La donna, cominciando a disarmarsi,
> s'avea lo scudo e dipoi l'elmo tratto;
> quando una cuffia d'oro, in che celarsi
> solean i capei lunghi e star di piatto,
> uscì con l'elmo; onde caderon sparsi
> giù per le spalle, e la scopriro a un tratto
> e la feron conoscer per donzella,
> non men che fiera in arme, in viso bella. (XXXII.79)

> [The woman, in beginning to disarm,
> had taken off her shield and then her helmet
> when a golden net, inside which her long hair
> usually lay hidden flat, came off with the helmet.
> Whence her tresses fell loose upon her shoulders,
> at once discovering her and revealing she was
> a damsel, no less fair of face than fierce in arms.]

We know that Bradamante's hair at times provides the only outward index of her femininity, just as Marfisa's does in her encounter with Guidone in canto XIX, octave 108.[42] Ariosto notes this function in canto XXV, in which Bradamante's twin brother remarks that when his sister's hair had once been cut short, he and she became indistinguishable. Conventionally described as golden and shining, the hair cascades down as a kind of reflective surface that sends back to those who look on it the idealized image of Woman, as both confirmation and object of desire.

In contrast with Bradamante's victory outside the castle, in fact, this sudden revelation of unsuspected femininity carries the poem's vocabulary into the lofty, lyrical register of Petrarchist hyperbole that often accompanies the appearances of Angelica. The epiphanic conceit describing Bradamante's gesture borders, in its architectonic elaboration, on the baroque:

Quale al cader de le cortine suole
parer fra mille lampade la scena,
d'archi e di più d'una superba mole,
d'oro e di statue e di pittura piena;
o come suol fuor de la nube il sole
scoprir la faccia limpida e serena:
così, l'elmo levandosi dal viso,
mostrò la donna aprisse il paradiso. (XXXII.80)

[As when the stage appears at curtain drop
amidst a thousand lanterns, full of
archways, proud structures, gilding, statues,
and paintings; or like the sun, which often
reveals its limpid, serene face from out of
a cloud: so the damsel seemed to open paradise
by taking off her helmet.]

The first, extended metaphor of spectacle rings strange, as it indicates the great gap between Bradamante's person and the contrivances of femininity, which appear here by analogy as no more real than the shiny trappings of courtly theater. The second figure oscillates in the other direction, lending the tones of cosmic nature to Bradamante's appearance as a woman. At the same time, this evocation's stringing of ill-matched metaphors, in which the vision of Bradamante is compared to an illuminated stage (surface on which light is projected), to the sun (source of light), and to paradise (environment pure with light?), seems to project a catachrestic failure of language to describe coherently the sublime effects of femininity's revelation.

At first the bedazzled company makes no further comment, in effect underlining Bradamante's association with speechlessness already noted in relation to her defeated opponents: speech itself, such instances suggest, depends on a psychic wholeness that is purportedly held intact by a clear gender opposition. Once this opposition becomes destabilized, the speaking subject seems to lose its location in relation to Bradamante; mouths drop open, but nothing comes out.

The lord of the castle eventually recovers to recognize his warrior guest with honor and shows her the superior courtesies due a knight of her renown. Yet soon a dilemma arises. Bradamante's host notes that *two* women are present: Ullania, the winner of the castle's most recent beauty contest, and Bradamante, whose revelation of her gender demands her placement in a category different from the one to which she seemed to belong at her arrival. Since the law of the castle states that women must compete as paragons of beauty in order to win their stay, Bradamante's host dutifully summons his judges. They are unanimous that Bradamante's beauty surpasses Ullania's; and Ullania, in observance of house rules, prepares tearfully to leave the castle and sleep outside, along with the three male opponents Bradamante defeated earlier.

These events foreground just the sort of oppositions and binary schemes Ariosto attenuates throughout the *Furioso:* Bradamante's companions are perplexed about how to classify her because they maintain only two categories for sorting out all the potential lodgers who come their way. The two contests are also incongruous in a way typical of medieval and Renaissance gender ideals, for the women's version mirrors the competitive code of men while at the same time leaving the female contestants mere spectators in their own cause. The women, that is, do not really compete; they offer themselves as objects for evaluation by others, in an inverted and emptied reenactment of male competition. This is not the woman warrior's usual league.

In a speech central to her characterization in the poem, Bradamante rejects this mere pretense of a contest and insists instead on a reconsideration of both the certainty and the significance of her gender. She first calls on her audience's conception of justice and fair treatment, framing her argument in a context that well exceeds the immediate disagreement over bed and board. She then reminds the group that her choice to compete martially has already indicated the category in which she wishes to participate, and she insists on maintaining her choice:

> Ma Bradamante con un saggio aviso,
> che per pietà non vuol che se ne vada,
> rispose:—A me non par che ben deciso,
> nè che ben giusto alcun giudicio cada,
> ove prima non s'oda quanto nieghi
> la parte o affermi, e sue ragioni alleghi.

> Io ch'a difender questa causa toglio,
> dico: o più bella o men ch'io sia di lei,
> non venni come donna qui, né voglio
> che sian di donna ora i progressi miei.
> Ma chi dirà, se tutta non mi spoglio
> s'io sono o s'io non son quel ch'è costei?
> E quel che non si sa non si de' dire,
> e tanto men, quando altri n'ha a patire. (XXXII.101.3–102)

> [But Bradamante, who pities the lady and does
> not want her to leave, responded with
> a wise opinion:—No decision, it seems to
> me, is good and just unless beforehand all
> that supports it and all that detracts from it is heard.

> I say, in taking up this cause, that whether I
> am more or less beautiful than she, I did
> not come here as a woman; nor do I wish my
> successes now to be those of a woman. But
> who will say, unless I undress myself
> completely, whether I am or am not what this
> woman is? And that which one knows not, one
> must not say, all the more if someone else stands to suffer from
> it.] [43]

Bradamante's position as Ullania's advocate revives the protective role she played on behalf of Angelica in canto I. This long speech, however, also focuses specifically on her own suspended gender identity in the poem. Her next remarks pose an ontological dilemma related to the deceptiveness of appearance, suggesting that because actions contribute more to one's being than anatomy does, she is in fact more warrior than woman.[44] She further observes the inappropriateness of comparisons across categories: a victory in one sphere ought not be weighed in another:

> Ben son degli altri ancor, c'hanno le chiome
> lunghe, com'io, né donne son per questo.

Se come cavallier la stanza, o come
donna acquistare m'abbia, è manifesto:
perché dunque volete darmi nome
di donna, se di maschio è ogni mio gesto?
La legge vostra vuol che ne sian spinte
donne da donne, e non da guerrier vinte.

Poniamo ancor, che, come a voi pur pare,
io donna sia (*che non però il concedo*),
ma che la mia beltà non fosse pare
a quella di costei, non però credo
che mi vorreste la mercè levare
di mia virtù, se ben di viso io cedo.
Perder per men beltà giusto non parmi
quel ch'ho acquistato per virtù con l'armi. (XXXII.103–4,
    emphasis added)

[There are plenty of others who have long
hair, like me, and that doesn't make them
women. Whether I gained entrance as knight
or as woman is clear: Why then do you wish to
call me woman, if my every gesture is
that of a man? Your law says that women
should be ousted by women, and not by warriors.

Let's suppose, yet, that as it seems to you,
I am a woman (*which, however, I do not
concede*) but that my beauty were not equal to
hers; I don't believe you'd want to deny me
the prize for my valor if I came second in beauty.
It does not seem just to me to lose for beauty
that which I acquired for valor in arms.]

By relegating to the level of hypothesis her participation in the category
of "woman," Bradamante does not *deny* her gender but rather defers it for
later establishment outside the question at hand. She contrasts, moreover,
not her membership in the categories "woman" and "man," but those of

"woman" and "knight," meticulously leaving the latter term ungendered throughout this speech ("guerrier," "cavallier") and attributing to others the preoccupation with her sex. Bradamante's aim in this argument (during which she adopts no gendered adjectival or participial endings whatsoever when referring to herself) appears to be not to persuade others that she is a man, but to decouple the categories "knight" and "man" for a possible re-alignment of the categories "knight" and "woman."[45] She thus encapsulates in this speech her efforts to hold open the terms in which to cast her historical and personal future, geared toward maternity though these may be.

Bradamante presents her quarrel in the fashion of a courtly diplomat adept at rhetorical maneuvers. Her defense employs such obvious forensic devices as reference to previous agreements, exclusion of unknown factors, appeal to precedents in similar contexts, pragmatic descriptions of the precipitating events, and citation of the law.[46] Finally, playing the last card of every diplomatic negotiator, Bradamante reminds her listeners that should reasonable persuasion fail, she retains the capacity for violent force. Her last lines note that if her eloquence proves insufficient to convince the assembled listeners, her physical powers will deliver a message they can readily understand:

> E quando ancor fosse l'usanza tale,
> che chi perde in beltà ne dovesse ire,
> io ci vorrei restare, o bene o male
> che la mia ostinazion dovesse uscire.
> Per questo, che contesa diseguale
> è tra me e questa donna, vo' inferire
> che, contendendo di beltà; può assai
> perdere, e meco guadagnar non mai.
>
> E se guadagni e perdite non sono
> in tutti pari, ingiusto è ogni partito:
> sì ch'a lei per ragion, sì ancor per dono
> spezïal, non sia l'albergo proibito.
> E s'alcuno di dir che non sia buono
> e dritto il mio giudizio sarà ardito,
> sarò per sostenergli a suo piacere,
> che 'l mio sia vero, e falso il suo parere. (XXXII.105–6)

[And yet if it were the custom that the one
defeated for beauty must leave, I would still insist on
staying; be the outcome of my stubbornness
what it may. Thus I must surmise that this is an unequal
contest between myself and this woman: by
competing with me for beauty she still has much
to lose, and she can never defeat me in arms.

And any game in which advantages are not equal among all
competitors, is unfair: hence let
lodgings not be denied her, either by rights or
as a concession. And if anyone should be
so bold as to say my judgment is not good and
right, I'll take him on as best he likes, and
show him my reason is true, his false.]

Bradamante wins the argument and passes the evening in the company of the grateful Ullania and other guests. By insisting that both she and Ullania stay, her performance at Tristan's Castle shakes up the traditional binary classifications for guests and literally makes room for other categories. Bradamante's revelation of the warrior inside the woman (inside the warrior), furthermore, suggests her political capacities may exceed those of the courtier diplomat she resembles. Her tactical unmasking of potential force recalls Machiavelli's invocation of the centaur in chapter 18 of *Il Principe* as the model for a head of state: half human and half beast, half reason and half animal force, Machiavelli's founder prince is, like the woman knight, a hybrid creature capable of showing whichever of these faces suits political necessity.[47] Bradamante's skillful control of her image before her host and judges suggests yet again her capacity for leadership in the role that awaits her in epic time.[48] This control is all the more evident given the intimate sufferings of Bradamante to which the reader has been privy in the earlier octaves of this canto (36–46), in which her brief flirtation with suicide brought on by her despair over Ruggiero is ultimately sublimated by a pledge to die with dignity and "honor" seeking revenge for Ruggiero's assumed betrayal of her with Marfisa. It is Bradamante's armor that prevents her sword from penetrating the flesh in a self-destructive impulse that recalls both Lucretia and Dido (44); and in this detail the poem underscores the crucial function of Bradamante's knightly identity in keeping her safe from the stereotypes of honor reserved for women. As it literally "points" with Bradamante's sword to the border of metal that separates the two roles she must reconcile, the scene of rejected suicide foreshadows Bradamante's next adventure, in which she will learn of a woman who lacked such armor in her time of despair, the paragon of feminine virtue and namesake of the Estense princess, Isabella.[49]

The next day, as she prepares for departure, the three kings she defeated the night before issue another challenge to Bradamante, whereupon she handily beats all three a second time. Not having been present inside the castle when Bradamante revealed her identity, the kings discover their victor's sex only after a second defeat by her. Their reaction is, like Sacripante's in canto I, shame. They lay down their arms for one year and withdraw from society to meditate on the humiliation of their defeat by a woman. Even Ullania, whose place in Tristan's castle was won through Bradamante's martial and verbal powers the night before, sees the woman warrior's performance not as a triumph of the best knight but as devastating proof of the kings' impotence; and she taunts them with their mortifying loss. The kings had set out from nordic lands to challenge Carlo Magno's finest knights as a way of establishing reputations in their own countries, but they abandon these designs when Ullania chides them:

> —Or che dovete (diceva ella) quando
> così v'abbia una femina abbattuti,
> pensar che sia Rinaldo, o che sia Orlando,
> non senza causa in tant'onore avuti?
> S'un d'essi avrà lo scudo, io vi domando
> se migliori di quel che siate suti
> contra una donna, contra lor sarete.
> Nol credo già, né voi forse il credete. (XXXIII.72)

> [—Now that a woman has beaten you (she said)
> how do you think you'll fare with
> Rinaldo or Orlando, do you think they boast
> their honors for no reason?
> If one of them takes to arms, I ask you
> if you'll be better against him

than you were against a woman.
I don't believe so; nor, perhaps, do you.]

Ironically, and despite Bradamante's exemplary *military* performance, Ulla-nia's taunting of the kings for their defeat at a woman's hands casts Bra-damante's victory in the derisive spirit of the medieval military parades I discussed in chapter 1, in which feminine victory signified not only de-feat but utter humiliation for the vanquished. In both scenarios, femininity connotes abjection and shame, a debasement of those it governs.

Bradamante shrugs off this group and continues on her way to Paris. After a short while she encounters a situation that presents new variations on her principal concerns in the poem: faith to her beloved and her fore-told destiny, and the question of her right to claim recognition as both woman and knight.

In canto XXXV Bradamante meets Fiordiligi, whose devotion to her hus-band, Brandimarte, echoes Bradamante's own faithful search for Ruggiero.[50] When Fiordiligi describes her husband, now held captive by Rodomonte, as "[il] più fedele d'ogni fedele amante" (XXXV.37.4) [the most faithful of all faithful lovers], Bradamante, who now believes Ruggiero has betrayed her, agrees to take up the woman's cause.[51] Her decision to aid Fiordiligi arises as much from the knowledge that Brandimarte is a faithful *man* as from her devotion to fidelity in general, for she registers no surprise at Fiordiligi's fidelity to Brandimarte:

> —Per quel ch'io vaglio, giovane amorosa,—
> rispose Bradamante—io m'offerisco
> di far l'impresa dura e perigliosa,
> per altre cause ancor, ch'io preterisco;
> ma più, che del tuo amante narri cosa
> che narrar di pochi uomini avvertisco:
> che sia in amor fedel; ch'a fé ti giuro
> ch'in ciò pensai ognun fosse pergiuro. (XXXV.39)

> [—For all I'm worth, oh loving young lady—
> Bradamante replied—I offer
> to do the hard and perilous deed,

for a number of reasons, besides those I mention.
But most of all because you say of your lover
a thing I find in few men:
that he is loyal in love. For in faith I swear to you,
I thought every one a perjuror in that regard.]

Along the way to Rodomonte's bridge, where Brandimarte is being held captive, Fiordiligi recounts to her rescuer the reason for Rodomonte's wrath at the world. Rodomonte's attempts to corrupt the beautiful Isabella's fidelity to the spirit of her dead husband had failed miserably because Isabella, Lucretia-like in her preference of death over dishonor, had cleverly contrived her own slaughter at Rodomonte's hands in order to escape him (XXIX). Rodomonte's shocked and grieved response includes the elaborate game wherein all who come to cross his bridge are challenged to defeat him or suffer capture. With this discovery of another woman's tragic death in fidelity, Bradamante's commitment to Fiordiligi's cause redoubles. When she meets the king of Sarza and Algiers, she roars her pride as a woman warrior in avenging Isabella's death:

> —Perché vuoi tu, bestial, che gli innocenti
> facciano penitenzia del tuo fallo?
> Del sangue tuo placar costei convienti:
> tu l'uccidesti, e tutto 'l mondo sallo.
> Sì che di tutte l'arme e guernimenti
> di tanti che gittati hai da cavallo,
> oblazione e vittima più accetta
> avrà, ch'io te l'uccida in sua vendetta.
>
> E di mia man le fia più grato il dono,
> quando, come ella fu, son donna anch'io:
> né qui venuta ad altro effetto sono,
> ch'a vendicarla; e questo sol disio. (XXXV.42–43.2)

> [Beast, why do you expect the innocent
> to do penance for your sin?
> With your own blood you ought to lay this lady to rest:
> you killed her, and the whole world knows it.

She will have a more welcome offering and victim
than all the arms and decorations
of the many whom you've thrown from their horses,
if I kill you to avenge her.

And the gift will be more pleasing from my hand,
since, as she was, I too am a woman:
I come here for no other purpose
than to take her revenge; and this is my one desire.]

Bradamante here reclaims her feminine identification, despite her insistence in the previous episode that it be excluded from the context of her martial exploits; and her reasoning is clear. In the earlier case, gender attribution was a matter of arbitrary discrimination and petrified custom. But here at Rodomonte's bridge, sexual difference is an element in the tragic determining events, because Rodomonte's aggressions extend from his abuse of the male-female relationship. Bradamante's uncommon declaration of her sex *before* a joust, in addition, heightens the thoroughly conventional effect this fact has on her treatment by her opponent; it thus keeps the issue of gender in the foreground.

The news prompts from Rodomonte an immediate diminution of Bradamante's stature as a knight and his displacement of their combat into the sphere of sexual conquest. Bradamante states her challenge in parallel with those of all former contenders for the bridge: "S'abbattuta sarò, di me farai / quel che degli altri tuoi prigion fatt'hai" (XXXV.43.7–8) [If I should be beaten, you'll do with me / as you have done with your other prisoners]. Rodomonte, however, alters his challenge significantly in the light of his opponent's sex. His boastful confidence trivializes Bradamante's valor with patronizing sexual innuendo:

Ma s'a te tocca star di sotto, come
più si conviene, e certo so che fia,
non vo' che lasci l'arme, né il tuo nome,
come di vinta, sotto scritta sia:
al tuo bel viso, a' begli occhi, alle chiome
che spiran tutti amore e leggiadria,

voglio donar la mia vittoria; e basti
che ti disponga amarmi, ove m'odiasti.

Io son di tal valor, son di tal nerbo,
ch'aver non dei d'andar di sotto a sdegno. (XXXV.46–47.2)

[But if it falls to you to be underneath,
where you belong, and I know it shall be so,
I don't want you to leave your arms or your name
undersigned there as vanquished:
I wish to offer my victory
to your lovely face, to your beautiful eyes, to your hair,
which all emanate love and gracefulness. Let it suffice
that you dispose to love me, where once you hated me.

I am of such valor, I am of such prowess,
that you needn't disdain to go under me.]

In Rodomonte's Petrarchist catalogue of Bradamante's delicate features, hostile intentions vie with the knight's obtuseness regarding women to produce a particularly exasperating reception of her martial challenge. Nowhere could clichéd references to Bradamante's feminine charms be less appropriate than in response to her seething demand for a warrior's bloody revenge. Rodomonte, moreover, exposes the intrinsic, paradoxical capacity of courtly love to subordinate women with a discourse of their superiority when he proposes that *his* anticipated victory over *her* might be construed as both a tribute and a gift. Juxtaposed with the strength and independence of the mighty Bradamante, the ideals of femininity lauded in courtly lyric here shrink into the meager substitutes for personhood they have always been. Petrarchan praise acquires a particularly sinister tone on Rodomonte's lips, as the power of attraction that is conventionally attributed to beautiful women confronts the sheer force ordinarily exercised by men—a force Bradamante has appropriated for herself. Apparently deeming his suggestion unworthy of reply, she says nothing. Instead she turns her horse to prepare for attack.

Aided by the magic golden lance she received from Astolfo in canto XXXII, Bradamante wins the match almost effortlessly.[52] Her parting remark to Rodomonte, left hanging upside down from his own bridge, volleys back to him his own crude sexual innuendo and restores their combat to the field of arms: "—Or puoi—disse—veder chi abbia perduto / e a chi di noi tocchi di star di sotto" (XXXV.50.3–4) [—Now you can see—she said—which one of us has lost / and whose turn it is to lie beneath]. Rodomonte, like Sacripante and the three kings at the Rocca di Tristano, is struck speechless:

> Di maraviglia il Pagan resta *muto,*
> ch'una donna a cader l'abbia condotto;
> *e far risposta non pote e non volle,*
> e fu come uom pien di stupore e folle. (XXXV.50.5–8,
>   emphasis added)

> [The pagan was left *mute* with wonder
> that a woman had brought him down;
> and *he could not and would not reply.*
> And he was like a man both stupefied and crazed.]

Like the mad Orlando, Rodomonte is here described as "folle" [crazed], for their furies share an origin in the eclipsing of another's will in the service of their own desires. Like Sacripante, Rodomonte loses his tongue when unhorsed by Bradamante; and like all the men she has thus far defeated, he suffers both a literal and a figurative loss of the ground from which males normally speak as dominant subjects. Rodomonte's case, the most severe of these losses, leaves him not simply toppled from his high horse to the ground, but topsy-turvey and hanging in the air, his world turned upside down by this inversion of conventional relations between the sexes. Rodomonte responds by retreating from his knightly identity altogether: he surrenders his invulnerable dragon-skin armor (which he is said to have inherited from the giant Nimrod) and goes off to live in a cave, vowing not to emerge for a year, a month, and a day. The kings in the Rocca di Tristano episode, two cantos earlier, acted in exactly the same way. Rodomonte's regression from civilization and into a cave, coupled with his troll-like behavior toward passers-by wishing to cross his bridge, emphasizes his kinship with the wild Orlando, with such classic figures of incivility as the troglodyte and the Cyclops, and with the sulking Achilles (with whom he is more than once assimilated in the poem).

Bradamante's supplementary relation to her conventional gender opposite appears most suggestively in the male double Ariosto provides for her. In canto XXII, while traveling with Ruggiero, Bradamante takes great interest in a story they hear about a young man sentenced to death for dressing as a woman in order to meet his lover secretly. Leaving unremarked the symmetry between Bradamante's dissimulation of her gender and the action of the man in the story, the narrator simply notes that the lady knight feels a bond of kinship with the unfortunate lover:

> Bradamante ode, e par ch'assai le prema
> questa novella, e molto il cor l'annoi;
> né par che men per quel dannato tema,
> che se fosse uno dei fratelli suoi. (XXII.42.1–4)

> [Bradamante hears, and this tale appears
> to weigh on her greatly and unsettle her heart.
> She seems to fear for that condemned man
> no less than if he were one of her brothers.]

Bradamante's identification with the youth, the narrator hints, is not unfounded. He next appears in canto XXV, in which Ruggiero, who has arrived to rescue him, mistakes him for Bradamante herself:

> Ruggier come gli alzò gli occhi nel viso,
> che chino a terra e lacrimoso stava,
> di veder Bradamante gli fu aviso,
> tanto il giovine a lei rassimigliava. (XXV.9.1–4)

> [As Ruggiero raised his eyes to (the youth's) face,
> which was bowed down and tearful,
> he had the impression that he saw Bradamante;
> so much did the young man resemble her.]

Ruggiero saves this person he believes to be Bradamante but remains perplexed and disturbed when, rather than the gratitude appropriate to a lover,

the youth renders him the more formal thanks customary toward a helpful stranger. A guessing game of names finally solves the puzzle. The young
man observes that he has a twin sister, whom Ruggiero may have met:

> —Che voi m'abbiate visto esser potria,—
> rispose quel—che non so dove o quando:
> ben vo pel mondo anch'io la parte mia,
> strane aventure or qua or là cercando.
> Forse una mia sorella stata fia,
> che veste l'arme e porta al lato il brando;
> che nacque meco, e tanto mi somiglia,
> che non ne può discerner la famiglia. (XXV.22)

> [—It could be that you have seen me—
> he replied—I know not where or when:
> for my part I too travel much of the world,
> seeking new adventures now here, now there.
> Perhaps it was one of my sisters you saw,
> who dresses in arms and carries a sword at her side.
> She was born along with me and resembles me so much
> that not even our family can tell us apart.]

When Bradamante once received a head wound that required her to cut her
hair, her brother recounts, "alcun segno tra noi non restò più / di differen-
zia" (XXV.24.5–6) [no outward sign of difference remained to distinguish
her from her male twin]. This incident in Bradamante's past is key, not only
as an illustration of her extreme gender ambiguity but also as a reevocation
of her original enamorment with Ruggiero, which occurred in Boiardo's
poem. The Saracen attack that dealt her the very wound that necessitated
the cutting of her hair was also the rude interruption to Bradamante and
Ruggiero's falling in love, indeed their first and only encounter before
canto IV of the *Orlando furioso* (*Orlando innamorato,* III.v.16–42, III.viii.52–
62).[53] Bradamante's earliest brush with her dynastic destiny, then, is related
in the two poems' narratives to her becoming *less* conventionally feminine,
and to a distinct emphasis on her capacity to confound gender expecta-
tions. In this reversed image of castration, Bradamante's wound, we might

say, paradoxically invests her with "the phallus," the symbolic assumption of superiority men enjoy in patriarchal societies.[54]

If Bradamante's armor serves as a device by which she suspends certainty of her gender, her twin brother, Ricciardetto, uses women's clothing to similar effect. Ricciardetto's functions, in the story that follows, are twofold. In his simultaneous identity and difference with Bradamante, he acts as a living extension of his feminine twin. He repeats and chiastically reverses the supplementary role potential in her suspension of the gender opposition, as both twins share a middle ground of indistinguishability. Second, he provides a poetic space for the absorption of Bradamante's masculine traits; for the anatomical difference of the otherwise twinned bodies ultimately maps both characters back into the gender relations the sixteenth century saw as appropriate between the sexes. Those relations, though "natural" in their orientation toward reproduction, are also displaced from strictly traditional masculine and feminine paradigms by each twin's demonstration of flexibility in gender identity and difference. Moreover, the phenomenon of identical twins of opposite sex—a "natural" anomaly—suggests a fusion of gender characteristics that is natural and not cultural. Since Bradamante and Ricciardetto are cast as identical *before* their cultural locations are assigned, their separation into gendered social roles for the closure of the poem appears as not an inevitable grounding but a culturally determined one, for epic resolution.

Ricciardetto tells Ruggiero how his sister one day (after having her hair cut short by the hermit who treated her head wound) stopped to rest in the woods and happened on a strange adventure.[55] After dismounting her horse and removing her helmet, Bradamante lay down in some tender grass and fell asleep. Bradamante's slumber was soon disturbed, however, when she was discovered by Fiordispina, a beautiful Spanish princess out hunting in the woods:

> E quando ritrovò la mia sirocchia
> tutta coperta d'arme, eccetto il viso,
> ch'avea la spada in luogo di canocchia,
> le fu vedere un cavalliero aviso.
> La faccia e le viril fattezze adocchia
> tanto, che se ne sente il cor conquiso. (XXV.28.1–6)

[And when she found my sister
all covered in armor except for her face,
with her sword in place of a distaff,
she thought she gazed on a knight.
She eyes this face and virile ways
so long that she feels her heart conquered by them.]

Fiordispina falls in love with Bradamante and eventually steals a kiss. Bradamante, not wishing to appear an unfeeling and discourteous fellow, reveals
her identity as a *femina gentile*. She confides to Fiordispina that although
she resembles a man, she is really an illustrious woman warrior in the tradition of the Amazons (XXV.31–32). Fiordispina's love, however, remains
unaltered. She laments her misfortune in falling into an attachment "contrary to nature," but she is no less smitten:[56]

Per questo non si smorza una scintilla
del fuoco de la donna innamorata.
Questo rimedio all'alta piaga è tardo:
tant'avea Amor cacciato inanzi il dardo. (XXV.32.5–8)

[Not one spark dies in the enamoured
woman's fire on hearing this.
The remedy is too late for her deep wound,
so far within had Love lodged his dart.]

A bewildered Bradamante accepts Fiordispina's offer of lodging for the
night. When the two women arrive at her city, Fiordispina has Bradamante
don feminine clothing, both in order to avoid scandal and to remind herself
that her budding passion is forbidden. That night Fiordispina's sleep is tormented by the fantasy that Bradamante's sex might change to "a better one":
"le par veder che 'l ciel l'abbia concesso / Bradamante cangiata in miglior
sesso" (42.7–8). Ariosto plays here on the slippage between dual usages of the
term *sex* as both a social and a bodily assignment (as both sex and gender, in
today's terminology), for in these lines Fiordispina's wish to legitimate the
love she feels for Bradamante *whatever* her official "sex" comes to focus directly on a desired transformation of the female paladin's body. Persuaded by
counterfeit dreams, she even tries several times to verify the desired trans-

formation, always observing the same result: "Si desta; e nel destar mette la mano, / e ritrova pur sempre il sogno vano" (XXV.43.7–8) [She stirs; and stirring she places her hand / (there), and yet she always finds the dream is empty]. Fiordispina's prayer that Bradamante's sex be changed may be, as Valeria Finucci argues, the desire for traditional male power and autonomy inherent in Freud's theory of penis envy, a wish that must, presumably, be understood as displaced onto Bradamante.[57] But Fiordispina does not appear to me to be concerned with power at all, either for herself or for Bradamante; rather she is caught in what the poem casts as a hopelessly thwarted desire. The name of the Spanish princess (which translates as "Thornflower") highlights the pain of this impasse: the flower rests atop a thorny stem that renders its blossom untouchable.[58] Most generally, Fiordispina's pain appears as a longing to overcome the unbridgeable gap between desire and its full satisfaction: a theme the poem has already visited in the story of Orlando. Whereas Orlando's desired plenitude with Angelica was ultimately blocked by the difference between his ideal projection of Angelica and her divergent personal desires, however, in Fiordispina's case this impasse is represented by the rigid social coding of physically sexed bodies.

Bradamante leaves Fiordispina and arrives at her family home, where she tells everyone the story of her unsettling encounter. Ricciardetto listens, rapt, to this narrative and recognizes Fiordispina from his sister's account as a woman he has seen and desired, but whom he never dared to hope would accept his love. His plan to present himself in Fiordispina's village as Bradamante, magically transformed into a man, reflects the mutual supplementarity the twins enjoy: neither twin suffices alone to satisfy Fiordispina's wish, but each is also more than herself or himself alone, for each can draw at will on the features of the other, magic or no.

Bradamante cannot satisfy Fiordispina's love (on the poem's horizon of possibility) for lack of that member whose absence traditionally marks woman's "insufficiency." Ricciardetto, nonetheless, is bound to assimilate qualities and gestures foreign to his masculine socialization if he wishes to gain the love of Fiordispina.[59] He recounts to Ruggiero how he presented himself to the Spanish princess in the guise of his sister. Fiordispina, under the impression that he is her longed-for lady warrior, carefully and lovingly dresses him in her favorite gown:

Poi fattasi arrecare una sua veste
adorna e ricca, di sua man la spiega,
e come io fossi femina, mi veste,
e in reticella d'oro il crin mi lega.
Io muovevo gli occhi con maniere oneste,
né ch'io sia donna alcun mio gesto niega. (XXV.55.1–6)

[Then after she had ordered brought to her one of her adorned
and luxurious dresses, she lays it out with her own hands
and dresses me as though I were a woman,
and ties my hair in a delicate golden net.
I moved my eyes about in modest manners,
and no gesture of mine denies I am a woman.]

Whether clad in armor or arrayed in women's gowns, the twins are indistinguishable. So persuasive is his outward projection of feminine mien that Ricciardetto arouses the desires of other men during the evening's social activities. Later that night—in a gesture that prefigures Bradamante's removal of her helmet in canto XXXII—he reveals his masculine body to a delighted Fiordispina, who believes her prayers for Bradamante's transformation have been answered. Unlike Bradamante's unmasking, which creates social uncertainty, however, Ricciardetto's presentation of the clear signifier of masculinity appears to resolve all confusion. Eventually, of course, Ricciardetto's disguise is discovered, and he is condemned to death for the couple's circumvention of marriage custom. It is from this execution that Ruggiero arrives in time to save Bradamante's twin.

Ariosto was presumably not so unaware as Fiordispina that she and Bradamante could have afforded each other sexual pleasure; but the *Furioso* suppresses that erotic question in preference for emphases on social constructions of gender and on Bradamante's reproductive future as a matriarch.[60] He comes extremely close to the matter, figuratively brushing up against it in Fiordispina's gesture as she seeks a metamorphosis in Bradamante's body by "putting her hand there": a movement halfway between investigation and caress. But the poet too draws back his hand with Fiordispina's, perhaps signaling his own disappointment or resignation before Bradamante's "lack"—her bodily determined limitation—in a culture of masculine rule. This episode precedes both the events at the Rocca di Tris-

tano and Bradamante's defeat of Rodomonte. It thus foreshadows early the
end to Bradamante's liberty to defer her gender by focusing on the limits
of her masculine masquerade. At least in Bradamante's case, physically embodied gender constitutes the epic rock on which romance errancy and
freedom must founder.

At the same time, however, Bradamante's and Ricciardetto's apparent interchangeability in every sphere except the sexual-reproductive one
stresses the capacity of Ariosto's heroine to exceed narrow notions of the
feminine: indeed she is arguably even a *better* warrior than her brother.[61]
Fiordispina acquires a lover whose sex is male but whose gender lies between the masculine and the feminine, at least insofar as he is able persuasively to "perform" femininity before public scrutiny. This lover's ability to
double for both genders, like Bradamante's own capacities in this regard,
goes beyond bipolar categories and allows a glimpse, however tentative, of
new ones that resist firm definition. Such is Ariosto's most suggestive attempt to figure poetically the noncorrespondence of conventional gender
categories with the desires and capacities of human beings. Bradamante and
Ricciardetto, in Fiordispina's eyes, are not *either/or* figures of gender: they
are *both/and,* or somehow between and beyond, admitting difference within
themselves. The episode leaves wholly undecided, furthermore, whether it
is not indeed the "femininity" of Bradamante *and* of Ricciardetto that is
essential to their erotic allure for Fiordispina, despite the socially necessary
decision in favor of the male twin as the "better sex."

This character who is Fiordispina's partner, however, is a confection
pasted together by Ricciardetto. Both he and his sister finally remain constrained by the physical and social "definitions" of their bodies: Bradamante
must crush Fiordispina's hopes that her anatomy will change to reflect her
masculine demeanor and legitimate a love between them; and Ricciardetto,
though he can dress to recall Bradamante, can only postpone the king's discovery that he is a man. Violation of the social rules governing heterosexual
sex, he learns to his great peril, brings swift and severe punishment too, a
fact that makes the danger of social transgression itself a possible message
of this tale.

The episode stands as Ariosto's fantasy exploration of gender's suscepti-
bility to doubling and displacement, a pattern that holds even in the tale's
telling. Both the twins' continued capacity to substitute for each other *and*

the future closing off of that capacity seem to be figured in Ricciardetto's role as transmitter of their story. The most persuasive witness to Bradamante's virtual manliness, her brother, relates her story to the man who will ultimately "make her" the woman she is destined to become in the Estense narrative. The tale of Bradamante's gender struggles turns, here, into a medium for relations between these two men, and it is men who will increasingly speak *for* her as well as *of* her as her story approaches heroic closure. As the tale of Fiordispina's love gives way to the story of Bradamante's and Ruggiero's inevitable union, the poem's brief flirtation with alternative sexualities serves only to cover the alternatives over, marking with fascination what the narrative perhaps most seeks to repress, including, perhaps, even Ruggiero's initial attraction to Ricciardetto when he believes him to be his beloved.[62]

This anecdote of doubling and desire, of desire that must be undoubled and re-sorted according to viable social institutions, foreshadows Bradamante's obligation to halt the suspension of her gender identity in order to fulfill her social and reproductive destiny as matriarch of the Este dynasty. Many readers express dismay over Bradamante's relinquishment of her autonomy in the last cantos of the poem.[63] This sacrifice is, however, inscribed in Bradamante's role as a character from the beginning of the *Furioso*. Bradamante's movement through the narrative is precisely the progress of a powerful individual figure into the hierarchical orders of family, class, and state: in short, into collective social and political structures. It is precisely this commitment by Bradamante that allows the poem to articulate its fictional historical link between her and the poet's contemporary Ferrarese patronesses. Moreover, if Ariosto meant for his poem to communicate to contemporary Italian leaders a moral (ambivalent or not) regarding the necessity of personal sacrifice in order to maintain a strong state, Bradamante represents his model leader.[64]

After participating in the overthrow of Marganorre's misogynist kingdom, Bradamante returns with her new ally and future sister-in-law, Marfisa, to Carlo Magno's camp (XXXVIII.7–9).[65] There her elder brother Rinaldo, who has learned of Bradamante's and Ruggiero's destiny, proposes the couple's marriage to his father, Amone. When Amone of Montalbano refuses to be denied his right to choose his daughter's mate, the last complex of obstacles to the couple's marriage enters the narrative. Bradamante's behavior in this crisis has struck many a reader, for it lacks her characteristic force and independence. In notable contrast to the first and second editions of the poem, in which the author did little to domesticate his heroine, moreover, the 1532 *Furioso* appears both more conservative (some have called it "bourgeois") in Bradamante's regard and increasingly pessimistic in its general political outlook.[66] This development is in my view part and parcel of the increasing conservatization of gender politics throughout the Cinquecento as economic and social conditions encouraged ever greater codification of the roles of men and women. Ariosto, it is true, draws his martial maid into a "domesticated," more conventional feminine role for the end of the poem. This feature of the *Furioso*'s narrative resolution, on the one hand, reflects standards of decorum and verisimilitude for a sixteenth-century audience, who would have found incongruous the combination of knightly activities with the motherhood for which Bradamante is destined throughout the poem.[67] Bradamante's shift away from knightly aggressiveness, however, also enacts a move from the feudal power relations of romance chivalry toward a politics of diplomacy that more resembles the workings of institutions Ariosto himself knew firsthand.[68] Thus Ariosto likens Bradamante increasingly to the public figures to whom the political allegory of the *Furioso* is addressed, even as he steers her into the ostensibly private realm of the family. Like those figures (and like traditional daughters) Bradamante will be constrained to achieve her aims while operating within hierarchical, institutional structures of power, wherein long-held alliances ("domestic" or foreign) are not to be impetuously discarded.

Despite her authoritative knowledge of a divinely ordained destiny, Bradamante cannot bring herself to defy her parents. Rinaldo assumes the role of diplomat, mediating between her and her father. When he argues that Bradamante is already betrothed to Ruggiero, her parents insist nonetheless that she must marry someone of a higher social station. Bradamante remains uncharacteristically silent:

> Sta Bradamante tacita, né al detto
> de la madre s'arrisca a contradire;
> che l'ha in tal riverenzia e in tal rispetto,
> che non potria pensar non l'ubbidire. (XLIV.39.1–4)

[Bradamante remains silent, nor does she
attempt to contradict what her mother says;
for she holds her in such reverence, in such respect,
that she could not think of disobeying her.]

If at first glance such behavior seems implausible in a character who has never before appeared submissive, it is also the case that at least two social institutions have undergirded Bradamante's actions throughout the poem: the chivalric code of honor and the family. In the light of this evidence (and of the dynastic genre of the *Furioso*), it is not surprising that her problem solving is cast *within* the bounds of these institutions. Bradamante's silence in these scenes, perhaps rhetorical insofar as it appears to be part of her strategy to escape the unwanted marriage without offending her parents, also recalls the earlier silence of her male opponents. While the loss of their privileged place in the Symbolic order of male superiority left them speechless, Bradamante faces here her own loss of autonomy as she is deprived of the masculine place she had appropriated within that order. At the same time, her subsequent response suggests that her silence—like her speech in canto XXXII—is diplomatic, a rechanneling of power from physical force into speech that importantly recalls, nonetheless, her martial prowess. Unwilling to disobey her parents (and in particular, the text specifies, out of reverence for her mother) Bradamante turns logically to the higher authority of the king.[69]

She asks Carlo Magno to grant her a boon: that no man be allowed to marry her who cannot *withstand* her—as distinct from defeating her—on the battlefield (XLIV.70). Bradamante's request is more than an ingenious elimination of virtually all possible contenders for her hand, given her established martial prowess. It also indicates her readiness to assume the role of the subordinate term in a gendered pair, albeit only under certain conditions and in a notably unladylike fashion: "he'll have to fight me." Bradamante makes her request to Carlo in the knowledge that she remains "defenseless" against her beloved, but the text is somewhat vague regarding whether her reasoning is based on a conviction of Ruggiero's martial superiority or on Bradamante's belief that she could never bring herself to harm him. Once alone, in a desperate apostrophe to Ruggiero, whom she mistakenly believes to be far away, she explains:

> Da Carlo impetrai grazia, ch'a nessuno
> men di me forte avessi ad esser data,
> con credenza che tu fossi quell'uno
> a cui star contra io non potessi armata. (XLV.91.1–4)

> [I implored grace from Carlo,
> that I not be given to anyone less strong than I,
> in the belief that you were the only one
> against whom I could not maintain defenses.]

The context of dramatic irony in which Bradamante utters her motivations underscores her enduring parity with her companion. She believes that another man has just won her in marriage, in a duel that ended not in victory for either contestant but in a tie between her and her opponent. What she does not know is that the masked knight who, alone among all contenders, was able to endure combat with her is, in fact, the disguised Ruggiero.[70]

Only in this hopeless moment of apparent obligation to marry Leone, a man she does not want, does Bradamante ponder breaking the rules of both familial and chivalric honor. Her willingness to reject those systems results, however, from her discernment of the highest value in Ariosto's moral system:

> —Basti che nel servar fede al mio amante,
> d'ogni scoglio più salda mi ritrovi,
> e passi in questo di gran lunga quante
> mai furo ai tempi antichi, o sieno ai nuovi.
> Che nel resto mi dichino incostante,
> non curo, pur che l'incostanzia giovi:
> pur ch'io non sia di costui tôrre astretta,
> volubil più di foglia anco sia detta. (XLV.101)

> [—Let it suffice that in keeping faith with my lover
> I be found firmer then any rock,
> and in this I surpass all women
> who existed in ancient and modern times.
> If they call me inconstant in all else,

I don't care, provided that this inconstancy be of use.
Provided that I not be forced to take this man,
let me be called more flighty than a leaf.]

As Ascoli has observed of these lines, Bradamante in effect promises here to
be both faithful and unfaithful, and she comes closer than the other characters to resolving the dilemma of conflicted allegiances that troubles so
many in the poem.[71] This instance is also a further demonstration of Bradamante's skill in political analysis, an ability to sort through the more and less
important elements of an unsatisfactory array of choices, and her readiness
to sacrifice certain public perceptions of her actions for a result she deems
more important. This rebellious spirit soon subsides, however. When Marfisa appears before Carlo and announces (in probable bad faith, for we have
no evidence of her claim within the poem) that Ruggiero and Bradamante
have already exchanged marriage vows and performed a private ceremony
in her presence, Bradamante appears meek and passive, just as she had been
in the earlier confrontation with her parents:

> Turbato il re di questa cosa molto,
> Bradamante chiamar fa immantinente;
> e quanto di provar Marfisa ha tolto,
> le fa saper, et ecci Amon presente.
> Tien Bradamante chino a terra il volto,
> e confusa non niega né consente,
> in guisa che comprender di leggiero
> si può che Marfisa abbia detto il vero. (XLV.106)[72]

> [The king, being most disturbed by this matter,
> has Bradamante called immediately;
> and he lets her know what Marfisa had tried to prove;
> and Amon is present.
> Bradamante keeps her face bowed to the ground,
> and confused, she neither confirms nor denies;
> in such a way that one can easily see
> whether Marfisa has told the truth.]

Bradamante's meekness in these moments of familial confrontation recalls
the crucial importance of her armor and knightly identity to the function-

ing of her autonomy. Without her armor she becomes a daughter, unwilling but obedient, resourceful but not openly rebellious. In this more than any other moment in the poem, as the "divested" knight stands listening passively to the testimony of others on her behalf, Bradamante's two roles reveal their irreconcilability within the traditional institutions of family and society. In Elizabeth Bellamy's terms, Bradamante's transformation when she lacks her chivalric accoutrements points to armor as the instrument that held together the "promise of psychic wholeness" enabled by her deferral of femininity and her recombination of gender attributes to serve her own ideals.[73] The poem's signal of Bradamante's disorientation in this moment of utter disarmament ("e confusa non niega né consente") underlines the armor's integrating, even prosthetic function for the woman warrior as subject. The poem's resolution of this momentary dispersal of identity will lie in Bradamante's abandonment of both her public persona as knight and her obligation of filial deference for a monarchical and wifely role that entails both reward and sacrifice.

The last canto of the *Furioso* presents Bradamante on the sidelines during the festive jousts commemorating her imminent wedding to Ruggiero. As she and others admire the wedding tent embroidered by Cassandra (which illustrates the Estense family's descent from Hector and which only Bradamante herself is able to decipher), Ruggiero wins most of the jousts of the day.[74] Rodomonte's arrival and challenge of Ruggiero to a fight to the death signal the approach of the poem's Virgilian closure. In the course of these events Ruggiero assumes a political responsibility lacking in his past actions. Poised momentarily between the two genres of romance and epic, he turns definitively toward the latter and destroys Rodomonte after only a brief moment of hesitation, the determined and brutal gesture of a man now reconciled to rule in the deceitful, violent world the *Furioso* has gradually laid open.[75]

Bradamante's presence in these stanzas is marginal, but it deserves scrutiny in connection with her earlier performance in the poem. Her plea to Ruggiero that she fight in his stead against Rodomonte distinguishes itself from similar unselfish and protective spousal requests because Bradamante alone among brides is capable of fulfilling such an offer (XLVI.114–15); she has in fact already defeated Rodomonte once (XXXV). Our last glimpse of her in the *Furioso* is, significantly, only a reflection conveyed through Ruggiero's eyes. As he fights Rodomonte in the final contest of the *Furioso,* he falls. He turns his gaze on Bradamante and summons courage out of his dismay at seeing her distress:

> Non fu in terra sì tosto, che risorse,
> via più che d'ira, di vergogna pieno;
> però che a Bradamante gli occhi torse,
> e turbar vide il bel viso sereno. (XLVI.125.1–4)

> [No sooner was he on the ground than he was up again,
> more filled with shame than with anger,
> for he had turned his eyes toward Bradamante
> and saw her serene face troubled.]

No longer the stunning warrior who sprang to life by charging into canto I, Bradamante now assumes the auxiliary office of the monarchical wife.[76] Spectator and inspiration to the public achievements of men, she might now be found among the balconied women pictured at the *palio* in Cossa's Ferrarese fresco discussed in chapter 1, or presiding over the *dame di palazzo* in a courtly "portrait" like Castiglione's. Like them, she now supplies to a man the sense of being looked at that helps to constitute him as a performing subject; and like them as well, she assumes the attributes of a femininity that is defined by its contrast with masculine action. While she assumes her place as spectator within the historical tableaux the poem has sketched describing Italy's future (cantos II, XXXIII, XLII, and XLVI), Ruggiero too locks into his destiny, stepping into those visual narratives as the partner projected by Bradamante's searching gaze throughout her quest in the poem.[77] Now protagonist and hero of Estense legend, a blur between political myth and fairy tale, Ruggiero plunges his dagger into the heart of Rodomonte, who has worn an armor not his own—and therefore not impenetrable—since his defeat by Bradamante.

If Bradamante's official entrance into Ferrarese "history" through her marriage to Ruggiero involves the sacrifice of her knightly independence and her acceptance of apparent gender dualities, Ruggiero will soon pay with his life for the same privilege. Moreover, since earlier defeat of Rodomonte contributed decisively to his death because it took away his dragonskin armor, she too is implicated in the violent culture the epic resolution embraces.[78] Because Ruggiero is destined to die shortly after he and Bradamante conceive their only son, she, presumably, will govern alone until Ruggierino reaches adulthood. Indeed, we learned in canto XLI (octaves 60–65) that Bradamante and Marfisa will venture out in search of the slain Ruggiero's body while Bradamante still carries the unborn child in her womb. Undaunted by the failure of this early attempt, Bradamante will later act on a dream in which Ruggiero reveals his slayers' identities; and the two women will seek out the Maganzesi fief, this time destroying it "by fire and sword" in bloody revenge (XLI.66).[79] This projected future, in my view, deeply undercuts the unequivocal domestication recent readers have insisted on in interpreting Bradamante's place in the *Furioso*.

In its turn from romance to epic narrative closure, Ariosto's poem moves from a realm of extravagant fantasy and magic toward institutional constraints and the imminence of death. This same movement requires the female knight to abandon her roving existence and observe the standards of decorum to which women of the sixteenth century were subject. As characters die and magic implements fade from use, Bradamante's and Ruggiero's converging narrative takes over as the principal one in the poem. Significantly, the closure of the *Furioso* leaves a dark cloud over their nuptials. The poem's last octave attends not to that ceremony of beginning—which readers never witness—but to the fatal stabbing of Rodomonte and the flight of his soul into hell. This death only briefly displaces the one it foreshadows by seven years: that of the young groom. Small wonder, in view of this cycle of sacrifices for the dynastic cause, that the first edition of the *Orlando furioso* bore the motto below its final lines that began this chapter.

That Bradamante does not mirror an ideal of twentieth-century feminism, it should go without saying, detracts nothing from her impact on the readers of the sixteenth century. For them her prowess and independence were either an exhilarating inspiration or cause for anxiety. Bradamante, as a powerful woman, alarmed those critics of romance who saw the genre as one that suggested politically perilous reversals of established custom. The debates following the poem's publication, as I discussed above, at times draw openly on the *Furioso*'s depictions of women in their theorization of the relations between epic and romance, and they relate the monstrosity of a hybrid literary form to potentially monstrous developments in the social frameworks of class and gender.

Ariosto's adoption of the romance form allowed him to construct a polycentric narrative that afforded opportunities to juxtapose, contrast, and mix numerous human "types" and potentially countless events. Such a structure gives fitting form to the thematics of the *Furioso,* which return consistently to the importance of loyalty to worthy commitments, yet revolve around the difficulty of interpretation and decision in the world where those commitments must operate. The romance tradition, imbued with magic, unsolvable riddles, and foreboding destinies, allowed extensive exploration of this difficulty. Its labyrinthine architecture also permitted the poet "the great aesthetic possibilities of digression and recurrence, and the feeling of · continuity and movement maintained throughout the vicissitudes of individual adventures."[80]

Ariosto carried this romance structure beyond itself, however. Elaborating the narrative line of Ruggiero and Bradamante as suggested (but not developed) by Boiardo, he connected his poem with events in contemporary history and demanded from the *Furioso* a relevance to its own time. Bradamante's place within this hybrid genre, as illustration of the insufficiency of predetermined schemes for human *or* literary definition, underscores Ariosto's engagement with the intricacies of the literary and social worlds. I suggest, finally, that no other character in the *Orlando furioso* is better suited to measure the distance between that fantasy structure of the poem and its historical moment, to reveal the ideological limitations of Ariosto's serious play with doubled genders and multiple genres, and to figure the sacrifices heroism exacts in its narratives of victory than Bradamante, for whom poetic closure coincides with recuperation and domestic containment. Importantly, however, Bradamante's past and projected "future" in the *Orlando furioso* work to undercut the moment of narrative closure and to resist her confinement to this role, as witnessed by her critics, either fearful or admiring, among Ariosto's first generation of readers. It is, finally, the character of Bradamante whose wandering adventures and undeclared gender allegiance best embody all that appeared transgressive and undisciplined in the *Orlando furioso* to the moralists and canon theorists of the latter sixteenth century. The poem's refusal to focus on a single hero and a unitary narrative action, its mixture of styles, and its epistemological and moral dilemmas all find convenient expression in the emblematic figure of Ariosto's wandering martial maid.

One sector of the *Orlando furioso*'s early audience took particular delight in the poem's treatment of Bradamante and other women. The association of Ariosto's literary-generic experimentation with women's attempts to exceed their traditional place extended strongly, in fact, into writings produced by women themselves in the latter sixteenth century. My next chapter turns to the reception and imitation of the *Orlando furioso* by one of its cleverest female readers, Laura Terracina.

4 Getting a Word in Edgewise:
Laura Terracina's *Discorsi* on the *Orlando Furioso*

I n canto XXXVII of the *Orlando furioso,* concluding a tempestu-
ous treatment of the contemporary *querelle des femmes* throughout
his poem, Ariosto offers a piece of advice that might figure in any
modern manual of self-liberation. He exhorts his "lady" readers to reverse
history's general neglect of their achievements by recording these on their
own behalf:

> Donne, io conchiudo insomma, ch'ogni etate
> molte ha di voi degne d'istoria avute;
> ma per invidia di scrittori state
> non sete dopo la morte conosciute;
> il che più non sarà, poi che voi fate
> per voi stesse immortal vostra virtute. (XXXVII.23)

> [Ladies, I conclude at last that in every age
> there have been many of you who were worthy subjects of
>   history;
> but due to the envy of writers,
> you were never known after your deaths.
> This will no longer be the case, once you
> yourselves render your virtues immortal.]

The poet's entreaty to the women of his day to take up writing each other's
praises and deeds so as to initiate a new history that includes women is, of
course, fraught with the same ironies that mark the rest of Ariosto's poem.
The careful reader may suspect that this "argument" is subject to the general
fate of simple solutions to complex problems in the *Furioso:* it will sooner or
later find its exact counterargument or founder on its practical but absurd

applications. Nonetheless, one woman writing in Naples less than a generation after Ariosto apparently took the advice of the Ferrarese poet to heart
and wrote a work that put his counsel into practice in an ingenious way.

Laura Bacio Terracina (1519–c.1577), a poet whose extraordinary popularity among her contemporaries has earned her only occasional mention
in literary history, published eight volumes of rhymes between 1548 and
1567.[1] As nearly all her critics have been quick to point out, Terracina's writing never approaches the eloquence or innovative distinction of the few
great Cinquecento lyricists: her poems are neither original nor technically
accomplished. This lack of star quality does not, however, distinguish her
from the vast majority of her versifying contemporaries, male or female,
for the sixteenth century produced several generations of poetasters. But
precisely because of its unexceptional character, Terracina's assiduous poetic
activity and the network of correspondents with whom she exchanged
poetic compositions provide important evidence of her generation's embrace of lyric forms. For Terracina and her cohort, lyric poetry was not only
a massive literary phenomenon, importantly facilitated by a publishing industry eager to capitalize on an expanding readership, it was also a favored
medium for personal communication among individuals. On this horizon
of poetic production, Laura Terracina stands out among her peers by virtue
of her exceptional popularity (evinced in the many editions of her poetry),
her conspicuously feminist poetic themes, and her work's unusual revisionary relation to the *Orlando furioso*.

In 1547, at the age of twenty-eight, Terracina published her first volume
of lyrics.[2] Like many other figures of the Neapolitan literary scene, she was
cultivated by the prominent bookseller and editor Marcantonio Passero,
who showed her verses to others, lauded her talents as the latest "mostro
del sesso femminile" [monster (or prodigy) of the female sex], and helped
her get this first collection published by the prestigious Venetian editor
Gabriele Giolito.[3] The volume features, among its other components, the
notable inclusion of four "lamenti" in the voices of characters from the
Orlando furioso. Passero also encouraged Terracina to adopt the laudatory
verse forms for which she became well known in Naples. She apparently
practiced often in this mode at the meetings of the short-lived Neapolitan
Accademia degli Incogniti, in which she enjoyed membership under the
name "Phebea"; and it is easy to imagine her poetry's passage from academy

to printed page in this supportive atmosphere. The ninth edition of this debut volume was published in 1694.[4]

Extremely rare today is the *Seconde rime*, which appeared in 1549, this time under the tutelage of Accademia member Leonardo Curz.[5] Curz seems, in effect, to have financed much of this second volume, since many of its verses were commissioned by him for addressees ranging from foreign dignitaries to his current love interest. The *Discorso sopra tutti i primi canti d' "Orlando furioso"* [Discourse on all the first cantos of the *Orlando furioso*], Terracina's third collection, was published in 1549 as well, and I will return to it in more detail below.[6] The fourth, fifth, and sixth volumes of Terracina's rhymes appeared in 1550, 1552, and 1558 and feature a conventional mixture of poems by the author in praise of others and poems written either in her honor or in dialogue with her. These collections were moderately successful for the time and were reissued twice, once, and twice, respectively. In 1561 Terracina published the only edition of her *Settime rime,* a collection of poems dedicated to all the widows of Naples.[7] A single edition (1567) appeared also of her eighth volume, which at the request of Venetian editor G. A. Valvassori revived the formal scheme adopted for the *Discorso.*[8] Finally, a manuscript of what would have been the ninth collection of Terracina's rhymes (again including compositions by others in her honor) resides in the Biblioteca Nazionale di Firenze.[9] Most of the poems authored by Terracina in this group are spiritual and laudatory verses written to men of the church.[10]

Two book-length monographs (1913 and 1924) and a couple of short essays by Benedetto Croce, a few bibliographic notices concerning rare editions, and a 1975 *tesi di laurea* constitute, to the best of my knowledge, the critical tradition of Laura Terracina.[11] My own entrance into this small company is prompted in part by Terracina's notable popularity during her lifetime. Still more significant than her success, for my interest, is her peculiar appropriation of the most widely read poem of her time, the *Orlando furioso,* as a platform for feminist criticisms of her society. Terracina's *Discorso,* I will argue, carries out within the dimension of the literary text a poetic errancy—and an ambivalent "occupation" of the "echo chamber" of canonical poetry—as her explicit response to women's lack of place in the literary tradition.

Female poets of the generation immediately preceding Terracina's (most notably Gaspara Stampa, Vittoria Colonna, and Chiara Matraini) had placed personal amorous suffering at the center of their poems and, through their use of mythological figures such as Echo, figured the low esteem accorded women's speech and desires.[12] Echo's story, as related by Longus, recounts her punishment for rejecting Pan, a god who both loved her and envied her ability to make beautiful music. Torn limb from limb by shepherds suffering from a madness Pan has sent among them, the ill-fated nymph is buried in scattered pieces throughout the woods, whence her voice continues to breathe in sounds that imitate all things heard. The more familiar Ovidian tale tells an alternative version of the story, that of Echo's hopeless love for the self-adoring and thus unresponsive Narcissus. Taking refuge from her misery in a rocky cave, Echo withers away until she remains nothing but a disembodied voice. Yet this voice, able to speak only by repeating the final phrases of utterances made in its presence, satirically fragments language in a way that makes audible the possible countermeanings hidden in the speaker's words. The phrases Echo repeats must originate in the mouth of another; yet they inevitably come back to their speaker inflected by Echo's divergent perspective, by her reception of their message, and by her wishes. The tale of Echo and Narcissus thus appears to question the possibility of a speaking subject fully in command of its words and to stage the emergence of subjects as a function of other speakers, other listeners, or what Jacques Lacan would call "the gaze."[13] Belatedness, derivation, disembodiment, fragmentation, turn, and return thus all come to be associated with the thwarted expression of Echo, a figure of interrelation "unable to originate discourse, unable to forbear from reply."[14]

Terracina's *Discorso* analogously submits Ariosto's poem to a formalized echo effect, a systematic mode of allusion and citation that allows her, like Narcissus's repulsed lover, to employ remnants of the earlier poet's own words in a way that questions their source and meaning. Doomed to repeat only the final syllables of what she hears from others, Echo acquires the ability to reveal truths unsuspected by those who utter them. Terracina as a woman poet found herself in a similarly secondary position, and she too employed the powers of commentary we recognize in Echo's belatedness. She derived forms and topics from Ariosto and others but reworked these to her own ends, sometimes becoming highly critical of the tradition in which she wrote.

In a new context of burgeoning print culture, moreover, unanticipated "echo effects" emerged as perils for Terracina herself. A creature of the printing industry's marketing strategies, the author of the *Discorso* experienced her fame at least partially as a loss of control over her own discourse. The assiduous requests she received from editors for more poems and the multiplication of error-ridden editions of her work appear to have tormented Terracina as an errant form of reproduction, an involuntary, even coerced, self-propagation in words. This frustration with the vicissitudes of mechanized printing was, of course, familiar to many published authors in the first generations of print culture and is even (in somewhat different form) famously immortalized in the second half of *Don Quixote*. The numerous textual variants that confront the readers of different editions of Terracina's work similarly illustrate her remoteness from the operations that brought her poems before a reading public, and underscore the perils inherent in this new medium for authors not admitted into the inner circles of the editorial process.[15] Terracina's thematic focus on women's speech and her structural relation to Ariosto thus intertwined with her peculiar situation as a female poet to produce a specifically feminine inflection of the authorial experience for sixteenth-century poets.

Writing on early modern women's love lyric, Ann Rosalind Jones describes Renaissance women poets as *bricoleuses:* improvisatory jugglers of found materials. Jones goes on to characterize Renaissance women's writings as "a literate kind of tinkering, the hybridization of disparate literary modes through which women produce new mixed genres."[16] It was through just this sort of tinkering with a single literary text that Terracina elaborated the form of her *Discorso*. Terracina explicitly configures her work in intimate structural and thematic relation to the *Orlando furioso,* composing each of her forty-six cantos to correspond with the identically numbered canto in Ariosto's poem. The *Discorso* solidifies Terracina's relation with the *Orlando furioso* (already initiated in the four "lamenti" of her first volume) and therein constitutes her small claim to fame, as this forty-six-canto poem was republished more times than any of her other works, at least ten before 1608.[17] Borrowing the opening octave from each of Ariosto's cantos, she breaks these purloined stanzas into pieces and intersperses them with new verses of her own devising and argument. Each line from Ariosto's octave reappears as the final line in an octave written by Terracina.[18] The result is a work of forty-six seven-octave cantos, each interwoven with the initial octave of Ariosto's respectively numbered canto. Adding also her own octave-length prefaces (to make a total of eight octaves per canto), Terracina stitches together a duet composition, a kind of coauthored *Furioso* in miniature, whose female-authored stanzas serve as echo chambers for the resonance of the canonical male poet's lines. Terracina's gesture appears to give Ariosto the last word in this scheme, but by controlling the middle space of each of her stanzas, she also turns the tables on him, forcing him to share with her the belated textual space of echoing refrain, and using her own lines to dictate the context in which Ariosto's verses will reverberate. Thus Terracina both appropriates the properties of Echo and keeps this figure of dependency at bay.

Her title for the composition (. . . *sopra tutti i primi canti d' "Orlando furioso"*) reflects a rigid architecture of dialogue and citation: Terracina dilates and disassembles the opening octave of each *Furioso* canto and employs Ariosto's lines as a structural device to anchor her own verses. This compositional strategy not only imposes a generative and formal constraint—committing the work to a precise pattern of citation and to the octave stanza—it also adds weight to the writings of the later female poet by association with an established male author. The *Discorso*'s kinship with the best-selling poem of the sixteenth century appealed not only to its author and its many readers, but especially to its publishers: Giolito capitalized on his numerous editions of the *Furioso* by using its woodcuts to adorn Terracina's cantos; and Valvassori did the same when he picked up publication of the *Discorso*. Through this merging of textual materials, editors accorded the *Discorso* advance prestige, but they also successfully marketed elegant editions of Terracina's work for relatively little money by recycling their stocks of illustrations. Terracina's *Discorso* thus suggests itself today as a remarkably inspired "spin-off" fostered by the same publishing industry that was already profiting so handsomely from Ariosto's poem.[19] It illustrates as well some of the material links in the Cinquecento production of literary works as cultural artifacts to be bought, sold, and circulated in relation to one another and to a common readership.

In addition to borrowing the *Furioso*'s octaves, Terracina retraces in miniature its shape by prefacing each canto of the *Discorso* with an eight-line introductory stanza of her own. These little exordia feature no systematic quotation from Ariosto, but like his proems in the *Furioso,* they function as dedications and introductions to the material in the canto they precede. At the same time, however, the *Discorso* cuts the *Furioso*'s cantos transversely rather than conforming to their flow into multiple narratives. This rejection of the earlier text's narrative direction constitutes a generic shift that allows Terracina to stage her arguments in the lyric forms more congenial to many sixteenth-century women's poetic practices. Dissolving Ariosto's narrative threads, she ties her work instead to the traditions of moral commentary and Petrarchism, proposing by both argument and example a new writing that might revive and refocus women's role in culture. Her strikingly mechanical variation of romance *entrelacement,* at once a violence and a tribute to its model text, thus provides a vivid example of women's detoured path of entry into the early modern literary scene.[20]

The topics discussed in the *Discorso* cantos often take up themes from Ariosto's corresponding proems or recall events narrated in the matching *Furioso* cantos. Terracina draws in this manner on the power and recognition of the earlier poem, but her evident aim is to bring attention to her own social concerns. Prominent among these concerns are the declining moral values of her generation, the violence that engulfs the age, and the historic injustices suffered by women in a world of male privilege. Her canto V, for instance, is, like the proem to Ariosto's canto V, an objection to violence against women. Terracina's eight-line preface to the canto, however, adds a distinctly feminine testimonial voice, which addresses as a related problem the general social complacency before slanderous attacks on women:

> Vorrei parlar, ma l'ira il dir m'intoppa
> Poi che sola difendo il nostro sesso.
> Gia il desiderio mio brama, e galoppa
> Di vendicarsi, e pur non m'è concesso,
> Contra costor c'han si la mente zoppa
> Appo noi Donne; in darne oltraggi spesso:
> Ma spero che dal ciel verrà saetta,
> Et credo che di noi farà vendetta.

> [I want to speak, but anger trips my tongue,
> for I alone defend our sex.

Of course my desire yearns and gallops
to take revenge; yet I'm not allowed,
against those whose minds are so lamed
from frequent insults against us women.
But I hope a fiery bolt will come out of heaven,
and I believe it will exact our vengeance.][21]

This proem addresses two of Terracina's most pressing interests: men's in-
justice to women and the social-psychological barriers to her own self-
expression. Her choice of the word *intoppa* in line 1, which connotes not
only impediment or entrapment but also oral stuttering, focuses this theme
of desire countered by verbal blockage and repetition from the outset. Hin-
dering Terracina's speech, however, is not the conventional subjection of
the poet before the daunting task of lyric expression. Instead the very topic
of her discussion (slander against women) seems to have induced an angry
paralysis of voice for which poetry may provide a remedy.

Canto V continues in dialogue with Ariosto's proem against domestic
violence. Here Terracina evidently overcomes her stutter, for she addresses
her words directly to men, telling them in octave 5:

Ti fe de la tua costa il buon fattore
Uscir la donna con si bel disegno
Acciò che d'una fede, e d'uno amore
Voi foste uniti in questo, et in quel regno.
Ma tu che nulla curi del tuo honore,
In loro spieghi il tuo si fiero sdegno.
Deh mira stolto a gli animai di terra,
L'Orsa con l'Orso al bosco sicuro erra.

[The good Creator made woman
emerge from your rib with such beautiful design
so that in one faith and one love
the two of you could be united in this kingdom and in the next.
But you, who care nothing for your honor,
unfurl on women your fierce scorn.
Oh, fool, look to the animals of the earth:
The she-bear wanders unafraid in the woods with her mate.]

Terracina's use of the octave stanza for poems of moral, political, and historical argument in this and other works is modeled, in part, directly on the *Orlando furioso*. The octave's uncomplicated rhyme scheme generally lends itself to discursive and narrative content, and Ariosto in particular employed his exordial octaves for regular *sententiae* on matters of ethical and political concern to his sixteenth-century readers.[22] Terracina adopts precisely this occasional moral and polemical spirit of the *Orlando furioso* for her *Discorso,* often matching the recipients of her canto dedications to the themes of the stanzas at hand, as when she dedicates canto II—on the sorrows of mourning—to the recently widowed Elionora San Severina.

Nevertheless, at first glance the *Discorso* eludes generic classification. Its title promises a treatise or dialogue, perhaps of literary criticism; yet it consists of octave cantos. It appears to be a miniature version of Ariosto's romance; but it develops no narrative. It coalesces instead as a sermonizing text made possible by Terracina's wandering through another work and effectively arming herself with its authoritative verses while launching her own social commentary from between the lines. The technical device employed in the work has been taken to be Terracina's own invention. Lina Maroi refers to the *Discorso*'s use of Ariosto's octaves as a "bizzarro trovato ed originale davvero" [a bizarre invention of true originality] and remarks that it "attirò l'attenzione delle menti cinquecentesche, avide di novità" [attracted the attention of sixteenth-century minds eager for novelty].[23] One established source for this technique was certainly the tradition of the Italian *centone,* which stemmed from the *cento* of late antiquity.[24] First adopted by Greek and Latin Homerists, this technique, wherein one author rearranges the verses of another into new, sometimes subversive compositions, achieved its first real success in what Jeffrey Schnapp felicitously terms the "patchwork poetics" of the fourth-century female poet Faltonia Betitia Proba.[25] Proba appears not only in Boccaccio's *De mulieribus claris* but in the very first feminist canon of writers, Christine de Pizan's *Book of the City of Ladies,* in which Christine lauds Proba's skill in rearranging verses from Virgil's *Bucolics, Georgics,* and *Aeneid* to effect a distinctly Christian composition. It is difficult to know whether Terracina could have recognized Christine *or* Proba as her forebears in this mode, though both women strike aggressive revisionary relations with their source authors not unlike that between Terracina and Ariosto. In other words, whether or not she knew them directly, Terracina's *Discorso* is in harmony with the earlier women's projects, particularly for its moralizing, Christian orientation. Terracina probably took more immediate inspiration from the Petrarchist *centone* compositions of her contemporaries (including some women), and from Petrarch's own poem, *Rime sparse,* number 70, which features stanzas ending with lines from his lyric models: Arnaut, Dante, Guido Cavalcanti, and Cino da Pistoia.[26]

Yet another tradition, already signaled in her first collection of poems, is even more likely to have inspired Terracina's citations from the *Furioso* than the lyric and feminist ones mentioned thus far. As I note above, among the poems in her first volume of *Rime* and reprinted following the *Discorso* in its 1565 Giolito edition is a series of four "lamenti" based on the complaints of Ariosto's characters Sacripante, Rodomonte, Isabella, and Bradamante. These poems exhibit parallels and direct connections with a lyric tradition that was both courtly and genuinely popularizing.[27] According to James Haar, as early as 1517, and most consistently from the 1540s through the 1580s, composers in Italy were setting Ariosto's verses to music.[28] The earliest and the most numerous examples of these compositions are madrigals based on the laments of characters in the *Furioso.* The fact that Terracina's first incorporations of material from the *Furioso* draw on the same stanzas that inspired these libretti suggests influence by a contemporary culture of music as well as of poetry.[29]

These interconnections stress again the *Orlando furioso*'s important crossroads position in a context of increasing exchange between elite and popular culture. Although the madrigals were composed for performances in the courts and academies, they drew on popular musical forms. In turn, such songs passed easily back into the *piazze* of Italy, where they inevitably underwent further changes in repeated oral and written transmission.[30] Giovambattista Pigna, one of the principal figures in the mid-century defense of the *Furioso* and of the romance genre, suggests that Ariosto himself revised stanzas of his poem after hearing them performed in the streets.[31] As I note in chapter 3, this popularity of the *Furioso* among a nonliterate audience, together with the poem's innovative structure and unconventional depiction of gender relations, was cited frequently by sixteenth-century critics in questioning its validity as a national literary classic. Terracina, who must have known this widely accessible song culture as well as, if not far better than she knew the learned roots of the *centone,* may have recognized the *Furioso*'s suitability for the *centone* technique through her exposure to the poem's musical tradition.[32] She seems in turn to have become a part of this citation network, as one contemporary Bolognese composer echoes Terracina's "Lamento di Sacripante" in a villanella libretto which also features citation from Ariosto.[33] One is tempted to see Terracina's influence also in the composition of Don Salvatore Cataldo, who in 1559 (ten years after the first publication of the *Discorso*) set to music all the opening stanzas of the *Orlando furioso*.[34]

Terracina's recasting of Ariosto's better-known text also played a part in the sixteenth century's ambivalent reception of the *Orlando furioso* itself. As Daniel Javitch notes, the *Discorso* served, in its own particular way, to enhance the moral value of Ariosto's poem in the years when it was an object of controversy.[35] One Venetian teacher even employed Terracina's *Discorso* to divert his pupils from the chivalric romances they preferred: "quelli che vogliono imparar lettere d'ottava rima li facio imparar el libro del Terrazina e alcuni altri" [as for those who want to learn literature in octave rhyme, I have them learn the book of Terracina and several others].[36] In this remarkable enlargement on Terracina's specific compositional scheme, a text that elbows its own lines between those of a more established poet actually displaced that poet's entire work out of a spot in the classroom! At the same time, however, Terracina's feminist initiative would appear ironically undercut. Her text may have figured prominently in the students' literary curriculum, but the Venetian schoolmaster appeared to think her a man (*del Terrazina*).

This dual role for Terracina's work—a conservative text in some respects and an innovative or even rebellious one in others—is, as Jones notes with regard to other poets, a typical feminist "negotiation" of forces on a cultural horizon. Indeed, we gain immeasurably in our understanding of these writings if we perceive them as instances of both rebellion and cooperation within a vastly complex scene of social change, rather than strain to sort out the women poets of early modernity (or any other time) to form strictly feminist and nonfeminist traditions. In the case of Terracina, aristocratic class affiliation, sympathies for the Spanish monarchy, and a strong Counter-Reformation religious conscience, together with an intense desire to participate in elite literary celebrity, formed a solid backdrop against which her ongoing interest in feminist concerns played itself out. Terracina's readers today are apt to note that her verses are filled with Petrarchist commonplaces and that "the prevailing tone of Laura's poetry is deprecatory and moralistic."[37] I would also suggest, however, that these features of Terracina's writing contribute to its interest for those who seek to understand the history of women's literary activity. Hindered by the lackluster education deemed sufficient for most women of her day and endowed with only modest poetic gifts,[38] fully enveloped in Counter-Reformation moralism and shaped by a highly conventionalized culture of writing, Laura Terracina labored nonetheless to be a political as well as a fashionable writer, *and* she wrote a good deal in defense and praise of women. Her combined participation in Petrarchism and in the tradition of moral writings by women suggests either that she was better informed about her feminine literary ancestors than we may know, or that women up to and through her time gravitated by historical circumstance to the lyric and moral modes. In her engagement with the most popular romance narrative of her time and with its particular attention to injustices against women, furthermore, Terracina gives us a view of early modern women's practices not only as writers but also as readers.

The *Discorso*'s dilation of Ariosto's text renders a graphic image of the expansion of a male-dominated literary tradition to accommodate the contributions of sixteenth-century women. Rather than write in opposition to that tradition, Terracina attempts to inhabit the space of established literature and to influence its direction quite literally from within. She seconds Ariosto's social commentary and at the same time corrects, or redirects, his views on women in her own recasting of his poem. The *Discorso* continuously discloses the bond between its innovative formal character, which we might say resides *between* literary genres, and its thematic intention to weave women's marginalized speech into the authoritative mainstream of public writing.

Such innovations enhance the significance of Terracina's title for the work: *Discorso*. This title ultimately suggests another kind of writing between the lines of an original text, for the term *discorso* commonly designated not only analytical discussion or persuasive argument in general — skills rarely cultivated by women of that period — but more particularly a systematic commentary or gloss on an earlier written work. The *Discorso* fulfills this commentary function largely through a process of rewriting.

Although it is broadly allied with Ariosto's sensibilities, however, Terracina's gesture is not the simple addition of a feminine voice to double the opinions of Ariosto's male narrator. It is an insinuation of her verses between the lines of an earlier text, a move that employs citation and displacement to clear a path for the later poet's project and for women's future writings.[39]

A broader look at the *Discorso* reveals this operation at work. Terracina responds affirmatively to Ariosto's suggestion that women write about each other by prefacing many of her cantos with dedicatory octaves to prominent women of her time.[40] Sharpening this focus on women are further dedications to "All Magnificent Women"; to "Men, the Enemies of Women"; to "Unstable and Inconstant Men"; and even to Ariosto's fictional heroine Olimpia.[41] Some cantos develop openly feminist themes, usually expanding on arguments made by Ariosto in his cantos of corresponding number. In canto XX, for example, which she dedicates to Isabella Colonna, Terracina admits her own shortcomings as a writer but repeats Ariosto's argument that women have accomplished many things for which they should be recognized. Similarly, in canto XXVII she defends the value of women's counsel (as Ariosto does in his proem), despite men's tendency to discount it. Canto XXVIII, which in Ariosto's poem offers a salacious story of female infidelity, is modulated by Terracina into a rebuttal of such themes. Instead she responds implicitly to the host who tells this story to Ariosto's character, Rodomonte, by observing that men are misguided to think they can find their own dignity in attacks on the honor of women.

The efficacy of Terracina's relation to Ariosto's poem comes into particular relief in several individual cantos of the *Discorso*. The *Furioso*'s canto XXXVII, as I noted at the beginning of this chapter, opens with the narrator's last explicit contribution to the debate over women that emerges as a prominent discussion topic in the poem. The poet observes that envy and ignorance have led men to neglect the recording of women's great deeds in their historical writings. He further asserts that since men have ignored women in their historical records, women must take responsibility for commemorating each other's achievements in their own writings.

But Ariosto's proem is closely bound to the narrative events of the canto to which it is attached, events that render questionable the narrator's confidence in women's superiority as the custodians of the law and public discourse. In canto XXXVII of the *Orlando furioso,* a band of knights—including prominently Ariosto's two female warriors—arrives in the kingdom of the violent tyrant Marganorre. Marganorre's sons are dead, arguably as a result of their own transgressions against women: one was killed by his unwilling bride, who also killed herself to keep from marrying him; the other died in a duel trying to steal a woman from her husband. Marganorre's view is that women have brought about the ruin of his family and taken away all he holds dear. In response, he has set up a code of laws requiring the total subjugation of women, beginning with their obligation to wear "dresses" humiliatingly cut off at the waist. Marganorre's dress code, which requires women's sexual difference to be always on display, clearly indicates Ariosto's interest in blatant, sexually based injustices.[42] Bradamante, Marfisa, and their comrades storm this kingdom and win it for rule by women. But the female rulers of the new order use their power to write laws that institutionalize yet another tyranny, a mirror image of their own familiar oppression. The women who create new laws for a nonmisogynist society thus project no renewed culture of mutual esteem—as Ariosto's narrator implies might be possible—nor do they build an atmosphere of even grudging tolerance. Instead they create a new slave society in which women may at long last subjugate men. Unable to devise an alternative outside the terms of the polarized logic of which they themselves are victims, the women commit themselves to a new regime of dehumanizing violence. Canto XXXVII thus culminates in dismal terms Ariosto's review of the contemporary *querelle des femmes*. It not only belies women's essential ethical superiority in the civil and social spheres; it also presents the binary terms of the *querelle* as the only visible horizon for gender relations in the future. This episode thus exerts sharp tension on the more optimistic view Ariosto's narrator voices about his contemporaries' good intentions toward women.

Terracina provides a direct response to Ariosto's expressed fears as well as the most explicit illustration of her poetic project in canto XXXVII of the *Discorso* (figs. 6, 7, and 8). There, like the poet of the *Furioso,* she urges women to leave off their traditional work with needle, thread, and cloth and assume the burden (*soma*) of intellectual training. Ariosto's stanzas cast this suggestion in a spirit of hope, observing that even a male monopoly on official discourse has not succeeded in extinguishing all memory of women's former glories (XXXVII.4–6). Terracina's opening lines for the *Discorso*'s canto XXXVII initially speak in direct assent to Ariosto's claims:

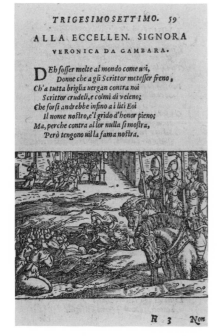

TRIGESIMOSETTIMO. 59

ALLA ECCELLEN. SIGNORA
VERONICA DA GAMBARA.

D*Eh foſſer molte al mondo come uoi,*
  Donne che a gli Scrittor meteſſer freno,
Ch'a tutta briglia uergan contra noi
Scrittor crudeli, e colmi di veleno;
Che forſi andrebbe infino a i liti Eoi
  Il nome noſtro, e'l grido d'honor pieno;
Ma, perche contra al lor nulla ſi moſtra,
  Però tengono uil la fama noſtra.

R 3   *Non*

Figure 6. Laura Terracina, *La prima parte de' discorsi sopra le prime stanze de' canti d' "Orlando furioso."* Venice: Valvassori & Micheli, 1584. Canto XXXVII. Courtesy of the Folger Shakespeare Library.

Non credo nò, che gli Scrittor; che in carte
Han scritto in biasmo nostro, e in poca lode,
C'habian si ben compito il mo(n)do, e l'arte,
Che non si possa oprar contra lor frode. (XXXVII.1)[43]

[No, I certainly do not believe that Writers who have written
slanders about us on paper, and said little in our praise,
have so well accomplished this manner and this art
that one can't operate against their fraud.]

Like Ariosto, Terracina argues that the views men have promulgated about women in history and literature need not go unanswered. But significantly absent from these stanzas is Ariosto's confidence in the new generation of male defenders of women among his contemporaries. Ariosto assembles a list of men he considers to be women's advocates, including Baldessare Castiglione, Pietro Bembo, and Galeazzo Flavio Capella (Capra), and

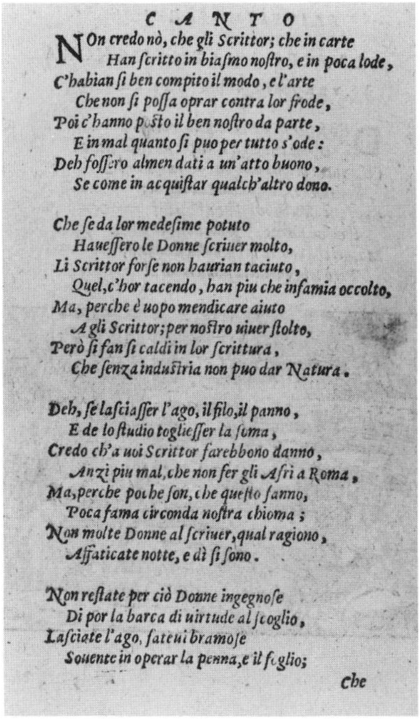
CANTO

NOn credo nò, che gli Scrittor; che in carte
Han ſcritto in biaſmo noſtro, e in poca lode,
C'habian ſi ben compito il modo, e l'arte
Che non ſi poſſa oprar contra lor frode,
Poi c'hanno posto il ben noſtro da parte,
E in mal quanto ſi puo per tutto s'ode:
Deh foſſero almen dati a un'atto buono,
Se come in acquiſtar qualch'altro dono.

Che ſe da lor medeſime potuto
Haueſſero le Donne ſcriuer molto,
Li Scrittor forſe non haurian taciuto,
Quel, c'hor tacendo, han piu che infamia occolto,
Ma, perche è uopo mendicare aiuto
A gli Scrittor; per noſtro uiuer ſtolto,
Però ſi fan ſi caldi in lor ſcrittura,
Che ſenza induſtria non puo dar Natura.

Deh, ſe laſciaſſer l'ago, il filo, il panno,
E de lo ſtudio toglieſſer la ſuma,
Credo ch'a uoi Scrittor ſarebbono danno,
Anzi piu mal, che non fer gli Afri a Roma,
Ma, perche poche ſon, che queſto ſanno,
Poca fama circonda noſtra chioma;
Non molte Donne al ſcriuer, qual ragiono,
Affaticate notte, e dì ſi ſono.

Non reſtate per ciò Donne ingegnoſe
Di por la barca di uirtude al ſcoglio,
Laſciate l'ago, fateui bramoſe
Souente in operar la penna, e il foglio;

Che

Figure 7. Laura Terracina, *La prima parte de' discorsi sopra le prime stanze de' canti d' "Orlando furioso."* Venice: Valvassori & Micheli, 1584. Canto XXXVII. Courtesy of the Folger Shakespeare Library.

encourages women to take heart from the philogynist writings of these authors. Terracina, in contrast, reiterates only that women must speak for themselves. She even raises the question of male self-interest in the current vogue of writings about women, thereby implicitly casting into doubt the motives of her model poet and his well-meaning exemplars:

> Ma, perche il tacer nostro assai piu spinge,
> Quel fervido desio, le menti ingorde,
> Ciascun come li pare, hor scrive, hor (s)pinge
> Tal contra a noi, che mille orecchie assorde.
> E cosi il nostro honor, sonando finge
> Ogni Scrittor con risonante corde,
> E si lietan di dare a lor piu altura
> Successo; n'è uscit' opra non oscura. (XXXVII.6)

> [But because our silence prods yet further
> that fervent wish, with greedy minds

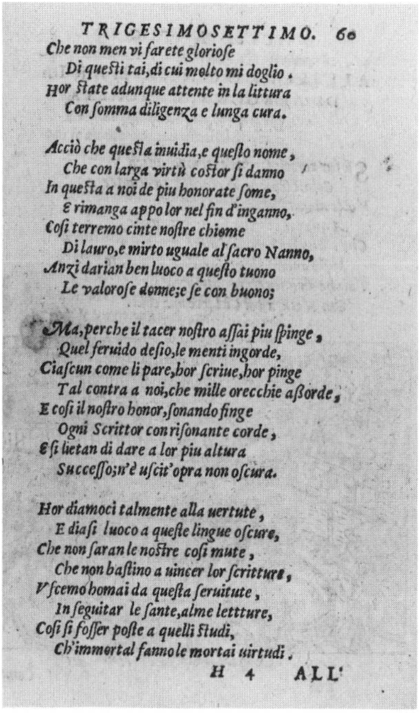

Figure 8. Laura Terracina, *La prima parte de' discorsi sopra le prime stanze de' canti d' "Orlando furioso."* Venice: Valvassori & Micheli, 1584. Canto XXXVII. Courtesy of the Folger Shakespeare Library.

each [man] as he likes now writes, now paints (incites)
such things against us that he deafens a thousand ears.
And so every writer feigns playing
the tune of our honor in resounding chords.
And they delight in elevating their own
success; nor once such work issues does it ever go dim.]

Significantly, Terracina directs almost all of canto XXXVII to women readers (*our* honor, *our* silence, etc.), as she insists on the necessity of their own writing. Her only address to the men in her audience appears in stanza 3, in which she warns them of women's potential discursive power:

Deh, se lasciasser l'ago, il filo, il panno
E de lo studio togliesser la soma,
Credo ch'a voi Scrittor farebbono danno,
Anzi più mal, che non fer gli Afri a Roma. (XXXVII.3.1–4) [44]

[Ah, if they put down their needle, thread, and cloth
and took on the task of study,
I think they'd do more damage to you writers
than the Africans did to Rome.]

As Terracina seeks an appropriate scale of repayment for men's misrepresentation of women, the verbal aggression she so often attributes to men prompts the menace of a feminine counterviolence figured as verbal war. Writing is here cast as an instrument of combat, adopted regularly by men against women, but up to now kept largely out of female hands. The bellicose retaliation evoked in these verses is sufficiently hyperbolic to shade them with irony (whether conscious or unwitting), as the prim Terracina threatens a response more credible from Marfisa or Bradamante than from a member of the Neapolitan academy. Yet such irony only contributes to the poignancy of Terracina's lines, written as they are in critical awareness unmatched by the power to alter society.

Her parallel between retaliating women and the warring Africans, moreover, inevitably recalls Dido, queen of Carthage.[45] In *Aeneid* 4 the bereft queen's final curse on a departing Aeneas appears to "predict" the Punic Wars, a long and bitter struggle between Rome and North Africa that was already part of Roman history when Virgil wrote in the first century B.C.E. Dido's curse on Aeneas for abandoning her in order to found Rome connects their personal relationship to an enduring narrative of colonization and subjugation for the sake of a patrilineal empire. Terracina's reference to the Africans in this octave threatening women's revenge thus entwines a history of struggle for military dominance with the record of men's oppression of women and projects these aggressions as parts of one large pattern. Hannibal's considerable and spectacular damage to Rome in the Punic Wars was followed, of course, by Roman victory. Terracina's threat that women might *exceed* the ravages brought to Rome by this war ("Anzi, più mal") thus implicitly projects a vindication and a desired overturning of history reaching all the way back to the injustices of antiquity.

Terracina's imagery for women's discursive retaliation against their historic mistreatment is, notably, not unlike the revenge Ariosto depicts for Marganorre. This canto also likens Terracina's poetic voice to that of the *Furioso*'s narrator, whose tone shifts with his response to narrative events and with his mood. If Ariosto's narrator tends to change his mind whenever the circumstances of his characters elicit from him new, sympathetic identifications with their troubles, Terracina loses her composure in moments of intense reflection on the plight of women. In these instances her anger gets the better of her, and, like the narrator of her model poem, she lashes out in hostile fantasies and violent wishes.

Many features of the *Discorso* point to its context of religious and political strife in Italy in the second half of the sixteenth century. A number of cantos explore moral themes of a general nature and reflect the anxieties of mid-sixteenth-century Catholics over the disintegration of their church's hegemony in Europe. Terracina often echoes Ariosto's comments on the difficulties of discerning true friendship or finding a faithful partner in life. But like other Counter-Reformation writers, she takes more seriously than Ariosto does the notion that the past was more innocent than the present. Ariosto famously dismisses the "great goodness of the knights of yore" and treats the idea of a lost moral rectitude as a nostalgic cliché. In contrast, Terracina appears to maintain that times must indeed have been much better once, especially where men and young people are concerned. Typical in its fervent embrace of Ariosto's darkest meditation on human conduct is her canto IV, addressed "To Traitorous Friends":

> Ov'è quel ben perduto, e quello amore
> Di quella antica etade, e quel soggiorno
> Tanto sincero, e tanto pien d'honore,
> Che rendea di vertudi il mondo adorno?
> Et hor sol biasmi trovo, e dishonore;
> Et sol'inganni, e fraudi d'ogn'intorno,
> In questa assai più oscura che serena
> Vita mortal tutta d'invidia piena. (IV.8)

> [Where are the lost goodness and the love
> of that ancient age, and that
> sincere, honorable life
> which made the world a virtue-adorned place?
> Now I find only slander and disgrace;

and only deceits and fraud at every turn
in this mortal life full of envy,
much more gloomy than it is clear.]

Ariosto's voice of foreboding holds particular, suggestive appeal for Terracina. In canto VII she meditates on the vanities of worldly struggles. Because people fail to grasp their destinies in eternity, she reflects, they lose sight of the utter brevity of earthly life, its transient sufferings and its ephemeral pleasures. In their oblivion, they remain unconscious even of their own actions:

> Se ben mill'anni avessi, hier nascesti:
> Ne piu si pensa nel tempo passato.
> Appena quello sai, c'hora facesti
> Tanto sei del viver smemorato. (VII.7.1–4)

> [Were you even a thousand years old, you were born but
>   yesterday:
> yet no one reflects on time passed.
> You barely know that which you've just done,
> so oblivious are you of living.]

She resumes this theme in canto XXV, "To Vainglorious Young Men and Women," arguing that a shortsighted desire for fame ruins young people and even hastens their deaths. In canto XXXIV Terracina rails against usurers; in XLII she attacks the iniquities of the courts.

Yet even in the more omnibus tirades, Terracina expresses interest in women's particular circumstances. Canto XI, "To The Libidinous Insatiables," begins with the poet's wish to shut out her perception of the sexual vice that surrounds her:

> Vorrei quest'occhi, e queste orechie ancora
> Serrar per sempre, e non sol per un anno
> Poi ch'io pur veggio in questa etade fuora
> Un stuol si brutto, e di perpetuo danno. (XI.1.1–4)

> [I'd like to close these eyes and seal these ears too,
> forever, and not just for a year.

> For I see truly, abroad in this age
> a wicked and perpetually harmful throng.]

Within this survey of moral decay she proceeds to consider women, who are among the most frequent victims of the behavior she condemns. Addressing her male readers, she asks:

> Quante matrone, e quante rie donzelle
> Le conducete svergognate a morte,
> Quante innocenti, e pure verginelle
> Vanno dolenti a ritrovar la sorte,
> Quanti gridi ne van sino a le stelle:
> Pur il vostro desio si folle, e forte
> Ogn'un lieto ne va del suo discorso [46]
> Raro è però che di ragione il morso. (XI.3)

> [How many matrons, and how many wicked girls
> do you lead in shame to their deaths,
> How many innocent maids and chaste virgins
> go sorrowing to meet their fate,
> How many cries rise from them all the way to the stars:
> Yet you all go happily recounting
> your desire, so crazed and strong,
> but rare is the one gripped by reason.]

When Terracina casts a critical eye on women, she often tempers her complaints with details of their difficult circumstances. In canto XXVI she regrets that there are many who seek only wealth, but she praises the women of her time who strive for virtue. Her canto XXII, which she instructs good women not to read (as Ariosto urges his female readers not to read his canto XXVIII), is an attack on wicked females who sully the reputation of the entire sex by taking lovers rather than contenting themselves with the pleasures of fidelity. Softening this criticism at the same time is the poet's regret that women are doomed to ruin if they falter but once in their judgment of matters amorous:

> Ma quante errando per il mondo vanno
> Et quante in li spitai si veggon strutte,

> Non pensamo nel fin, del nostro danno
> Corremo cieche al precipitio tutte.
> Or di un breve voler, si lunge affanno,
> Peggio è, dipoi, che siam nomate putte. (XXII.7.1–6)

> [But how many women go erring through the world
> And how many are seen ruined in the hospitals.
> We think not of the end, of our detriment;
> we all run blind to the precipice.
> Now, from that brief desire stems such long suffering;
> and what is worse, we come to be called whores.]

Here Terracina admonishes women that society will be pitiless in labeling their sin if they overstep the sexual limits set for them, evoking a variation on the circular definition of femininity I discussed in chapter 1. This path from virtue to promiscuity to ruin, she cautions, is marked by the onset of venereal disease. In the syphilis wards of the hospitals and prisons of the time, infected women of all classes languished beside prostitutes and suffered the same ostracization.[47] But critical as she is, Terracina's adoption of the first-person plural in lines 3, 4, and 6 suggests her solidarity with the victims of this narrow margin for female error. As she distances herself from the reckless behavior some women adopt, she acknowledges that crippling social strictures limit the activities and threaten the well-being of her entire sex.

Terracina's combination of political allegiances is most apparent when she writes about war. A sympathizer with the Spanish rulers of Naples, she dedicates the entire *Discorso* to Charles V and writes repeatedly in support of his military campaigns.[48] In many octaves she celebrates prominent soldiers of the day, whom she often compares favorably with the ancients. Her canto XIV is dedicated to Pope Julius III, in praise of his war efforts in alliance with the king of Spain. More aggressively, she addresses canto XLII to Sultan Suleymen, king of the Turks. Accusing Suleymen of knowing Christianity to be the true faith but persisting cynically in his own religion, she predicts that both he *and* his faith will meet an end worse than that of Ariosto's defeated pagan king, Agramante.[49] In canto XL she taunts the king of France:

Il nostro Re gli è assai di te più forte
La verità de cio fa chiaro segno,
E miglior genti, di battaglia, e accorte
Tien questa Italia, e Spagna, e di piu ingegno. (XL.1.3–6)

[Our king is so much stronger than you are;
and clear signs show that this is true.
And shrewder folk, better in battle
and more ingenious, belong to Italy and Spain.]

Yet even this topic is inflected with Terracina's concerns for women and their experience of state politics. Although she praises Julius III in canto XIV as a warring monarch, she wonders whether her pen is virile enough ("Sarà le penna mia tanto verile"—a line that, as printed, includes a pun on "true enough") to allow her to write about war, which is far outside her sensibilities and experience as a woman ("Che'l sesso feminil, d'arme non sente"). Indeed, she shifts the ground of war poetry—and of the historically masculine epic mode—to consider at length the victims of such violent glory.[50]

Canto XV, "A li crudeli e sanguinosi capitani" [To cruel and bloody captains], begs military officers to curb the violence of their troops against women, children, and the elderly, even as Terracina excuses this behavior and concedes (perhaps with irony) that every man thinks first of his own fame ("Bench'io vi scolpo; che ne la vittoria / Ogn'un pensa sua fama, & a sua gloria"). Although she appears to pardon these combatants, Terracina questions a military leadership that permits the ravaging of towns and civilians:

Qual Capitan, qual conduttier che regge
Un giovenile esercito, e gagliardo
De la impieta crudel, ritiene e fregge
Il furor sanguinoso, e il crudel dardo,
Qual sia soldato pur ch'osservi legge,
Che non sia contra *Donne* un Leopardo,
Giudicio sano gliè, ch'in ogni cosa
Fu il vincer sempre mai laudabil cosa.

Ma che colpa di questo hanno i figliuoli,
E tanti vecchi, e *tante afflitte donne,*

Che de l'altrui fallir, patiscon duoli;
Qual pensier, è che tanto vi disdonne,[51]
Che di noi fate i nostri padri soli
Lasciando empii trophei, di *veste, e gonne.* (XV.2–3.1–6,
   emphasis added)

[Whatever Leader, what mercenary charged
with a young and vigorous army
holds back from its pitiless cruelty
the bloody furor, the cruel arrow;
Whatever soldier too observes the law,
and will not be a Leopard against *women*
shows good judgment, for in every matter
victory has always been a praiseworthy thing.

But what fault is this of children
and the aged, and *so many afflicted women*
who endure the pains of another's defeat?
What thought so overtakes you
that you deprive our fathers of us,
leaving behind unholy trophies of *dresses and skirts.*]

As Terracina develops this canto, she asks the same questions women have
always asked from their position on the margins of men's wars.[52] Is there no
glory in letting one's opponent live? Is there no conflict between religious
devotion and the military ravages perpetrated by the faithful? Her conclusion is a grim one befitting her times: Insatiable war is not about God or
the welfare of the world or honor. It is about blood and rage and desire:

Ne a Dio, n'al mondo, ne a l'honor pensate,
O dispettosa, e insaciabil guerra,
Che via piu il sangue, che lor beni amate.
Il sangue, l'ira, e il desiderio pregno
Spesso far suole, il capitan men degno. (XV.5.4–8)

Laura Terracina returned to the *Orlando furioso* in her later writings, once
again filtering her political and moral concerns through Ariosto's poem. Her

Seste rime features a suite of octaves entitled "A istantia del signor Girolamo di Costanzo sopra d'una stanza del Furioso," in which Terracina evokes Rodomonte's complaint against Doralice (XXVII.118), already visited in her first collection of rhymes. In 1567 she resumed her relation with Ariosto on the large scale with a sequel to her earlier *Discorso*, the *Seconda parte de' discorsi sopra le seconde stanze de' canti d' "Orlando furioso."* Returning to many of the themes of the first *Discorso*, she elaborates again in the *Seconda parte* on topics derived from the *Orlando furioso*'s forty-six proems. The generative device structuring the *Seconda parte* differs only slightly from that of the first. The second octaves of Ariosto's cantos here supply the final lines for each octave by Terracina, just as the first octaves were distributed over cantos of the earlier work; and just as in the first *Discorso*, each canto begins with an octave of Terracina's own. But octave 1 of the canto proper in the *Seconda parte* almost entirely reproduces octave 1 of Ariosto's corresponding canto, with only line 7 belonging to Terracina. The first line from Ariosto's octave 2 becomes Terracina's line 8, initiating the final-line citation pattern that incorporates all of the *Furioso*'s second octaves.[53] This compositional scheme allows Terracina partly to "reassemble" the *Orlando furioso* stanzas she broke apart in order to write the first *Discorso*, suggesting a very large operation in which the entire Ariostan poem might dilate and contract under the poetic hand of Terracina.[54] The *Seconda parte* as a result of this reassembly also required Terracina herself to compose fewer lines of poetry.

Terracina writes in her preface dedicating this work to Franco Larcari—with what degree of sincerity we cannot say—that she had no desire to write another *Discorso* but was prevailed on by the prominent Venetian publisher Luigi Valvassori, and was even constrained to write by her husband when she resisted.[55] She claims to be old, uninspired, and weary of "i fumi del mondo." If indeed Terracina's verses in the *Seconda parte* witness the passage of eighteen years since the *Terze rime*, it is not only in the exhaustion she attributes to her poetic voice but in the growth of her disillusionment with fame and love. The writer of the later work is a seasoned poet—author of seven lyric collections—and a married woman of middle age.[56] Moreover, the coercion by her husband and Valvassori, together with the apparent solicitation of the Rodomonte lament in the *Seste rime* (prominently flagged in the composition's title) point to Terracina's disenchantment with the fame she had earned through the wide distribution of the *Discorso*.

Already in the *Quarte rime,* which followed by just a year the publication
of the *Discorso,* Terracina's prefatory letter to Giovanni Alfonso Mantegna di
Maida complains that the *Discorso* came out with errors from the printer in
addition to her own, the latter of which Ludovico Dolce had promised—
but neglected—to correct. "Dolce forse ad altrui, a me amarissimo" [Sweet
perhaps to others, to me quite bitter], she quips, punning on the unzeal-
ous editor's name as she remarks his violation of her trust in him. Terracina
places her confidence for the *Quarte rime* in Mantegna, whose expertise as a
speaker of Tuscan qualifies him especially, in her view, to oversee a Neapolitan's emergence in a print market thoroughly dominated by the Florentine
tongue. In a postscript letter appended to the *Rime quinte,* also addressed
to Mantegna, Terracina remarks that she would not be writing at all any
more, were it not for Valvassori's assiduous requests for more poems and
her own knowledge that Mantegna watches carefully over the production
of her work.

Mantegna's responses to Terracina's expressions of gratitude insist that
her verses are already so perfect as not to require any interference from him
as editor. While such is undoubtedly the response—created for print—of a
gracious and generous collaborator, these exchanges also underline the context of linguistic standardization in which virtually any non-Tuscan poet
had to rely on editors expert in the new, "official" language of print advo-
cated by Pietro Bembo's *Prose della volgar lingua.* Terracina's biographers have
been far more eager to assume that her poems were virtually rewritten for
her by helpful editors than to acknowledge the atmosphere of intense poetic
collaboration reigning among all poets of the period, male and female. The
burden of linguistic revision enforced for nearly *all* poetic publication of
the sixteenth century, moreover, was real, especially for non-Tuscans, and
included Ariosto himself.[57] Significant here is Terracina's apparent sense of
estrangement from the processes that brought her poetry into print on the
Venetian market once she gave it over to those who solicited work from
her. In a market economy for literature, Terracina's poems seemed to reappear to her as strangers rather than the children of her imagination. At
the same time, her husband and her sponsoring press exhorted her to keep
as many of these alienated texts as possible in circulation.

The *Seconda parte* features more open self-reference as well as more aggressive and ambivalent handling of Ariosto's material than the *Discorso*

does. In canto IX, octave 5, Terracina remarks wistfully on the pangs of love she felt in her own youth; in canto XXIX she performs the unusual aggression of directly revising Ariosto's line, "parlò contra il dover" [he spoke as he shouldn't have], to read "parlò contra di noi" [he spoke against us]. In canto XXVIII, "A le triste, et malegne mogliere" [To wicked and malicious wives], Terracina assumes the reluctant voice of Ariosto's narrator, who claims to be constrained to write about unpleasant topics. Ariosto directs his apologies in canto XXVIII to women who might be offended by the story of female lust that Rodomonte is about to hear from an innkeeper. Terracina, in a very different spirit, borrows this poetic persona of ambivalence to describe her own conflict between solidarity with her sex and her desire to criticize the morals of adulterous wives. Claiming that she too is a woman and that she considers herself among the faithful wives whom she addresses ("Ch'anch'io son Donna, et come voi mi estimo"), she copies Ariosto's gesture of blaming his feigned source, Turpin, insisting it was Turpin who obliged her, too, to include such unsavory material in her text. The canto's final couplet, which according to the work's generative pattern must reproduce the final two lines of Ariosto's octave, rings with the shift of the speaking voice from male to female as Terracina echoes, "N'ho fatto mille prove, et v'ho dimostro, / Ch'io son nè potrei esser se non vostro." [I've given a thousand proofs and shown to you / that I am, and could be nothing but, your own.]

Most aggressive of all is Terracina's canto XXX, in which she turns Ariosto's verses against him and lets loose her fury as woman and as poet. Canto XXX corresponds to the apology by Ariosto's narrator for his earlier bitter outburst of disappointment over Angelica's escape from the mad Orlando. Terracina echoes with a similar outburst and recovery, but she turns her hostility toward Ariosto himself:

> Ser Lodovico ha il torto, se vuol dire
> Mal de le donne, e porle in ciò a comune.
> S'alcuna l'amor suo non può patire,
> Deve perciò sua sola opinion
> Dar caccia a l'altre, e farle al basso gire?
> Se quella sola è del suo mal cagione?

Ma il suo sparlar m'ha fatto a questa volta
Che dopo molta patientia, e molta,

Non ho potuto a tanto mal tacere
Che contra noi senza ragion ei dice,
Nè quelle rime legger, nè vedere
Più posso, anchor ch'io pur ne sia amatrice.
Per esserne tanto acre, e cosi fiere,
E certo opra crudel d'un'ira ultrice.
Ma mi bisogna far come l'infermo
Quando contra il dolor non ha più schermo.

D'altra parte io lo scolpo, e l'escuso,
Che quando un di cor ama, e non è amato
Si grave dolor sente, che confuso
Nè sa detto formar ch'altrui sia grato,
Nè trovar loco può vivendo escluso
Il suo voler da l'amoroso stato,
Di cui vedendo ogni speranza folta
Cede a la rabbia, e a bestemmiar si volta.

Io quanto a me perdono al dolor troppo.
Ma sì convien le donne rispettare:
Et non correr col dir bugiardo, e zoppo
Per una, che sia rea, l'altre a biasimare.
Che di carrera tutte, e di galoppo
Sozzopra le vedo io per l'aria andare,
Benche tacendo, il dir suo non confermo,
Manca il dolor, ne l'impeto sta fermo.

Che buon ciò sappia a chi è toccato al vivo,
Non credo anchor, nè crederollo mai:
Chi de l'honor senza ragione è privo
Con ragion dee sentir tormenti, e guai.
Però sempre col buono ho scritto e scrivo
Che merta l'huomo honor, e lode assai,
Tenendo nel mio stil la man raccolta,
Che la lingua al dir mal facea si sciolta.

Hor l'odio qui lasciam da parte e l'ira,
D'honor, e di piacer formando rime,
Ch'a dir il ver chi con giust'occhio mira,
Fu degno sempre l'huom d'honor sublime.
La lingua sempre nel mal dir ci tira
E giorno, e notte, con dolor ne opprime,
E si ravvede, e pente, e n'ha dispetto,
Ma quel che ha detto, non può far non detto. (XXX.3–8)

[Ser Ludovico is in the wrong, if he wants to speak
ill of women and place a common blame on them all.
If some lady cannot suffer his love,
must his opinion of her, alone, for this reason
dismiss all other women and bring them low?
If only she is the cause of his suffering?
But his criticism has brought me to the turn,
where after a great, great deal of patience

I was not able to keep quiet before so much wrong
which he speaks against us for no reason.
And I can no longer bear to read those verses or see them,
though I am still their admirer.
To be so acrid and so fierce [about the matter]
is surely the cruel product of an ulterior ire.
But I must do as a sick person
who has no more defense against the pain.

On the other hand, I forgive him and excuse him,
for when one loves from the heart and is not loved back,
one feels such deep pain that he is confused.
And knows not how to fashion a word pleasing to others,
nor can he find himself a place,
since his desire lives excluded from the amorous state.
Hence, realizing that there is no hope,
he gives in to rage, and he resorts to cursing.

For my part I forgive him in his exceeding pain.
But it is proper to respect women,

and not rush to telling lies and lamed
by one who may be wicked, criticize the others.
Because I see them all of a sudden violently
tossed in the air and fallen to the ground.
If I keep silent, I'm not confirming his words;
pain fails, nor does vehemence endure.

That one touched to the quick knows this well
I don't believe now and I never will:
Whoever is deprived of honor for no reason
must rightly feel troubled and tormented.
But I always wrote and write in good spirit
for (the)[58] man deserves much honor and praise,
restraining with my style the hand
that my tongue so loosened to speak ill.

Now let us leave hatred and anger aside,
making rhymes of honor and pleasure.
For verily, if one looks with a straight eye
(the) man appears ever worthy of sublime honor.
The tongue always draws us to speak ill,
and day and night it oppresses us with sorrow.
And we reconsider, and regret, and feel vexed,
but what one has said one cannot unsay.]

Clearly, Terracina is not concerned here with subtle distinctions between Ariosto's narrator and the poet himself. Implicitly recognizing the poet's fiction, however, she assumes a position similar to that of the *Furioso*'s mad speaker, who lets his anger run away with his reason, then recovers to suggest conciliation with potentially offended readers. As in her earlier attacks on adulterous wives and violent soldiers, here too she oscillates from open criticism back to sympathy for the position of the poet spurned in love. Highlighting what her poetry has systematically both mobilized and struggled against—the inevitable echoes in history of words already pronounced—she proposes nonetheless a move beyond old differences. That Terracina's own poetic voice would now be released for similar irreversible resonance appears to have been both her comfort and her torment. Surely her project was to inject her own commentary into the historic discussion of women's faults and virtues; but her contributions had already come back to haunt her in the unfamiliar shapes of misprinted words.

Terracina's formal system for the *Discorso* and her other poems deriving from the *Furioso* is immediately evident: she borrows Ariosto's lines to complete her own stanzas. In the service of her distinct project, however, Ariosto's verses—like those repeated by Echo—often come out altered, distorted to give entirely new meanings. In canto XXXVII, for example, Ariosto's words "n'è uscit'opra non oscura" refer to women's labors over centuries past, which have resulted in works *not without brilliance*. Terracina's reworking of the line to fit her argument revises its punctuation to produce a homophonic phrase of quite different meaning: "Nè uscit'opra, non oscura." Here the line invokes the works men write to slander women, which, *once circulated, never fade into obscurity*. In other instances Terracina's layering of a feminine speaking voice over the masculine one of Ariosto's narrator produces ironic distancing, such as we find in the *Seconda parte*'s canto XXVIII discussed above, in which Terracina's direct citation of Ariosto, her echo of his line in her own voice ("Ch'io son, nè potrei esser se non vostro"), inevitably questions Ariosto's advocacy for her sex. How, she seems to ask, her women readers, is the author of the *Furioso* your poet—*vostro*—in the same way that I am *vostro/a*? Here Terracina submits Ariosto's lines to an echo effect that suggests its own greater authenticity when compared with the original. Finally, the more sophisticated assault of canto XXX in the *Seconda parte* employs both of these devices and adds to them an ironic appropriation of the inconstant narrative persona we find in the *Furioso:* Terracina aims to beat Ariosto at his own game while calling his poem to account for all its criticisms of women, retracted or not.

These equivocations resulting from the transposition of speakers and of grammatical cues effect a double voicing in Terracina's text that orients the *Discorso* constantly back toward the *Orlando furioso,* but in the same sort of polemical relationship that Jeffrey Schnapp has noted lies at the heart of all *cento* literature.[59] By their very nature secondary and subservient at the same time they are critical, such texts both affirm and diminish the stature of their sources. Oscillating between intertextual consonance and dissonance, they cast ironic reflections on established works and expose nuances in the meaning, function, and ideology of their models. Schnapp observes that female authors' predominance in *cento* writing "coincides with one of the genre's most salient attributes: its self-denigration as a belated, derivative and/or 'nonserious' form of writing." [60] This rhetoric of humility, he notes, emerges even from the name for the poetry itself, as the *centonarius,* or "dealer in *centones,*" was the ragpicker or the beggar at the lowest level of Roman society. Terracina's participation in this humble ragpicker's poetry — in what Jones would identify as the practice of the *bricoleuse*—allows her to accomplish her aim of entering the (largely male) company of poets without betraying her origins in the community of women. Abandoning her needle and thread she picks up the writer's pen. With that instrument, however, she performs the labors of the seamstress as well as those of the poet, "patching" together an unevenly colored, irregular, but protective cloak to wear in the chilly air of the male literary tradition.

5 From Insult to Injury:

Bandello's Tales of Isabella de Luna

On 27 July 1564 a Spanish woman living near the church of San Salvatore alle Coppelle in Rome dictated her last will and testament to an official notary, comforted by the additional presence of several clergymen.[1] The señora was evidently of considerable means and independence, for at this late date in her life she retained substantial properties (including her own house) and enough disposable income to distribute among numerous beneficiaries. When she died ten months later (22 May 1565), she had carefully arranged for the payment of all her debts and for the collection of sums owed to her by others. In addition, she bequeathed generous funds to monasteries and convents as well as to her loved ones (her mother, two sisters, an uncle, and friends). She sponsored several dowries; freed and provided for her African slave, Scilla; pledged fifty scudi to a woman named Nicolosa if the latter agreed to abandon a life of sin and began to live as a decent person; and named Cardinal Alessandro Farnese her universal heir. To him she gave instructions to have her buried in the convent of the Minimi in Trinità dei Monti, in a chapel to be built from the proceeds of her estate (a request that was never carried out). Finally, she asked Farnese, as her executor, to dedicate her remaining assets to pious deeds.[2] It comes as only a mild surprise that all these good works were made possible by a far from holy labor. For Isabella de Luna, the testator in question, practiced virtually the only profession that allowed women of her day the freedom to earn and dispose of their own income as she does in the document at hand: she was a courtesan.[3]

The narrative of conversion this information suggests was not unusual among certain ranks of Isabella's profession. Relations between the prostitute community and more "legitimate" elements of urban life were quite fluid and sometimes contradictory, so that passage from one way of life to the other was, at least for some, an option. As I discussed in chapter 1, sexual commerce was legal and indeed actively administrated by most early modern municipalities. Prostitutes of all ranks had regular contacts with representatives of the official government, the various professions, and the overseers of the dowry market, as well as with the church. They maintained relations with many members of the business community in the normal exercise of their trade and could be counted among the regular patrons of cloth merchants, sellers of food and wine, and other purveyors of goods and services.

On the other hand, women active in the sex trade were urged by the clergy on at least a yearly basis to mend their ways and return to the Christian fold.[4] To this end there were special sermons addressed to prostitutes on many occasions, including the annual feast day of their patron saint, Mary Magdalene. Local charities that ran houses for repentant prostitutes offered them incentives to give up their truck in flesh; and occasionally generous charitable donors even furnished dowries for prostitutes, thus making them attractive marriage prospects for men who were otherwise too poor to aspire to a dowried bride. Similar dowries might be assigned as well to poor girls who had not prostituted themselves but were considered to be at risk, thus enabling young women to marry rather than enter that trade. Elite courtesans, on the other hand, often sought to balance out the wages of sin by making donations to charities and cultivating pious relations with the church, especially in their mature years.[5]

In his history of sixteenth-century Rome, Pio Pecchiai numbers Isabella de Luna among the most important courtesans of her generation.[6] Born in Moorish Granada, she left Spain at an early age to follow the fortunes of a man in the army of Emperor Charles V. She traveled much of Europe with the imperial forces and even witnessed their 1535 action in Tunis before settling down in the Eternal City to practice the oldest profession. This same information reaches us also through one of Isabella's contemporaries, Matteo Bandello, who declares in the opening to *Novelle,* part II, novella 51, that among the countless courtesans of Rome,

> ce n'è una detta Isabella da Luna, spagnuola, la quale ha cercato mezzo il mondo. Ella andò a la Goletta e a Tunisi per dar soccorso ai bisognosi soldati e non gli lasciar morir di fame; ha anco un

tempo seguitata la corte de l'imperadore per la Lamagna e la Fian-
dra e in diversi altri luoghi, non si trovando mai sazia di prestar il
suo cavallo a vettura, pure che fosse richiesta.

[there is one called Isabella da Luna, a Spaniard, who has traipsed
over much of the world. She went to Goletta and to Tunis to aid
the needy soldiers and make sure they didn't starve. She also at one
time followed the emperor's court through Germany and Flanders
and in various other places, never satiating her desire to lend out
her horse for rides, as long as she was asked.]

Another commentator on sixteenth-century life, Pierre Brantôme (1540–
1614), was also struck by Isabella. Placing her among the women of Rome
who "are often seen sleeping together, in the fashion called in imitation
of the learned Lesbian Sappho, *donna con donna,*" Brantôme observes in *Les
Dames galantes* (1566):

J'ay cogneu une courtisanne à Rome, vielle et rusèe s'il on fut
oncq, qui s'appelloit Isabelle de Lune, Espagnole, laquelle prit en
telle amitié une courtisane qui s'appelloit la Pandore . . . et cou-
choit ordinairement avec elle; et, comme debordée et desordonée
en paroles qu'elle estoit, je luy ay ouy souvent dire qu'elle la ren-
doit plus putain, et luy faisoit faire des cornes à son mary plus que
tous les rufians que jamais elle avoit eu.[7]

[I knew a courtesan in Rome, old and knowing if ever there was
one, called Isabella de Luna, who took another courtesan named
Pandora as lover, one of the loveliest of the time in the whole of
Rome, who had just been married to a butler of the Lord Cardinal
d'Armagnac, though without relinquishing her old trade, and she
was kept by this Isabella and regularly slept with her, and, unre-
strained and disorderly in her speech as this Isabella was, I often
heard her say that she had made Pandora more of a whore than
before and caused her to put the horns on her husband's head more
than any other roisterer with whom she had made love.][8]

If Brantôme is to be credited, then Isabella, perhaps like many prostitutes
through the ages, violated contemporary mores for women's sexual behav-

ior in more ways than one, exercising erotic as well as economic freedom in the course of her relations.[9] She was in any case a typical member of the superior ranks of her profession. Like all highly successful courtesans, she had a principal patron, a Mantuan nobleman named Uberto or Roberto Strozzi, a relative of the renowned Florentine banking family and nephew to Baldessare Castiglione. Noting that the information given by Bandello in his two novellas featuring Isabella is "fully confirmed" by archival documentation, Pecchiai also cites evidence that Isabella purchased her house in 1544, with Strozzi mediating the sale; and that she was respectfully welcomed by her neighbors when she took up residence in that home.[10] Her attendance by a notary and no fewer than seven Augustinian friars when she dictated her will further suggests her standing in the Roman community.

As every student of the Renaissance knows, the term *cortigiana* refers to a specific category among women in sixteenth-century society. The most famous of these women were the *cortigiane oneste,* whose combination of sexual freedom, learning, and cultural sophistication made them indispensable participants in the courtly social life of the Italian Renaissance. The *cortigiane oneste* were also among the first women to participate in the writing of vernacular love poetry in Italy; and their achievement has earned them a prominent place both in current studies of women's cultural history and in scholarship devoted to the Cinquecento lyric tradition. Important as these celebrities were for their participation in the cultural elite, however, the image they cultivated for themselves is far from representative of the many women who practiced in the sex trade, even at its highest levels.[11] Alongside the accomplished poetry of courtesans such as Veronica Franco and Tullia d'Aragona exists another, less genteel but much more voluminous tradition of "courtesan literature" in the legacy of writings that speak *about* courtesans. This tradition has much to tell us regarding sixteenth-century culture, both "high" and "low," for it gives us a view of courtesan life that is at once less decorous, more troubled, and often more revealing about Cinquecento attitudes than the writings of the acclaimed women poets. The lyric poetry of honest courtesans constitutes several extraordinary women's highly stylized attempts to sketch the interior, mental spaces of desire. Standing in tension with these women's writings is the (largely male-authored) prose, verse, and theatrical literature in which courtesans come alive as characters; this tradition recalls the bawdy, dangerous, and thoroughly exterior dimensions of life as a "public woman." Neither strain, certainly, furnishes a direct view of courtesan life, for both are to some degree products of the literary-cultural imagination, and both are separated from us by historical distance and the individual perspectives of various authors. The latter set of texts, however, complements the courtesans' own self-depictions, and together with pictorial and documentary materials contributes to a richer understanding of the prostitute's place in the archive of sixteenth-century cultural images.

Most courtesans and prostitutes of lower rank did not, of course, produce writings of their own and thus do not speak to us about themselves. Their presence in literary and archival texts assembled by others makes them nonetheless one of the most "visible" groups of women in early modern culture. This visibility alone would justify their prominence in studies of early modern women, given the paucity of information about women of the period in general. Of more compelling interest from a historical perspective, however, is the prostitute's (often quite literal) location outside the space of proper society.[12] Because the prostitute was by definition exempted from traditional female imperatives of chastity, silence, and obedience to a husband, her exceptional status helps define by contrast the parameters of behavior for ordinary women of the period. As I illustrate in my discussion of one example in the following pages, literary texts about courtesans are especially suggestive in their staging of relations between prostitutes and other sectors of society; and in this regard they open our view generally to the dealings of social marginals and subalterns with mainstream culture. Indeed, the compromises and contradictions between official morality and its transgression in early modernity are rarely so evident as in the stories, plays, and dialogues in which these objects of desire and contempt, of fascination and ambivalence, appear as protagonists.

Alongside major works by Aretino, Delicado, Coryat, and others, Bandello's *Novelle* include several tales of courtesans, two of which feature the figure of Isabella de Luna.[13] Matteo Bandello (1480–1561) was a Dominican friar. He is best known to students of the English Renaissance as an earlier source of materials appearing in Shakespeare's *Much Ado About Nothing, Twelfth Night,* and *Romeo and Juliet.*[14] Selections from his 214 stories circulated in free translations in France in the 1550s and again in the 1570s, and others soon appeared in English among the tales in Painter's *Palace of Pleasure* and the *Tragical Discourses* of Fenton.[15]

Bandello scholarship in the early part of the twentieth century was long bogged down in discussions of how much of his material was "original," how much of it he "stole" from Marguerite de Navarre (in whose court he served for a time), and how much of it was "merely" documentary. Bandello's tales are perhaps most striking to readers familiar with those of Boccaccio, because they often lack the structural symmetries of earlier works in the novella tradition.[16] Few of his stories have the shape we find in the classic novellas of Boccaccio, in which, for example, Andreuccio da Perugia sets out for Naples to buy a horse, has three unexpected encounters, and returns home a rich man; or Frate Alberto convinces a woman that he is the archangel Gabriel, sleeps with her numerous times, and is roundly punished by his religious order once he's found out. Bandello confesses in his collection's preface that he has "no style" and that he writes simply in the belief that history [*l'istoria*] and narrated events such as those he recounts will be of interest, no matter what their stylistic merits.[17] In the dedicatory letter to the collection's first novella he adds that he writes "neither to teach others nor to increase the ornament of the vernacular, but only to keep record of the things that appeared to me worthy of being written."[18] The subject matter and structure of many of his tales bear out his quasi-documentary claims, as they appear to resemble the chronicle style—or today's tabloid journalism—more than the edifying storytelling of an earlier tradition.

Bandello also shunned the large frame-tale structures that had bound together many major collections of novellas from the *Arabian Nights* to Boccaccio's *Decameron,* Chaucer's *Canterbury Tales,* and even the *Heptameron* of his contemporary Marguerite de Navarre.[19] He opened his assembly of tales instead to a messier and simpler logic of accumulation, abandoning in the process any "redemptive" connotations for the act of narration itself.[20] Ostensibly based on conversations he engaged in during his travels and later wrote down and gathered together, the *Novelle* cast Bandello as a collector of news—which is, after all, what *novelle* means—about the sundry exploits of his contemporaries. Descriptive titles of the tales thus promise to report how "La Contessa di Cellant fa ammazzare il conte di Masino e a lei è mozzo il capo" (part I, novella 4) [The Countess of Cellant has the count of Masino killed and then her own head is cut off]; or how "Galeazzo ruba una fanciulla a Padova e poi per gelosia e lei e se stesso uccide" (I.20) [Galeazzo steals a girl from Padua and then out of jealousy kills both her and himself]. Several of these stories indeed feature sufficient oddities to make them plausible candidates for inclusion in the "strange but true" rubric of today's tabloids: "Una simia, essendo portata una donne a sepellire, si veste a modo de la donna quando era inferma e fa fuggire quelli di casa" (III.65) [An ape, seeing a woman being carried to her grave, dresses up in her sick-bed garments and chases off all the people of her household].

Bandello's tales make especially fitting material for any study of the inter-actions between imaginary and factual narratives because they famously confound distinctions between fictional and historical writing, and freely mix the conventions of the novella with those of the chronicle.[21] The pref-ace to each story sets its telling in a separate conversational context, at which the author claims to have been present. Crafted as dedicatory let-ters and as memoirs of the occasions on which the author heard his stories, these prefaces are apparently afterthoughts, perhaps written to support their publication. It is not at all clear that Bandello ever sent his stories to the ad-dressees he invokes, because he gathered the *novelle* together for publication only late in his career. This structure nonetheless raises the historical ques-tion of patronage within our considerations of Bandello's work and adds an additional "documentary effect" to his tales as a collection.

Moreover, whatever the documentary status of the prefaces, Bandello abandoned the relatively comfortable, overarching sense of place that binds more traditional story collections and oriented his book instead toward effects of fragmentation, digression, aporia, and displacement. Consistent with his many declarations of this poetics, he clearly favors inconclusive or disconsolate endings and often chooses grimly sensational material as the basis of his narrations.[22] His further insistence that whether or not his tales are true he reports them as they were told to him by his sources is a familiar storyteller's disclaimer that gestures toward both literary and documen-tary writing. As all these elements attest, the historico-literary character of Bandello's writing prompts us to consider how literature can function as a source of information about the past and at the same time implies the au-thor's own consciousness regarding the literary organization of historical writing.[23] The tales of Isabella de Luna are exemplary in their interweaving of these concerns.

Bandello offers us two encounters with the famous Spanish courtesan (see appendixes 1 and 2 for complete translations). In the first (part II, novella 51), he pays tribute to his character's wit and verbal deftness in a classic *novella di beffa*. Describing her as "la più avveduta e scaltrita femina che stata sia già mai" [the most cunning and clever woman there ever was], he introduces Isabella with undisguised admiration: "Ella è di grandissimo intertenimento in una compagnia, siano gli uomini di che grado si vogliano. . . . È piacevolissima, affabile, arguta, e in dare a' tempi suoi le risposte a ciò che si ragiona, prontissima." [She is enormously entertaining in company, no matter what the social rank of the men. . . . She is delightful, affable, witty, and ever ready to respond in her turn to whatever people are talking about.] Noting that Isabella speaks excellent Italian, he adds, "È poi tanto sfacciata e presuntuosa che fa professione di far arrossire tutti quelli che vuole, senza che ella si cangi di colore." [She is also so brazen and bold that she claims she can make blush whomever she wants, without herself ever changing color.]

The novella hinges on this last detail, as Bandello recounts an instance in which Isabella appears to have met her match in the person of a certain Rocco Biancalana, a man in the employ of an unnamed "illustrissimo e reverendissimo cardinale." Rocco, we learn, is a friend of Roberto Strozzi, but unlike Roberto, who (as we know), "[d]'essa Isabella era . . . un poco, come si dice, guasto . . . e volentieri la vedea" [was, as the saying goes, a bit stuck on this Isabella . . . and he was always eager to see her], Rocco finds himself in continuous conflict with the Spanish courtesan. Rocco regularly dines with Roberto and several other men, on which evenings "di continovo si suona e si canta e si ragiona de le lettere così latine come volgari, e d'altre cose vertuose" [there is continuous playing of music and singing, and people discuss literature—both Latin and vernacular—and other virtuous things], but in Rocco's eyes Isabella has no place in such company. "E insomma tra la Luna e la Lana era crudel nemistà, non potendo Rocco sopportare che una sì publica e sfacciata meretrice, che aveva avuto più ferite ne la vita che non sono fiori in primavera, praticasse con quei gentilissimi spiriti." [And so, between Luna and Lana (literally: "Moon" and "Wool") there was cruel enmity, since Rocco could not bear that such a public and shameless prostitute, who had received more wounds from life than there are flowers in spring, should frequent those most gentle spirits.]

With a touch of irony perhaps directed at the pretensions of "quei gentilissimi spiriti," Bandello foregrounds as part of the novella's situation a tension between the narrator's view that Isabella makes fine company for any man and Rocco's sense of class distinctions. Rocco's discontent over matters of social place increases when his cardinal sends to the city another man in his service, Antonio Romeo, who outranks Rocco: "Come egli fu venuto a Roma, Rocco mancò alquanto del suo grado, perciò che stava sotto al Romeo." [As soon as he came to Rome, Rocco lost a certain degree of his stature, since he was Romeo's subordinate.] Rocco spends more and more evenings with Roberto and his friends, complaining often of Romeo's stinginess with food. In his bad humor he quarrels one day with Isabella and threatens to say things to her that will make her blush with shame. Isabella reminds Rocco of her invulnerability to conventional slanders against women: "E che mai puoi tu dire—soggiunse Isabella—se non ch'io sono una puttana? Questo si sa già, né io per questo arrossirò." [And what can you say to me—responded Isabella—other than that I'm a whore? Everybody already knows that, and I won't blush over it.]

Exasperated beyond his limit, Rocco announces that he will sponsor a sumptuous dinner for all their friends, if Isabella agrees to attend as well and listen to all the things he plans to say to her. He then sets about (in a gesture that mirrors Bandello's own pastime) collecting anecdotes about her behavior from everyone he knows, and recording all of these in "un lungo memoriale di tre fogli di carta" [a long memorandum on three sheets of paper]. On the appointed evening, Rocco's superior, Antonio Romeo, who is feeling a little under the weather but has heard of the planned entertainment, also shows up for dinner, hoping to raise his spirits in this amusing company. Rocco arrives, hot under the collar, and begins immediately to insult Isabella: "Puttana sfacciataccia, questa è la volta che non solamente ti farò arrossire, ma ti farò crepare!" [Shameless, dirty whore, this time I'll not only make you blush, I'll make you croak!] Since Rocco will not hear of sitting down to dinner first and saving the insults for afterward, an apparently resigned Isabella requests permission to read the first page of Rocco's text aloud herself. She keeps her promise not to tear up the pages or burn them, but in Rocco's consent lies his downfall nonetheless; for once Isabella has the text in hand, she takes control.[24] She holds the paper before her eyes, but rather than read out Rocco's carefully crafted enumeration of her flaws, she recites all the complaints *he* has made night after night about Romeo, carrying off her performance so well that "[p]areva proprio che ella ciò che diceva lo legesse su la scrittura" [it looked just as if she were reading from the page all the things she was saying]. Given the presence in the room of precisely the man he had targeted with these bitter criticisms, Rocco is speechless with shame. He leaves to Isabella and the rest of the party the lavish dinner he had hoped to consume in victory, and Isabella savors an extravagant meal and the last laugh, both at Rocco's expense.

Rocco Biancalana's resentment of Isabella's contacts with his peers points to the problematic social mobility of courtesans, who were conditionally welcome but never fully accepted into proper society. The story centers on Isabella's popularity, her resourceful wit, and her dismissal of Rocco's attempt to capture the "truth" about her in writing. Bandello also highlights the degree to which Rocco's anger arises from his frustrations with his own subordinate status, as Isabella becomes the surrogate object of a rage he is unable to direct toward his superior. The clever Isabella understands this about Rocco's dismay, and she turns his resentment back on him in the theatrical and amusing fashion for which she was apparently well known. In this tale, the target of Bandello's irony seems to be Rocco, as the narrative presents Isabella in an almost entirely positive light. Bandello's companion novella to this one returns, significantly, to Isabella's defiance and abuse of textual authority; but in the second instance she will not so easily escape the wrath of her social superiors.

Novella IV.16, like II.51, revolves around Isabella's wit and audacity, but in this instance she is far less able to control the spectacle she stages. In this tale, Isabella first scoffs at but then submits to a jail sentence as punishment for not paying one of her debts. She soon makes good on the obligation and is released from prison, but finds she must also endure a further, unexplained punishment in the form of a public whipping. If here too Isabella walks away without so much as blushing, the reader is less amused than amazed at her composure before "mezza Roma" [half of Rome] as she heads home, her buttocks stinging, "senza monstrare in viso uno minimo segno di vergogna" [without showing the smallest sign of shame in her face].[25]

In this story, Isabella appears distant indeed from the women we associate with idealized scenes in the great courts and literary salons of Italy. A tough, foul-mouthed woman of the streets, she is not likely to be found strumming a lute or penning poetry for soirées among the prelates of Rome.[26] The court sergeant who serves her the order to pay her bill finds her not keeping elite company in some luxuriously appointed interior but "nella strada publica, che si interteneva a parlamento con alcuni compagnoni" [out on the public street, where she was amusing herself in conversation with several of her fellows in the trade]. We learn something more about the flavor of Isabella's rhetorical gifts when the narrator informs us that "tra l'altre sue notabili parti bestemmia crudelissimamente Iddio e tutti li santi e sante del paradiso" [among her other notable habits she is wont to cruelly curse God and all the male and female saints in paradise], a skill the author allows Isabella herself to illustrate in response to the arrival of the court official: "Pesa a Dios, que quiere esto borrachio vigliaco?" [What in God's name does this drunken coward want?][27] The histrionic flourish with which she follows this question—tearing to pieces the sergeant's court summons, using it to "wipe" her derriere, and giving it back to the officer before shocked and delighted onlookers—achieves, in its way, an even greater expressive eloquence than her suggestion to the outraged official that he go to hell.

This behavior lands her in court, where even during her hearing "al tutto rispondeva di modo che pareva che si burlasse e che il fatto non pertenesse a lei" [she responded to everything as if she were joking and as if the affair had nothing to do with her].[28] Finally she is sentenced to remain in jail until she comes up with the money she owes. "E considerando ella che dimorando dentro la prigione la sua bottega grandemente perdeva, non possendo in quello luogo il suo molino macinare, ebbe, non so come, modo di pagare il mercatante." [And when she considered that if she stayed in jail her business would take a great loss, as there she wouldn't be able to grind her mill, she found a way—I don't know how—to pay the merchant.] The narrator's coy "non so come" [I don't know how] suggests that Isabella must have earned the money in her usual way, and the possibility that she used the jail as a brothel may be the reason for the puzzling turn of events that follows. The moment of payment, the moment in which Isabella finally concedes authority to the law, is also a point of reversal in Bandello's narrative, for it is strangely on fulfilling her contract to pay that Isabella receives the more humiliating punishment of the public whipping. The logic of this outcome becomes apparent only on closer examination of the novella in relation to its preface and to the broader context of sixteenth-century prostitution.

Most of this tale focuses on Isabella's defiance not only of her station but also of the law, as the story's comic machinery builds her impudence to an amusing extreme. The novella achieves a typically Bandellian "chronicle" or "reality" effect at its closure, as it breaks off without restoring the comic tone that had governed it up to the moment of the whipping. The surprise punishment delivered in the last paragraph instead reins the figure of Isabella violently back into the orbit of official power and provides a disquieting finale to Bandello's otherwise playful narrative, chastening both Isabella and any readers who had up to this point taken delight in her actions.

The preface to this tale foreshadows Isabella's punishment by recounting the treatment of another prostitute, the heroic military meretrix Margaritona. It opens, typically for Bandello's collection, in the apparent middle of an ongoing conversation, as a group of soldiers in the papal army discusses the "sharp punishment" mysteriously delivered to Margaritona, despite her celebrated success in capturing soldiers from the enemy Spanish forces. The soldiers' vague and bewildered speculations about why Margaritona was burned at the stake give rise to the telling of Isabella de Luna's punishment in Rome, which immediately follows.

Bandello's spare portrait of Margaritona offers a rare and sympathetic literary glimpse at one of the women who routinely accompanied early modern armies in their campaigns. As I discussed more fully in chapter 1, military prostitutes usually provided itinerant troops not only with sexual services, but also with practical assistance ranging from the collection of spoils after battles to spying and actual combat. These women were also important players in the "theater of insults," the taunting games that originated in the spectacles one army performed to offend another on the battlefield and which were later reenacted in various guises for the home populace on the troops' victorious return.[29] Being marginal both to the norms of the civic society and to the male military community, their position was also most precarious. The domestic community that cheered the military prostitutes was also known to turn against them, especially if the army's undertakings had been less than successful. Chronicles recount occasions in which prostitutes died in public tortures [*supplizi*], apparently in punishment for having reaped financial gain from the now-devastated local forces. Such reversals of fortune stress the extreme ambivalence and complexity of attitudes converging on the figure of the prostitute in early modern city life. Both desired and scorned in a culture that placed high value on feminine chastity, the prostitute occupied two polar positions, sometimes simultaneously. Before external enemies, she represented the lowest social rank within the community itself. In this regard she was useful for addressing insults to hated outsiders precisely because directing the blow "from below" increases its leverage. Within her own urban community, however, the prostitute might be cast as the internalized representative of the foreign enemy. In this case she could be punished in substitution for the unavailable foreigner and thereby facilitate the community's return to equilibrium.

Isabella de Luna herself must have performed at least some of these same military functions while traveling with the army of Charles V, just as Margaritona had carried out similar duties for the anti-Spanish papal forces a few years later. Other details emphasize further symmetries between the story and the preface. Most notably, the two narratives feature parallel breaks at the last paragraph, where in each case we confront an abrupt gap into which any justification for the subsequent events disappears. Both arrive at the other side of this gap to recount the infliction of violence on the story's protagonist rather than her expected reward (Margaritona) or release (Isabella). In each case, the humor deriving from the actions of these forceful women dissipates and is replaced by sober confusion. The preface especially foregrounds this shift: A sentence that basks in amusement over Margaritona's embarrassed captured soldier—a topos that recalls the comic dismay of Ariostan knights defeated by Bradamante and Marfisa—lurches temporally forward to a moment *after* the heroine's annihilation: "La cagione poi di far abrusciare essa Margaritona variamente fra li soldati si diceva." [The reason for later burning this Margaritona at the stake was recounted variously by the soldiers.] It is this metaleptic gap—this elimination of a central term in the causal chain of reasoning—that leaves the men (and Bandello's readers) to supply for themselves an acceptable explanation for Margaritona's end.

Another contemporary reference to Margaritona suggests the type of disturbing events that may exert their force in this ellipsis. Marino Sanuto reports in his *Diario* entry for 5 February 1529:

De qui si ha come una femina, qual era ne la compagnia del conte
di Caiazo et andava vestita da homo, nominata Malgarita, femina
valente ma ben di partito; la qual in questi zorni passati havia ama-
zato 12 ragazi, li qual per lei a uno a uno li faceva morir nel suo
alozamento et li soterava lì in casa, perchè li parea che dicti ragazi
li tolesse el guadagno, inteso questo, il signor conte la fece pren-
dere et torturata confessò il tutto, et li fece apichar per il colo con
il lazo largo, et sotto li fece far un gran focho, per modo che cussì
viva apichata si brusò, ma con tanta forteza et constantia che più
non si potria dir.[30]

[From here comes the news of how a female named Malgarita,
who was in the company of the count of Caiazo and went about
dressed as a man — a valiant woman but certainly a prostitute —
in these past days had killed 12 boys. She put them to death one
by one in her lodgings and buried them there at home, because
it appeared to her that the said boys were depriving her of her
profit. On hearing this, the lord count had her taken in and, under
torture, she confessed it all. And he had her hanged by the neck
with a loose knot, and below he had a great fire made, in such
a way that thus hanged alive she burned. But she showed such
strength and constancy that one could not say more (i.e., put it
into words).]

Sanuto, like Bandello, mixes admiration with his wonder at the valor of
Margaritona (Malgarita); but the discrepancy between the two writers' accounts raises several questions. Is Sanuto's account a faithful rendering of
Margaritona's crimes and punishment? If so, what are we to make of the
absence from Bandello's tale of Sanuto's details — details that present Margaritona as nothing less than a serial killer — in favor of a narrative that
presents her only "offense" in her valorous capture of the enemy soldier?
Or is the report recorded by Sanuto a sensational product of military gos-
sip, exaggerated in its description of Margaritona's crimes? In what way did
Margaritona suspect the boys were stealing from her: by taking her money
or — as is more likely — by stealing her clients?[31] Finally, if the Sanuto account was in any way embellished in its passage from soldier to soldier
before being recorded on the chronicler's page, were the extra details added

before her execution and used to help convict Margaritona (as happened commonly to victims of the Inquisition, for example), or were they added after the fact, to conceal another (perhaps even less savory) truth as the story passed from camp to camp?

These are questions that might be answered by careful examination of further documentary evidence, but they exceed the scope of this chapter. The two accounts, in any case, illustrate the difficulty of assessing "real" events from the past, given the narrative and textual forms through which we are constrained to view history.[32] What we can say is that Bandello interweaves the stories of Margaritona and Isabella, effectively placing Margaritona between the two Isabella tales in a position of mediation that allows her story to shadow both parts of Isabella's. If we may see the second Isabella story as the resolution of the first—see part IV, novella 16 as the conclusion in which Isabella is finally punished for her trick in part II, novella 51—then Margaritona's story functions as an "intermezzo" commentary, drawing over the Isabella tales an atmosphere of anxiety and violence regarding the power not of lawbreakers in general, but of highly sexualized and transgressive females.[33]

Indeed, the issue of the "foreign" threat, which may have suggested Isabella's tale as an allegory of Spanish-Italian hostilities, is displaced by the execution of Margaritona, who was a papal ally (and a heroic one at that) *against* Spain. Bandello distances and mystifies the theme of male impotence by substituting for Sanuto's twelve boys a single Spanish (and thus foreign) soldier. Yet Sanuto's account haunts both versions with the unspeakable dread that the prostitute soldier (perhaps the most foreign figure of all, no matter where her homeland) not only challenges male power and homosociality, but may prove literally fatal to it. These forces backed by institutional muscle inevitably prove more powerful than she, however, as Margaritona herself becomes the final victim in the series. In Sanuto's account, the prostitute strikes back at boys she thinks are commercial competitors, and the *donna publica* becomes the femme fatale over questions of market and profit. The captain's letter cited by Sanuto records the swift response of official power to the prostitute's rash rebellion; but by the time this story has circulated to the camp depicted in Bandello's preface, its moral of "just punishment" has disappeared along with all the details of Margaritona's crimes.

In the opening of the novella proper, Bandello notes that Isabella served the soldiers who "are always willing to go the wet way" (that is, to have vaginal intercourse with a woman), and this claim implicitly reverses the image we receive from Sanuto of an army whose men were also tempted to go "the dry way,"[34] whether with young boys or with the cross-dressed prostitute herself. The story of Margaritona's unexplained execution may be another such reversal, this one implicitly setting "straight" the role of women in the army, both sexual and military. In any case, given its reticence about the reasons for Margaritona's execution, Bandello's preface contrasts with Sanuto's tale of multiple murder duly avenged and presents to readers instead a parable of the army's arbitrary power of capital punishment. Bandello alleviates this chilling effect by closing his preface with another slight shift in tone, returning to the amiable context of male sociality in which such stories—and such women as Margaritona and Isabella—were shared. Figuratively repeating the exchange of the two women "between men," he makes a gift of the preface and tale in which they are contained as characters to Bernardo da San Bonifacio.[35] The conventional complimentary closure, "State sano," stands in ironic contrast to the condition of the two women in the preface and story, who are handled roughly indeed.

Isabella's and Margaritona's stories foreground the role of the prostitute as example to the community, but such stories as theirs occupy a specific place in the literature of exemplarity for women.[36] Exemplary Renaissance tales for women, as distinct from their more varied masculine counterparts, often center on the integrity of the female body, and they conventionally relate this corporeal integrity to the strength of institutions such as marriage and the state. Stephanie Jed argues in *Chaste Thinking,* for example, that the myth of Lucretia and its recurrence as topos in Renaissance narratives of liberation disturbingly project rape (and its vengeance) as "a prologue to republican freedom."[37] According to Livy's narrative, Lucretia's rape by Tarquin and her subsequent heroic suicide serve as the dual catalysts for Brutus's demand that his compatriots take up arms. Their celebrated retaliatory struggle results in the foundation of Republican Rome. Jed's audacious reading explores the renewed fascination with Lucretia's story in the period of Florentine republicanism, highlighting both the self-destructive notion of female heroism Lucretia inaugurates and the link between violence against women and the establishment of a legitimate male citizenry in myths of foundation.

Susanne Wofford has similarly studied marriage *cassoni* depicting rape or abduction scenes, which were especially fashionable in late Quattrocento Florence.[38] One of the most popular sources for images depicting "the emergence of marriage, and, by extension, civilization, from violence, conquest, and rape," notes Wofford, was Boccaccio's novella of Nastagio degli Onesti. Botticelli's painting depicting the phantoms encountered in the woods by the lovelorn Nastagio was copied often on the panels of these wedding chests and thus presented itself as a frequent didactic exemplum to new brides in Florence. In Boccaccio's tale (*Decameron* V.viii) a brooding Nastagio beholds in the forest the ghost of a woman who in life had refused to reciprocate her knight's affections. Now condemned to repeat for eternity a scene of courtly *contrapasso,* this female spirit's fate is to flee in vain from the knight's hounds as they chase her through the woods, to fall to their teeth, and to submit while her lover cuts her heart and other organs out of her body to feed to his dogs. Attributing an edifying value to this spectral scene, Nastagio invites his friends and his unresponsive lady to witness it for themselves over a rich woodland banquet. At the sight of the coldhearted woman's divine punishment, Nastagio's beloved and all the other women present readily agree henceforth to do the bidding of men: "[T]utte le ravignane donne paurose ne divennero, che sempre poi troppo più arrendevoli ai piaceri degli uomini furono che prima state non erano." [All the women of Ravenna became fearful at this, and ever after they were much more submissive to the pleasures of men than they had been before.][39] Wofford is careful to appreciate the levels of irony in Boccaccio's tale, which preclude any simple reading of this novella's sexual politics. Her greater interest lies in the circulation on marriage *cassoni* of this and other narrative images (the rape of the Sabine women, the rape of Lucretia, the story of Susannah and the elders, Boccaccio's tale of Griselda) in which "violence against women is figured as a necessary originary moment of male control and domination that makes possible the ensuing benefits of civilization which are brought by and symbolized by the women, but only after they are subjected to their husbands."[40]

Both Wofford and Jed focus on narratives in which women are imagined as catalysts or key figures for disruptions of the social order. This instability, according to the logic of such stories, must be brought under control if cherished institutions—and proper relations of authority within them—are to survive and flourish. Wofford's attention to scenes of narrative closure that in their projection of violence as a source of moral order "lead readers to feel that some aspect of the conclusion remains unaccounted for" speaks also to the ends of the two parts of Bandello's part IV, novella 16.[41] Both Margaritona's and Isabella's stories figure the punishment of their crimes as a restoration of social and legal, if not moral, order. Bandello's preface remains pointedly ambiguous, however, about the reason for Margaritona's execution, as the soldiers themselves grope for explanations that might warrant her end. If the withholding of explanation at precisely this point in the story exposes Bandello's discomfort with Margaritona's crimes, real or supposed, it also parallels the lack of justification for Isabella's whipping and casts her as the return of what was repressed in Margaritona's preface, a fear of feminine (or subaltern) power to derange the social, sexual, and civil order.

Violent forms of humiliation and executions—like their more positive festive counterparts, the pageant and the triumph—were in Bandello's day considered by the authorities to be especially effective illustrative spectacles for the populace. Unlike the protagonists of positive exemplary tales for women—the virgins who sacrifice their lives rather than their family reputations, or the good women who finally learn to submit to their husbands' authority—prostitutes often functioned as *negative* exemplars in spectacles as well as in stories.[42] We see this thinking in the lieutenant and governor, who agree that Isabella's boldness is "di pessimo esempio" [a bad example] and that "alcuna dimostrazione" [some kind of illustration] ought to be made of it. A central concern of the tale is indeed the *public* nature of Isabella's actions, which amount to a kind of theater of disrespect in which she turns the sergeant and the judge into unwitting straight men for her comedy. The recurrence of the word *public* in the tale (as in II.51) underscores the difference between Isabella and other women as well as the dilemma the governors face, given that her exceptional status is condoned by the state. The sergeant who serves her the official summons finds her on a *public* street, where honorable women were rarely seen but where prostitutes moved freely as a matter of course. He commands her before a crowd, "a la presenza di tutti quelli che con lei erano" [in the presence of everyone there with her], to appear at the appointed place and time. Her subsequent responses, both verbal and corporal, are thus important not only for their contemptuous message but also for their performance in front of the same audience who witnessed the serving of the summons. In the chain of communications among the authorities, the lieutenant represents Isabella's affront in terms of example to the community, clearly attributing to it a public significance. There follows an anxious series of exchanges among officials about the gravity of Isabella's behavior. The sergeant is concerned that he looks foolish, while the lieutenant impresses on the governor that a bold female has insulted his office. The governor has her taken "publicamente" to the bargello and then to the prison. Later, after serving her time in jail, she is sentenced further to be given fifty lashes "su la publica strada." The sentence is made public, and once a crowd has gathered, the executioner lifts up her clothes "ne la via publica" and "le fece mostrare il colliseo all'aria."

The action of the executioner who lifts up Isabella's skirts recalls her original gesture of pretending to clean herself with the summons, a repetition surely not lost on witnesses to both events. The second punishment is important, however, not only because it repeats from the ironic perspective of the law the very gesture the offender had used to defy legal authority, but also because it represents a regression of the legal system to Isabella's insistence on a corporal and spectacular rhetoric of justice rather than a textualized and abstracted one. In the earlier Bandello tale, Isabella subverts the power of Rocco's punctiliously written "indictment" by turning it into a mere stage prop in her comic theater. If in the first story she successfully turns into farce the "documented" accusations against her, in the second she aims to repeat this subversion in a more serious legal context. Isabella insists on her own performative, bodily message — "written" in gestures and "signed" in excrement — in response to the written condemnation presented to her as a legal code. If at first the Roman authorities are puzzled by the missive she sends them, they attempt to decipher it nonetheless: the sergeant carries the torn and sullied summons back to be examined dutifully by his superiors. Their final action is to supplement the consensual legitimacy of the one law (of the text) with the coercive force of the other law (of the spectacle), in a punishment in which writing reverts to ritual in the marking of the offender's body with scars. Isabella thus joins a crowd of female characters in literature and myth who attest to "the cultural writing on the body of woman — her disfigurement — as a sacrifice necessary to guarantee the continuation of society."[43] At stake in Isabella's narrative is not, of course, the fate of society as a whole, or the foundation of a new state, or even the institution of marriage, which is reinforced in Boccaccio's tale. But her story does concern crucial aspects of civic order: the legitimacy of the modern legal code and its enforcers, and women's place in relation to that authority.

In Isabella and Margaritona we confront the popular female body, only tenuously controllable by the regulatory and penal power of the state. Both provide spectacular occasions for the display of judicial violence, as public objects of punishment in an age before the relocation of retribution to the closed spaces of prisons, asylums, and hospitals in the "Great Confinement" of the seventeenth century. As Michel Foucault observes in his classic study of the prison system, the shift over the course of the late seventeenth to the nineteenth centuries from external, spectacular forms of torture and execution to concealed punishments delivered in closed spaces, away from public view, marked a turning point in modern legal institutions as such. In this shift, "the body as the major target of penal repression disappeared" and justice was relocated in punishment of "the soul."[44] Isabella's tale appears indeed to capture not simply a moment *before* that nineteenth-century abstraction of punishment away from the body; it illustrates an instance of the unsuccessful attempt to *achieve* that abstraction. Power presents itself to Isabella as the half-man, half-beast centaur invoked by Bandello's contemporary, Machiavelli:

> Dovete, adunque, sapere, come sono dua generazioni di combattere: l'uno con le leggi, l'altro con la forza: quel primo è proprio dello uomo, quel secondo è delle bestie: ma perché el primo molte volte non basta, conviene ricorrere al secondo. Pertanto, a uno principe è necessario sapere bene usare la bestia e l'uomo.[45]

> [You must know, then, that there are two ways of fighting: one with laws and the other with force. The first is appropriate for man and the second is for animals. But since many times the first does not suffice, it is useful to fall back on the second. Thus, a prince must know how to use the ways of beast and man.]

In Isabella's insistence on the spectacle of her public, performative actions—even at the price of humiliation and injury—we measure her distance from the idealized and interiorized images of courtesans we receive from the lyric and portrait traditions. Isabella's type of resistance to power is akin to that of the jester or the fool. To the officer's bureaucratic manner and his legal summons to court, she responds with scatological theater. Before her judge she affects incomprehension and performs burlesque. Finally, as though regretting the insufficiency of Isabella's fine and imprisonment (nonpublic forms of retribution), the Roman officials supplement the one system with the other, employing spectacle to underline for a broad public the costs of not consenting to treat the law as legitimate, of forgetting that behind the written law stands the power to inflict pain or even death. Nonetheless, she (like Margaritona) towers over all the other figures in Bandello's tale for the integrity with which she faces her ordeal.

As Foucault (and Nietzsche before him) [46] observes, public punishments rely not on the immediacy of spectacle but on the creation of impressive memories for an observing audience: repetition and the figural resemblance of the punishment to the crime committed are crucial in the efficacy of such displays. Bandello's figurative substitution of the Colosseum for Isabella's backside condenses the sexual and juridical themes that run through the Isabella and Margaritona narratives, but it also triggers a set of collective historical "memories." The most public space of Rome, the Colosseum was a popular meeting place for lovers of all kinds over the centuries, reputed in undocumented stories even to house individual brothels in its lower arcades. It was also a common figure for the prostitute's body itself, with its many openings, which—as the saying went—any man in Rome could enter for a fee (hence the bawdy pun on *culo*: *culisseo*). The Colosseum's greatest claim to infamy, however, was surely not its use for sexual encounters ("wet," "dry," or otherwise) but its function as the theater for games in which early Christians were executed for the sport of Roman citizens. As Isabella's punishment "[mostra] il colliseo all'aria" [puts the Colosseum on display in the open air], it also recalls a form of arbitrary power directed regularly against outsiders as an exhilarating demonstration of sheer sovereign force. As was the case for the early Christians, the decisive advantage lies with the state in this struggle between Isabella's insistence on theatricalized justice and the governor's attempt to impose a codified, written alternative. Ironically, then, this conflict ends with a performance in Isabella's mode, but taken literally out of her hide.

In both Margaritona and Isabella the law meets its own creations, for they are the incarnate products of an ambivalent moral and economic system that requires some "wayward" women to move freely in the public sphere in order to keep the majority of females available for circulation in a private marriage economy hinged on female chastity.[47] The governor takes into account that Isabella is after all a woman and a public prostitute, suggesting that for these reasons she should not be punished with excessive force. But her public recognition is precisely the reason why Isabella can serve as an example to other potential transgressors of the governor's authority. In legal parlance as well as in everyday language, the prostitute is a "public" woman. This language underscores the strenuous early modern effort to keep marriageable woman strictly confined to the most private sphere of child rearing and household management. It also suggests that Isabella—as a woman removed from that private sphere—is available to the authorities for a public production of meaning. Isabella is authorized to exercise her trade within the limited parameters where the state permits prostitution: her offense is not her status as a *donna publica*. Instead she suffers that final, humiliating penalty because paying her monetary debt fails to compensate for her open mockery of official power—a mockery in which she persists even before her judge.

Isabella's last will and testament, cited at the beginning of this chapter, suggests that she was not so irresponsible regarding all of her debts as she chose to be with the merchant of Bandello's story. Her prosperity and her apparent success in business project her, indeed, as a prototype for the individual capitalist, rising from the humble ranks of the army to the ownership of her own palace, able to generate theoretically unlimited profit, and ever at odds with regulatory institutions: a far less tame version of the individual male entrepreneur represented by the unpaid merchant in IV.16, who exhibits such faith in the fairness of the courts to guarantee him justice. Bandello's paired Isabella stories proceed from Rocco's resentful recording of Isabella's offenses in II.51 through the legal documentation of more serious violations in IV.16; but they end with the abandonment of words and papers in favor of the blood and scars of an executioner's whip. Not surprisingly, for Isabella, the public woman "who [has] been dealt more wounds by life than there are flowers in spring," the painful occasion of ritual punishment becomes a moment of stubborn resistance. In the last lines of Bandello's tale we see her pull herself together, defiantly reintegrating a self momentarily shattered on the stage of public torture. A different legal philosophy will one day carry out the aim to abstract the law's inevitable violence away from this "spectacular visible body."[48] But Isabella de Luna, it seems, prefers the theater of public memory, where the crimes of both sides may be witnessed by all.

Appendix 1: Bandello to His Magnificent Nephew Messer Gian Michele Bandello

Women, when taken by surprise, usually have a ready response; and in an instant they are able to furnish whatever the situation requires. And since this faculty comes to them by nature, there should be no doubt that those women who have more experience will be the most provident and astute. But what women have more experience than the courtesans at the Roman court? All the beautiful and most elevated intellects of the world commonly gather here, for Rome is everyone's fatherland. Here good literature of all sorts flourishes, whether in Latin, Greek, or the vernaculars; here are excellent legal scholars and the most consummate of both moral and natural philosophers; here one sees miraculous painters. There are sculptors who draw out living faces from marble, and molders of metal who cast whatever they fancy. But not to recount the arts one by one, they are all here in all their perfection. Hence whoever wants to achieve excellence in any sort of skill goes to learn in Rome. And since—as the wise Sulmonese[1] says— it often occurs that the same field produces both the rose and the nettle, there are both good and wicked men in Rome.

But leaving all else aside, I will speak of courtesans who, to give some honest title to their practices, have usurped this name of "courtesans." They are as a rule all greedier for money than flies for honey. And if some young downy-bearded type falls into their hands who is not sufficiently cunning, I can tell you for sure that without touching a razor they will shave him to within an inch of his life and carry out his dissection. Now, as an honored company of many gentlemen was conversing in Milan about several courtesans and about the ways they so often practice, the captain Gian Battista Olivo—a most witty and courteous man—told a little story that had taken place in Rome. And I, having written it down according to his narration, wanted it to be yours. And so I send it to you and give it to you as a present, all things that are mine being yours. Be well.

Part II, Novella 51   *The Spanish Isabella da Luna Plays a Wonderful Joke on Someone Who Expected to Play One on Her*

Whoever set out to catalogue all the things courtesans do in all the places where they are found would in my opinion have too much to do; and when he thought he was finished, there would be just as much left to say as had already been said. But let us come to some specific instance, and tell one of the jokes that these barbers play.[2] Among the others who live in Rome, there is one called Isabella da Luna, a Spaniard, who has traipsed over much of the world. She went to Goletta and to Tunis[3] to aid the needy soldiers and make sure they didn't starve. She also at one time followed the emperor's court through Germany and Flanders and in various other places, never satiating her desire to lend out her horse for rides, as long as she was asked. She has of late returned to Rome, where those who know her hold her to be the most cunning and clever woman there ever was. She is enormously entertaining in company, no matter what the social rank of the men, since she knows how to adapt herself to everyone and give every man his due. She is delightful, affable, witty, and ever ready to respond in her turn to whatever people are talking about. She speaks Italian very well; and if she is stung, don't think she becomes dismayed and lacks the words to sting back the one who has it coming. Because she has a biting tongue, and she looks no one in the face. Instead she lashes out blindly with her piercing words. She is also so brazen and bold that she claims she can make blush whomever she wants, without herself ever changing color.

Gathered in Rome were some of our most virtuous and courteous Mantuan gentlemen, among whom were Messer Roberto Strozzi and the brothers Capilupi, Messer Lelio, and Messer Ippolito. Messer Roberto is in Rome for his own pleasure and Messer Ippolito is employed in the business of our most illustrious and most reverend cardinal of Mantua.[4] They all live in one house, but each has his own private quarters there. It is quite true that most of the time they eat in company, each one bringing his own portion, and thus they lead a gay and happy life. Very often they are joined by others, because they are such good company. And in their lodgings there is continuous playing of music and singing, and people discuss literature—both Latin and vernacular—and other virtuous things, in such a way that they never fall out of good spirits.

A certain Rocco Biancalana frequented these men with great familiarity and ate with them often. He had a job as the agent of a most illustrious and most reverend cardinal; and having been in Rome quite some time and being likable and no less sharp-tongued than Isabella, every day he had clamorous words with her. Now, Messer Roberto was, as the saying goes, a bit stuck on this Isabella, who also was often found in the company of the above named men; and he was always eager to see her. But between Rocco and her there was perpetual rivalry, and they argued together over which one of them was the more slanderous, more aggressive, and more presumptuous, in such a manner that they were always at each other. On which account those gentlemen took marvelous pleasure, seeing the readiness of both of them to speak the most sinister insults. And often, to goad them into trading rude remarks, they would set them at each other as one does with dogs. And so, between Luna and Lana there was cruel enmity, since Rocco could not bear that such a public and shameless prostitute, who had been dealt more wounds by life than there are flowers in spring, should frequent those most gentle spirits. And he often squawked about it to Messer Roberto.

Now the most illustrious and most reverend cardinal who was keeping Rocco in Rome, perhaps having some business of great import to negotiate, sent also to Rome Messer Antonio Romeo, a man of great abilities and capable of managing every difficult and delicate kind of business, no matter how tangled it might be. And in effect Romeo would have been an impeccable gentleman, if it weren't for one flaw that spoiled him completely: he was mean and stingy beyond measure. As soon as he came to Rome, Rocco lost a certain degree of his stature, since he was Romeo's subordinate and could negotiate no more and no less business than Romeo dictated. So that it seemed he worked for Romeo and not for the cardinal. And at home he lived with Romeo not as a companion, but almost as a servant. But nothing weighed on Rocco more than Romeo's stinginess; so much that he would have happily given up every little advantage he enjoyed and—as they say— ditched his cardinal. And he was ready to set himself up with anyone, even in the private sector and no matter what their station; for this Rocco was quite the parasite and he always liked to have his table well stocked.

In this bad humor of his, he often found himself lunching and dining with the above mentioned gentlemen, and among them he often gave vent to his anger over the extreme stinginess of Messer Antonio. And even if Isabella was there, he didn't care. He would start to tell how Romeo bought such hard bread that you couldn't chew it with your teeth or cut it with a knife; and that it had mold, and that he very often let it be baked twice, claiming that it helped dry the catarrh. That before bringing the wine to table, he watered it down so much that someone with a thousand head wounds could have drunk it. That they saw no other meat than beef, which before being finished off had been used for three or four soups. That there was a piece of shank that had been put on the table more than twenty times without anyone's touching it, because it was just a naked bone with no meat on it and which, as soon as the table was set, would jump up on the plate all by itself.[5] He told how the cheese was all gnawed by moths and rotten, and how the fruit was bought unripe and brought to table five or six times. These things Rocco would say with no caution at all, and he never cared if everybody heard him.

It came about one day that between him and Isabella cruel words were exchanged, and they started to launch accusations, at which point Rocco told her that if it hadn't been for his respect for Messer Roberto, he would have said some things to her that would make her turn crimson. "And what can you say to me," responded Isabella, "other than that I'm a whore? Everybody already knows that, and I won't blush over it." In the heat of his anger, Rocco offered to host a sumptuous and magnificent dinner, where in addition to other dishes there would be two pairs of pheasants, if she would allow that in her presence he would tell each and every one of the awful things he knew about her. And they agreed on the following Thursday for this. In the meantime, though Rocco knew many a lewd tale about Isabella, he nonetheless heard a lot of things he had never known from many others who were acquainted with her. And so they wouldn't escape his memory, he made a long memorandum of them on three sheets of paper. He was a fine calligrapher, and he wrote everything down in very beautiful order.

Now when the night of the dinner arrived, Messer Antonio Romeo, who had heard about it and was feeling a little under the weather, went over to the Mantuans' house to raise his spirits with the match that was supposed to take place. Everyone was there with Isabella in a great room, gathered around the hearth. Rocco reached for his notebook and said to Isabella, "Shameless dirty whore, this time I'll not only make you blush, I'll make you croak!" Isabella looked a bit melancholy and said, "Rocco, is it possible that you wish me dead? Let us dine in peace, and after dinner you can read your criminal trial." "No, no," responded Rocco, "I want to make your dinner taste more bitter than gall!" And since she could see that he was quite determined to read before eating, Isabella pleaded at length with those gentlemen that they do her the favor of letting her be the one to read at least the first page of what Rocco had written. And she promised not to run off with it or tear it or burn it, but after having read the first page to render it back to this Rocco. The request did not appear unreasonable, so everyone urged Rocco to comply; and he did.

As soon as she had the writing in hand, Isabella slowly read eight or ten lines. Then she said, "Listen, gentlemen, and you will hear if there ever was in all the world a more slanderous tongue than that of Rocco." And then where she was supposed to read off these evils about herself, she made as though she didn't know Romeo was present and instead recited in perfect order all the things Rocco had said so many times in vituperation of this Romeo, bitterly criticizing the stinginess of that man. And indeed it looked just as if she were reading from the page all the things she was saying. And when she had said quite a lot, she folded the paper and said, "Gentlemen, what do you think of this knave? Don't you think he deserves a thousand hangings? I don't know this Romeo, but I've heard that he's a most courteous person and that in his house they live quite well. And this ribald is not ashamed to speak ill of a decent man, a man in whose house he lives. Think what a wretch." Rocco was completely beside himself, half stunned, and he didn't know what to say for himself. In the same way Romeo, who knew that the things said about his stinginess were true, left without saying good-bye. And Rocco did likewise. So luck had it that neither the one nor the other tasted a mouthful of the prepared dinner; and it was said that Rocco had made the soup—as the saying goes—for the birds.[6] Those who remained dined and laughed long with Isabella, for she had known so well how to trick Rocco and save herself.

Notes

1   Publius Ovidius Naso (43 B.C.E.–17 C.E.), born in Sulmona. Bandello cites from Ovid's *Remedia amoris* 44–46.

2   Cf. Bandello's claim in the preface to this novella that courtesans will "shave" unsuspecting men to within an inch of their lives and then dissect them. Barbers often performed as surgeons in Bandello's time.

3   Goletta is the port at Tunis. Delmo Maestri speculates in his note that Isabella must have been at Tunis when the city was briefly occupied by the Spanish under the command of Andrea Doria. See Maestri's edition, *Bandello. La seconda parte de le novelle* (Alessandria: Edizioni dell'Orso, 1993), 478, n. 13.

4   Cardinal of Mantua: Ercole Gonzaga, son of Isabella d'Este Gonzaga and Francesco Gonzaga.

5   Payne's translation notes here, "Meaning apparently that it was alive with maggots." See volume 5 of *The Novels of Matteo Bandello Englished by John Payne* (London: Villon Society, 1890), 68.

6   Bandello's phrase here is "per le gatte" (literally, "for the she-cats"). Maestri explains: "aveva preparato la beffa non per gli altri, ma per se" (*Seconda parte,* 481, n. 39); Payne translates, "wherefore it was said that Rocco had, as the saying goes, made soup for the cats" (70).

Appendix 2: Bandello to the Magnificent Lord Count Bernard of Saint Boniface, Field Master of the French Army in Piedmont: Greetings

The very same day that the Lord Count Guido Rangone sent you to Chieri, while many good soldiers were still gathered together, we began to discuss the sharp punishment that had been given in the Venetian camp to Margaritona, a woman of little honesty but great courage, who in the company of Gaiazzo earned her cash by riding in the light cavalry.[1] And certainly there were men who picked up their pay at the bank without deserving it as much as she deserved hers. Like the time when the league's army was at Cassano, and Antonio Leiva[2] was holding out at Inzago, little more than two miles away. This Margaritona, armed and on horseback, got almost inside the Spanish fort near Inzago, and by means of several good blows she captured a Spanish soldier and conducted him before the illustrious Lord Gian Maria Fregoso, who was general governor of the *serenissima* signory of Venice. This Spaniard, realizing he had been taken prisoner by a female, was on the verge of despair.

The reason for later burning this Margaritona was recounted variously by the soldiers. There were those who affirmed she had been justly burned and others who blamed Messer Paolo Nani, the prosecutor, along with the count of Gaiazzo. And so as we talked of this, Messer Giovanni Salerno, who, as you know, is very talkative and often interrupts the conversations of his companions in order to say what he wants, told a little story that happened not long ago in Rome. This novella has been taken down by me. Thinking then to whom I should give it, I decided to send it to you; and so I send it to you as a gift and consecrate it to your name. Be well.

Part IV, Novella 16   *Punishment of the Whore Isabella Luna*
for Disobedience to the Commandments of the Governor of Rome

Who the Spanish woman Isabella de la Luna is, I think most of you know, since for a long time she trooped through Italy and abroad in the army of the emperor, in which many of us here have also fought in other times. Among her many whoresome ways, she has this about her: that her every action is as haughty as one will find. After her tour of duty in service to the needy soldiers, who are always willing to go the wet way,[3] she headed for Rome, where as usual she planned to lend out her body for rides to whomever paid her best. Now it came to pass that she owed a certain sum of money to a merchant for goods she had accepted from him; and she put him off at length, deferring her payment with words from one day to the next, to the point where she would happily have worked off the debt in so many rides of her personal carriage. But the merchant, who wanted money and not the peace of Marcone,[4] wouldn't lend her his ear; he only kept soliciting her to settle the debt. For her part, she played deaf to the matter of payment.

The merchant saw this and realized that if he didn't resort to other means he might never be paid; so he went to the governor of Rome, Monsignor de' Rossi, bishop of Pavia. On telling his story to the bishop, he obtained a citation for Isabella which demanded that she appear personally before the tribunal of this governor on a certain day at a specific time. The sergeant of the court went to Isabella's lodgings and found her out on the public street, where she was amusing herself in conversation with several of her fellows in the trade. The sergeant gave her the summons and then also verbally commanded, in the presence of everyone there with her, that she appear at the specified time as is customary. She, who among her other notable habits is wont to cruelly curse God and all the male and female saints in paradise, on receiving the citation in her hand, turned to the sergeant with disdain in her face, and brimming with rage and anger said, "Pesa a Dios, que quiere esto borrachio vigliaco?"[5] After which words, carried away by her overwhelming fury, she tore the papyrus citation into little pieces. Then with an air of insolence and ridicule, in front of everyone there, over her gown and on her derriere parts, as if she had just relieved herself, she wiped that unclean orifice with the citation. And then she contemptuously gave back the torn paper to the sergeant, telling him to go to hell.

The sergeant took the torn papyrus with him and presented it to the lieutenant of the lord governor, minutely recounting to him Isabella's response and all of the actions she had performed to make him look foolish. The lieutenant, on hearing of such enormous temerity and presumption in a shameless prostitute, referred the entire matter to the lord governor, arguing that the boldness of this female was a very important act and a bad example, in most serious contempt of his office, and deserving of bitter punishment so that others might learn not to put themselves so brazenly in contempt of the magistrate's officers and not to treat his orders so lightly. To the lord governor as well it seemed that such excess should not be passed over lightly, and that rather it was necessary to make some sort of illustration out of it. At the same time, considering that the offender was a woman and a public prostitute, he preferred not to treat the case with the full severity and harshness it deserved. Nonetheless, in order that the presumption of Isabella not go unpunished, he had her taken publicly from the bargello and conducted to the prisons at the tower of Nona.

When she was examined by the judge who took her preliminary statement, she responded to everything as if she were joking and as if the affair had nothing to do with her. Then she confessed to the debt she owed the merchant and demanded that she be allowed many months to pay it off. But since it had already been a year since she took the goods from him, she was sentenced to pay the entire sum before she could leave the prison. And when she considered that if she stayed in jail her business would take a great loss, as there she wouldn't be able to grind her mill, she found a way—I don't know how—to pay the merchant.

Then when she thought she was free and about to return home without further penalties, the judge pronounced a [second] sentence against her: that in the public street she be given fifty good lashes by the executioner on her bare ass. The sentence was made public; and on the day it was carried out half of Rome came to see such a noble spectacle. She was lifted up over the shoulders of a sturdy sergeant. And in the public street the executioner raised her clothes up over her head and made her put the colosseum on display in the open air, and with a stiff whip he began to strike her fiercely on the buttocks, so that the colosseum, which at first had appeared candid and healthy, in little time turned sanguine in color. After receiving such a fierce and humiliating beating and once her clothes were lowered again, Isabella made like a hound dog that, when it sets foot out of the kennel, shakes off all the straw and walks away. She did just the same. And though her buttocks were hurting, she walked away toward her house without showing the smallest sign of shame in her face, as if she were just coming back from a wedding feast.

Notes

1   Euphemism for prostitution. Francesco Flora's note in *Tutte le opere di Matteo Bandello* (Verona: Mondadori, 1966), 1302, here glosses: "Cioè vendeva se stessa."

2   Antonio Leiva (a.k.a. Antonio da Leva, 1480–1536) was the most famous of Charles V's generals, winner of the battle of Pavia and Marignano, and governor of Milan.

3   Bandello's phrase is "volentieri cavalcano per lo piovoso." The *Grande dizionario della lingua italiana* (Turin: UTET, 1981) cross-references *piovoso* to its entry no. 13 under *nave,* "Andare in nave per il piovoso" [To go by ship in the rain]: to have sexual relations according to nature (contrasts with "Andare in zoccoli per l'asciutto" [To wear clogs on dry ground]: to have sodomitical, or also homosexual relations). "Clogs" here may refer to the wooden shoes worn in Venice during periods of high water to keep feet from getting too wet. The image is thus one of appropriateness or inappropriateness to weather conditions, but also of wet (vaginal) versus dry (anal) sex. The citation offered by the *dizionario* as illustration also comes from Bandello, I.6: "Era il sommo suo diletto [del Porcellio] d'andar in zoccoli per l'asciutto. . . . La moglie, ch'era donna molto costumata, s'accorse in breve che il marito mal volentieri andava in nave per il piovoso."

4   Euphemism for sex.

5   Isabella speaks in a hybrid of her native Spanish and Italian: "What in God's name does this drunken coward want?"

Notes

Introduction

1   Giuseppe Verdi, *Rigoletto* (libretto by Francesco Maria Piave), 2 sound disks and notes (Middlesex, England: Hayes, 1989), act 3. Unless indicated otherwise, all translations in this volume are mine.

2   Gilda will in fact sacrifice her life for the Duke, thus revising the impact of this song on any listener aware of the opera's conclusion.

3   Scholarly works that provide overviews of this literature include Ruth Kelso, *Doctrine for the Lady of the Renaissance* (Urbana: University of Illinois Press, 1956); Ian Maclean, *The Renaissance Notion of Woman: A Study of the Fortunes of Scholasticism and Medical Science* (Cambridge: Cambridge University Press, 1980); Marina Zancan, "La donna," in *Letteratura italiana: Le questioni,* ed. R. Antonelli and A. Cicchetti (Turin: Einaudi, 1986); Constance Jordan, *Renaissance Feminism: Literary Texts and Political Models* (Ithaca: Cornell University Press, 1990); Margaret L. King, *Women of the Renaissance* (Chicago: University of Chicago Press, 1991); Pamela Joseph Benson, *The Invention of the Renaissance Woman: The Challenge of Female Independence in the Literature and Thought of Italy and England* (University Park: Pennsylvania State University Press, 1992); and Mary E. Wiesner, *Women and Gender in Early Modern Europe* (Cambridge: Cambridge University Press, 1993). For further references, see the individual chapters of this book.

4   Akin, if perhaps remotely, to my thinking here are Rosi Braidotti's discussions advocating a feminist "nomad subjectivity" in our postmodern age. See the introduction to her *Nomadic Subjects: Embodiment and Sexual Difference in Contemporary Feminist Theory* (New York: Columbia University Press, 1994), 1–39.

5   See Wiesner's chapter 3, "Women's Economic Role," on the difficulties faced by women travelers and merchants who were suspected of being prostitutes and bawds (*Women and Gender,* 82–114), and her discussions of similar responses to women's efforts to educate themselves (117–45) and participate in artistic and political (146–78) and religious (179–217) cultures.

6   Following a scholarly tradition that views Christine de Pizan as the first woman writer to formulate a systematic critique of misogynist literature and historiography, I adopt the French name for this centuries-long quarrel.

7   This is not to say that class differences were not also perceived as significant among women. See Constance Jordan, "Renaissance Women and the Question of Class," in *Sexuality and Gender in Early Modern Europe,* ed. James Grantham Turner (Cambridge: Cambridge University Press, 1993), 90–106.

8   My theoretical guides in these discussions include Mikhail Bakhtin, whose language of "prosaics" I borrow here and below. See *The Dialogic Imagination: Four Essays by M. M. Bakhtin,* ed. Michael Holquist, trans. Caryl Emerson and Michael Holquist (Austin: University of Texas Press, 1981); *Problems of Dostoevsky's Poetics,* ed. and trans. Caryl Emerson (Minneapolis: University of Minnesota Press, 1984); *Rabelais and His World,* trans. Hélène Iswolsky (Cambridge: MIT Press, 1968); *Speech Genres and Other Late Essays,* ed. Caryl Emerson and Michael Holquist, trans. Vern W. McGee (Austin: University of Texas Press, 1986). See also Gary Saul Morson and Caryl Emerson, *Mikhail Bakhtin: Creation of a Prosaics* (Stanford: Stanford University Press, 1990); and Katerina Clark and Michael Holquist, *Mikhail Bakhtin* (Cambridge: Harvard University Press, 1984).

9   Cf. Guido Ruggiero's proposal for a rereading of the Renaissance, which "to be successful, will need a cooperative effort between those who study the texts of literature and those who read the texts of history, especially in the archives— an interdisciplinary effort in terms of the boundaries currently drawn perhaps, but one that shares an interest in the close analysis of texts in their historical perspective common to much of the new social history and the new cultural poetics of criticism" ("Marriage, Love, Sex, and Renaissance Civic Morality," in Turner, *Sexuality and Gender,* 10–30; I cite from 10).

10   Bakhtin, *Speech Genres,* 7; emphasis in original. See also, for details regarding my discussion here, his *Dialogic Imagination,* 259–422; and Morson and Emerson, *Mikhail Bakhtin,* 272–305.

11   The first edition of the *Orlando furioso* was published in 1516, followed by a slightly revised edition in 1521. The 1532 edition, "Tuscanized" and expanded from forty to forty-six cantos and including several entirely new episodes, has come to be regarded as definitive. Although I am well aware that a sustained comparison of the final edition to the earlier ones would yield interesting information about Ariosto's development of the issues I take up, I leave that investigation to others. Because what concerns me most is the *Furioso*'s role as a text of mass consumption, I concentrate here on the most widely distributed edition. See Santorre Debenedetti and Cesare Segre, eds., *Orlando furioso. Secondo l'edizione del 1532 con le varianti delle edizioni del 1516 e del 1521* (Bologna: Commissione per i testi di lingua, 1960). My citations refer overwhelmingly to the edition of Emilio Bigi (Milan: Rusconi, 1982), which relies on (and in some instances corrects) the Debenedetti and Segre text. Among the many works on the history of the *Furioso*'s three redactions, see Alberto Casadei, *La strategia delle varianti: Le correzioni storiche del terzo "Furioso"* (Lucca:

Pacini Fazzi, 1988); and his *Il percorso del "Furioso": Ricerche intorno alle redazioni del 1516 e del 1521* (Bologna: Il Mulino, 1993). I refer readers to these works for additional bibliography on the question.

12   See Marina Beer, *Romanzi di cavalleria: Il "Furioso" e il romanzo italiano del primo Cinquecento* (Rome: Bulzoni, 1987).

13   Calvino's relation to the *Orlando furioso* may be less evident to readers unfamiliar with Ariosto's poem. In addition to the obvious *"Orlando furioso" raccontato da Italo Calvino* (Calvino's witty prose retelling of the sixteenth-century poem), allusions to the *Furioso* abound in Calvino's writing: from the chivalric satire of *Il cavaliere inesistente,* to the portrait of Viola in *Il barone rampante,* to the *Cosmicomiche*'s opening tale, "La distanza dalla luna," to his essays on the classics and on narrative technique; to the wildly interrupted, tour-de-force narrative of *Se una notte d'inverno un viaggiatore,* Calvino's debt to Ariosto runs through his work as a whole.

14   As I discuss in chapter 3, Ariosto's innovations in the techniques of suspense narration were pathbreaking.

15   Erich Nicholson, "Romance as Role Model: Early Female Performances of *Orlando Furioso* and *Gerusalemme Liberata,*" in *Renaissance Transactions: Ariosto and Tasso,* ed. Valeria Finucci (Durham: Duke University Press, 1999).

16   I develop this line of argument in greater detail in "Of Women, Knights, Arms, and Love: The *Orlando Furioso* and Ariosto's *Querelle des Femmes,*" MLN 104.1 (1989): 68–97.

17   Kelly's 1977 essay is reprinted in her *Women, History, Theory* (Chicago: University of Chicago Press, 1984). For an important assessment of Kelly's impact and of developments in early modern Italian historiography since her essay was published, see chapter 1 in Samuel K. Cohn Jr., *Women in the Streets: Essays on Sex and Power in Renaissance Italy* (Baltimore: Johns Hopkins University Press, 1996). Cohn notes that while Kelly's question "begged for new research of a social character" (5), her methods remained essentially those of the Burckhardtian tradition she sought to upset, thoroughly immersed in the representations of women offered by high intellectual culture. Cohn himself mixes the narrative and quantitative methods of economic history and microhistory, respectively, "placing and testing the extraordinary within the context of the ordinary" (99), and calls for a careful and regionally comparative combination of these methods among historians, with cautious attention to the clues offered by literary and other more figurative sources (including study of the rhetorical gestures contained in court records and archival documents themselves).

18   Ottavia Niccoli surveyed male and female Italian authors among the British Library's incunables and sixteenth-century editions (one of the largest and most comprehensive collections available) and found no more than twenty-four women, compared with an indefinite number of men, surely more than

one thousand, but prudently estimated to be around three thousand. See Ottavia Niccoli, "Forme di cultura e condizioni di vita in due epistolari femminili del Rinascimento," in *Les Femmes écrivains en Italie au Moyen Age et à la Renaissance* (Aix-en-Provence: Publications de l'Université de Provence, 1994), 13–32. As Margaret King, Albert Rabil, and others have indicated, while the Quattrocento fostered several isolated but vocal female humanists who wrote extensively in Latin and on many subjects, by the Cinquecento such figures were absent. As we celebrate the activities of sixteenth-century women writing in the vernacular, then, we should also ask why their numbers remained so small compared with those of men, and why so many of these women expressed themselves exclusively in lyric poetry. See Margaret L. King, "Book-Lined Cells: Women and Humanism in the Early Italian Renaissance," in *Beyond Their Sex: Learned Women of the European Past,* ed. Patricia H. Labalme (New York: New York University Press, 1980), 66–90; and idem, "Thwarted Ambitions: Six Learned Women of the Renaissance," *Soundings* 59 (1976): 280–304; and King and Albert Rabil Jr., eds. and trans., *Her Immaculate Hand: Selected Works by and about the Women Humanists of Quattrocento Italy* (Binghamton: Medieval and Renaissance Texts and Studies, 1983).

19   See the economic analyses of Cohn, *Women in the Streets;* and Wiesner, *Women and Gender;* as well as the literary/cultural discussion of Peter Stallybrass, "Patriarchal Territories: The Body Enclosed," in *Rewriting the Renaissance: The Discourse of Sexual Difference in Early Modern Europe,* ed. Margaret W. Ferguson, Maureen Quilligan, and Nancy J. Vickers (Chicago: University of Chicago Press, 1986), 123–44.

I   Circular Definitions

1   "Eye and Mind," in Maurice Merleau-Ponty, *The Primacy of Perception,* trans. James M. Edie (Evanston: Northwestern University Press, 1964), 159–92; I cite from 162–63.

2   See in particular the section entitled "Of the Gaze as *Objet petit a,*" in Jacques Lacan, *The Four Fundamental Concepts of Psychoanalysis,* ed. Jacques-Alain Miller, trans. Alan Sheridan (New York: Norton, 1978); and Juliet Mitchell and Jacqueline Rose, eds., *Feminine Sexuality: Jacques Lacan and the École Freudienne,* trans. Jacqueline Rose (New York: Norton, 1982).

3   I am indebted to Harry Berger Jr. for his lucid and far-reaching discussion of early modern subjectivity in an unpublished essay entitled "Graphic Imperialism." For discussions of the appropriateness of psychoanalytical critical practices to early modern texts, see the introductions to Juliana Schiesari, *The Gendering of Melancholia: Feminism, Psychoanalysis, and the Symbolics of Loss in Renaissance Literature* (Ithaca: Cornell University Press, 1992); and Lynn Enterline,

The Tears of Narcissus: Melancholia and Masculinity in Early Modern Writing (Stanford: Stanford University Press, 1995).

4   The Sala dei mesi is unofficially reputed to have been a banquet room. There were no kitchens in the Schifanoia palace, whose name derives from *schivare* [avoid, shun] and *noia* [cares, boredom, annoyance]; but chroniclers tell of banquets being brought there from the ducal palace for serving.

5   On the Sala dei mesi, see Ranieri Varese, "Il ciclo cosmologico di Schifanoia: Un momento nella civiltà cortese in Europa," in *The Renaissance in Ferrara and Its European Horizons,* ed. J. Salmons and W. Moretti (Cardiff: University of Wales Press, 1984), 309–20; and idem, "Novità a Schifanoia," *Critica d'arte* 17.113 (1970): 49–62; Aby Warburg, "Arte italiana e astrologia internazionale nel Palazzo Schifanoia di Ferrara," in *La rinascita del paganesimo antico. Contributi all storia della cultura raccolti da Gertrud Bing,* ed. Gertrud Bing (Florence: La Nuova Italia, 1966), 247–72; Giacomo Bargellesi, *Palazzo Schifanoia* (Bergamo: Istituto italiano d'arti grafiche, 1945); Ludovico Zorzi, "Ferrara: Il sipario ducale," in his *Il teatro e la città. Saggi sulla scena italiana* (Turin: Einaudi, 1977), 3–60; F. Mercier, "L'organization de l'espace dans les fresques du palais Schifanoia a Ferrara," *L'information d'istoire de l'art* 13 (1968): 82–84; and A. Venturi, "L'arte a Ferrara nel periodo di Borso d'Este," in *Rivista storica italiana II* (Rome: Fratelli Bocca, 1885), 689–749.

6   On such festivities in general, see Peter Burke, *Popular Culture in Early Modern Europe* (1978; reprint, Hampshire, England: Gower, 1988); and Peter Stallybrass and Allon White, *The Politics and Poetics of Transgression* (Ithaca: Cornell University Press, 1986), especially the introduction. Stallybrass and White's first chapter, "The Fair, the Pig, Authorship," though concerned primarily with market fairs in England and not state-orchestrated games, is also very informative. For Renaissance official pageantry, see Charles M. Rosenberg, "The Use of Celebrations in Public and Semi-public Affairs in Fifteenth-Century Ferrara," in *Il teatro italiano nel Rinascimento,* ed. Maristella de Panizza Lorch (Milan: Edizioni di Communità, 1980), 521–35.

7   On the rise of the Estensi in Ferrara, see Richard M. Tristano, "Vassals, Fiefs, and Social Mobility in Ferrara during the Middle Ages and Renaissance," *Medievalia et Humanistica,* n.s., 15 (1987): 43–64.

8   Mikhail Bakhtin, *Rabelais and His World,* trans. Hélène Iswolsky (Bloomington: Indiana University Press, 1984), 246. Much recent work on the "carnivalesque" seeks to temper Bakhtin's optimism regarding the subversive possibilities of masquerade, carnival, and traditions of festival role reversal (e.g., Stallybrass and White, *Politics and Poetics*). Nevertheless, the *palio* appears distinct from such events as market fairs and mardi gras festivals, as participation in it by Ferrara'a populace was minimal and apparently highly controlled. See Louise Olga Fradenburg's full-scale study of the related tradition of the tournament,

City, Marriage, Tournament: Arts of Rule in Late Medieval Scotland (Madison: University of Wisconsin Press, 1991).

9   G. A. Facchini, *Il palio di San Giorgio a Ferrara* (Ferrara: Società anonima tipografica emiliana, 1939), 6–7. Facchini supplies a photo reproduction of the relevant page from the 1279 statutes, which are held in the Archivio di Stato di Modena. See also Nino Franco Visentini, *Il palio di Ferrara* (Rovigo: Istituto padano d'arti grafiche, 1968). Visentini's principal source is Facchini's work. Both volumes have as an explicit aim the restoration of the Palio di San Giorgio as an annual event in Ferrara; thus they tend to elide the unsavory aspects of the early *palio*. It is possible that the second-place prize, the pig, was considered the "booby prize" for the race's loser. On second place being last, see Alan Dundes and Alessandro Falassi, *La Terra in Piazza: An Interpretation of the Palio of Siena* (Berkeley: University of California Press, 1975), xi. For extensive reflection on the cultural significance of the pig, see Stallybrass and White, *Politics and Poetics;* but also John J. Winkler, *The Constraints of Desire: The Anthropology of Sex and Gender in Ancient Greece* (London: Routledge, 1990), 188–209.

10 *Diario di Ugo Caleffini (1471–1494),* ed. Giuseppe Pardi (Ferrara: Premiata Tipografia Sociale, 1938–XVII), series: Monumenti, vol. I, pt. I, 87.

11 Emphasis added. Caleffini, *Diario,* 251 (23 March 1500). It is not clear whether the apparent change in the order of the contests signals a flexibility in the *palio*'s diachronic structure or simply a mistake in the chronicler's record. This discrepancy forestalls me from insistence on rigid "pairings" in the sequence of the races, but a certain symmetry emerges from both of these structures. Steeds–asses–men–women suggests (perhaps) that asses are to steeds as women are to men (i.e., inferior, laughable imitations); the late chronicle's recorded sequence of steeds–men–women–asses might establish the same set of relations, this time in chiasmus. Such a reading requires assigning to the male runners the sign value of "masculinity," however, a reading regarding which I have many doubts.

12 See Victor Turner, *The Anthropology of Performance* (New York: Performing Arts Journals, 1987), 99; and idem, *The Ritual Process: Structure and Anti-Structure* (1969; reprint, Ithaca: Cornell University Press, 1977); also Harry Berger Jr., "Bodies and Texts," *Representations* 17 (1987): 144–66; and idem, "From Body to Cosmos: The Dynamics of Representation in Precapitalist Society," *South Atlantic Quarterly* 91 (1992): 557–602.

13 In most contexts, *donna* constitutes a term of respect (or at least lack of disrespect), carrying with it the noble connotations of the Latin etymon *domina*. The meaning of *femina* (which derives from the same Latin root as *fecundus*) ranges from that of simple biological sex (e.g., in animals) to its common use as a denigratory reference to woman. This small slippage proves more significant as the *palio*'s history becomes clearer.

14 A reputed source dated 1371 (and perhaps known to Facchini) provides further encouragement for such a reading, as it too records a race in the Palio

di San Giorgio by *mingarde,* the Ferrarese equivalent of the Italian *meretrici* [prostitutes]. See *Enciclopedia dello spettacolo* (Rome: Le maschere, 1958), 5:174. Discussions of Cossa's fresco panel regularly note that the women represented in that image are the prostitutes of Estense Ferrara and that the men are either Ferrarese Jews or members of some other marginal social group, but they present no documentation on this point. Even the *Enciclopedia* does not identify this source directly, and unfortunately, all other secondary sources settle on this question by referring back to the *Enciclopedia.* My own efforts at tracking down the original citation have thus far been unsuccessful.

15 Richard C. Trexler, "Correre la Terra: Collective Insults in the Late Middle Ages," *Mélanges de l'École française de Rome moderne* 96.2 (1984): 845–902. This rich and perceptive essay has been a principal guide to my *palio* explorations; without it many of the interpretations offered in the discussion that follows would have remained unsubstantiated conjectures. See also E. Rodocanachi, "Les Courses en Italie au vieux temps," *Revue des études historiques* 66 (1900): 241–52; and Martine Boiteux, "Les Juifs dans le Carneval de la Rome moderne," *Mélanges de l'École française de Rome moderne* 88 (1976): 745–87.

16 On games as "repetition" of future loss in preparation for its psychological impact, see Sigmund Freud, "Beyond the Pleasure Principle" (1920), in *Standard Edition of the Complete Psychological Works,* ed. James Strachey (London: Hogarth, 1953–74), 18:3–64.

17 Trexler, "Correre," 872–73.

18 See, e.g., Giovanni Villani's entry in capitolo 132 for the Palio di San Giovanni run outside Arezzo in 1288: *Croniche di Giovanni, Matteo, e Filippo Villani* (Trieste: Sezione Letterario–Artistico del Lloyd Austriaco, 1857), 162–63. For further examples, see Trexler, "Correre," 862–64.

19 G. Villani, *Croniche,* book 10, 167 (355). *Baracane bambagino,* or goatskin cloth, was the third-place prize in the women's race in Ferrara's Palio di San Giorgio of 1496. The first-place women's prize was the *palio verde;* for second place a piece of *pignola,* or cloth suitable for making mattresses and flour sacks; for third place the *bambasina;* for fourth place a pair of shoes and cloth for making simple headcoverings; and to each of the other runners a coin worth 36 quatrini. Food prices listed in this same chronicle during the same year indicate that sausage cost 8 quatrini per pound, fish 5–6 quatrini, ricotta 4 quatrini, and oil 9 quatrini. See Caleffini, *Diario,* 148, 191. Machiavelli too records one of these races in his *Vita di Castruccio Castracani:* Castruccio, "[fece] in dispregio de' Fiorentini battere monete, correre palii a cavagli, a uomini e a meretrici" (623), from Niccolò Machiavelli, *Tutte le opere,* ed. Mario Martelli (Florence: Sansoni, 1971).

20 Villani, *Croniche,* 11.97. See Trexler, "Correre," 863, for further examples.

21 Giovanni di Pagolo Morelli, *Ricordi,* ed. Vittore Branca (Florence: Felice Le Monnier, 1956), 308.

22 Trexler, "Correre," 863–64.

23   In Ferrara as elsewhere, the races became progressively more "wholesome," but they continued well into the nineteenth century. See Facchini, *Il palio,* 43–47. Trexler indicates that prostitutes were still running races in Germany toward the end of the seventeenth century and in Lucerne up until the French Revolution; and as late as 1519, prostitutes raced in the Pauline races of Rome ("Correre," 885ff.). Facchini (*Il palio,* 36–37) recalls the Ferrarese boat races of 1598 on the occasion of Pope Clement VIII's visit, for which thirty women were recruited from another city: "Le barchette furono sei e corsero tre alla volta. In ciascuna stavano quattro donne che remavano e una sedeva a poppa suonando il cembalo. Tutte erano inghirlandate di fiori e indossavano succinte vesti a sei colori, secondo le barchette. Durante la corsa alcune di esse, per maggior divertimento, fingevano di cadere nell'acqua e poi nuotando si rimettevano sui legni." Facchini's allusive term "succinte vesti" and the women's comic antics, as well as the fact that they were brought in from another town, suggest the women's profession, although the boat races described above appear more akin to chorus girls' slapstick—or perhaps mud wrestling?—than to derisive moral display.

24   E.g., a Mantuan edict of 23 April 1496 (the same day on which Francesco also issued regulations for prostitutes) requires Jewish men to wear a yellow cord around one shoulder. An edict of three days later specifies that Jewish women must wear "segnali gialli sulla testa" (Archivio Gonzaga Serie F.I.3, busta 2038–39, fasc. 8, fol. 2v). See also Attilio Milano, *Storia degli ebrei in Italia* (Turin: Einaudi, 1963); Cecil Roth, *The Jews in the Renaissance* (Philadelphia: Jewish Publication Society of America, 1959), 25, 77, 211, 217, 289; Diane Owen Hughes, "Distinguishing Signs: Ear-rings, Jews, and Franciscan Rhetoric in the Italian Renaissance City," *Past and Present* 112 (1986): 3–59; and Leah H. Otis, *Prostitution in Medieval Society* (Chicago: University of Chicago Press, 1985), 70. On the Jews' role in derisive festivals, see Alessandro Fontana, "La scena," in *Storia d'Italia* (Turin: Einaudi, 1955), 1:794–868, esp. 828, n. 2; Boiteux, "Les Juifs"; and Paolo Toschi, "La giudiata," in *Le origini del teatro italiano* (Turin: Einaudi, 1955). Roberto Bonfil's learned *Jewish Life in Renaissance Italy,* trans. Anthony Oldcorn (Berkeley: University of California Press, 1994), presents itself as a major revision of Roth.

25   Trexler, "Correre," 848–57, provides an extended discussion of the ribalds' military and civic role, with helpful reflections on the etymology of their name.

26   For provocative reflections on this figure, see Roger Caillois, "The Sociology of the Executioner," in *The College of Sociology 1937–39,* ed. Denis Hollier (Minneapolis: University of Minnesota Press, 1988), 233–47.

27   Trexler, "Correre," cites a number of references to the scant clothing ribalds wore into battle (849 n. 7). For the statutes, see A. Pertile, *Storia del diritto italiano* (Turin, 1984), 3:229. I cite from Trexler, 853.

28   Condemnations of sodomy are frequent in the chronicle and legal sources I

have cited throughout this chapter. Among the secondary sources, see Elizabeth Pavan, "Police des moeurs, société et politique à la fin du Moyen Age," *Revue historique* 536 (1980): 240–88; Richard C. Trexler, "La Prostitution florentine au XV siècle: Patronage et clientèles," *Annales: Economies, sociétés, civilisations* 36.6 (1981): 983–1015; Guido Ruggiero, *The Boundaries of Eros: Sex Crime and Sexuality in Renaissance Venice* (Oxford: Oxford University Press, 1985); and idem, "Vizi, e virtu nel Rinascimento," in *La storia della prostituzione* [*Storia e dossier* 4] (Florence: Giunti-Barbera, 1989), 25–39; Werner L. Gundersheimer, "Crime and Punishment in Ferrara, 1440–1500," in *Violence and Civil Disorder in Italian Cities, 1200–1500,* ed. Lauro Martines (Berkeley: University of California Press, 1972), 104–28; and John Boswell, *Christianity, Social Tolerance, and Homosexuality* (Chicago: University of Chicago Press, 1980).

29   Trexler, "Correre," 882, cites the Statuti . . . Ivrea, 2:12.

30   Again I rely on Trexler, "Correre," 882, which cites *Rerum italicarum scriptores,* vol. 11, pt. 1, p. 40.

31   Trexler, "Correre," 898, cites the *Rerum italicarum scriptores,* vol. 33, pt. 2, p. 62. As Trexler notes, the "productivity" of the prostitute was in fact a principal motive for the reversal of fortune and the beating of the Bolognese women. The chronicle relating this account specifies that the women's flogging was triggered by their bragging about how much money they had made in their trade in spite of the army's defeat. Oddly conscious of the sacrifices and contradictions prostitution imposed on women, the chronicler offers that the woman who died expired from the pain of the flogging, *or perhaps from shame at having her breasts exposed* (my emphasis). Matteo Bandello's preface to his novella (part IV, novella 16) alludes to a similar reversal of fortune and is the subject of chapter 5.

32   See Otis, *Prostitution;* Jacques Rossiaud, *Medieval Prostitution,* trans. Lydia Cochrane (Oxford: Basil Blackwell, 1988); Romano Canossa and Isabella Colonello, *Storia della prostituzione in Italia dal quattrocento alla fine del settecento* (Rome: Sapere 2000, 1989); Paul Larivaille, *La vita quotidiana delle cortigiane nell'Italia del Rinascimento* (Milan: Rizzoli, 1983); Ruggiero, *Boundaries;* and idem, "Vizi," 25–39. Though all these studies are valuable, none contains specific information about Ferrara. For insights regarding the ancient precedents for medieval prostitution practices, see David M. Halperin, *One Hundred Years of Homosexuality and Other Essays on Greek Love* (New York: Routledge, 1990), 88–112; and idem, "Atene. Il corpo violato," in *La storia della prostituzione* [*Storia e dossier* 4], 4–24.

33   The persistence of this urban map is evident in any modern city, where prostitution is typically concentrated in the outermost perimeter of streets. The alternative area surrounding train and bus stations substitutes for the ancient crossroads (*trivio*) in this function, while today's drug traffic supplants the earlier versions of contraband mercantilism that also characterize these urban zones. A Mantuan *grida* issued on 11 April 1496 by Isabella d'Este specifies that city's

"luogo destinato alle meretrici"; see Archivio Gonzaga Serie F.I.3, busta 2038–39, gride, fasc. 8, fol. 1v. On early modern Ferrara, Luigi Napoleone Cittadella observes the designation of prostitution districts in Ferrara and the institution of the bells (*sonagli*) in 1382. The city imposed the yellow armband in 1438. Cittadella adds, "Nel 1482 fu loro dato luogo fra s. Agnese e s. Clemente; nel 1569 si cangia la loro località; nel 1610 loro viene proibito andare in carozza od in calesse; nel 1598 vi era già imposto *un Dazio* sul loro esercizio" (291, Cittadella's emphasis); Cittadella, *Notizie amministrative, storiche, artistiche relative a Ferrara* (Ferrara: Domenico Taddei, 1868), 1:290. A Ferrarese proletarian culture magazine includes in its local history column the notice: "Le «Gance» o luoghi di prostituzione, furono per molto tempo confinate fuori della città, oltre il fiume Po. . . . In seguito furono poste a s. Agnese e a s. Clemente; e dovevano pagare un Dazio nel loro commercio!" "Effemeridi ferraresi," 23, 15 April 1977. The same column in an earlier volume (18. 48, 2 December 1917) recalls, "In un tempo lontano passato [via Romiti] era denominata «strada del Postribolo»; poi prese il nome di «via dell'Inferno»; mutò nome la terza volta e prese quello di «via del Bordelletto»; con questa ultima denominazione si appellava il tratto che da via Spronello (or delle Scienze) va a via Buonporto"; *La domenica dell'operaio. Periodico popolare settimanale*. See also Hughes, "Distinguishing Signs."

34   Rossiaud, *Medieval Prostitution,* observes: "It was between 1350 and 1450 that the cities institutionalized prostitution, setting up a *postribulum publicum* when the city did not already have one. The Castelletto in Venice opened its doors in 1360 (not long after the municipal brothel in Lucca). . . . Florence took a similar decision in 1403; Siena in 1421" (59).

35   In Rome, these measures were directed also at the celebrated courtesans. See Larivaille, *La vita quotidiana,* 184–201; and Georgina Masson, *Courtesans of the Italian Renaissance* (New York: St. Martin's Press, 1975), 132–44. History would be well served by a revaluation of the much romanticized lives of early modern courtesans, for which project the studies of Larivaille and Rosenthal make an excellent beginning. See Margaret F. Rosenthal, *The Honest Courtesan: Veronica Franco, Citizen and Writer in Sixteenth-Century Venice* (Chicago: University of Chicago Press, 1992). Veronica Franco's letter to a friend on the pains and dangers faced by common prostitute and courtesan alike provides a sobering first-hand corrective to the popular view of the courtesans' carefree liberties and honors. See her *Lettere,* ed. Benedetto Croce (Naples: Ricciardi, 1949), 35–38.

36   The first chapter of Rossiaud's book provides some chilling statistics on the frequency of gang rapes in fifteenth- and sixteenth-century Dijon. He adds, "Literature, legend, and popular mythology have retained only the more benevolent aspects of these youth solidarities. The champions of a popular culture largely defined by laughter and what is called the Gallic tradition would do well to look twice, for these groups of grotesque maskers who resemble the comic

characters of farces and *sotties* lead us to forget the victims, most of whom were 'abandoned' to a life of vagabondage and prostitution" (*Medieval Prostitution*, 26).

37 Trexler, "La Prostitution," provides in n. 12 a relevant passage from the *Statuta populi et communis Florentiae* of 1415, printed in a modern edition (Frieburg, 1778–83): "Nefandi facinoris ipsique naturae contrarii, et enormis criminis putredinem abhorrentes, quale est vitium sodomiticum, et volentes in hoc pro extirpatione huius modi criminis in augmentum aliorum ordinamentorum possetenus providere, discernimus quod" (*Statuta*, 3:41). It bears noting that the documents refer not to a sexual orientation but to an act. Halperin's remarks on the ahistorical use of the term *homosexuality* in our references to practices predating the nineteenth-century theorization of "sexuality" are pertinent. See his *One Hundred Years*, 15–40.

38 Cittadella, *Notizie*, 291, 296.

39 Pietro Aretino includes cross-dressing among the techniques taught by the aging whore, Nanna, to her apprentice, Pippa: "subito che il messere ti vede diventata di femina maschio, te si avventarà come la fame al pan caldo." *Sei giornate* (1536), ed. Angelo Romano (Milan: Mursia, 1991), 190.

40 Trexler, "La Prostitution," 995. More than a century later a similar scandal over androgynous dress would break out in England with the publication of the pamphlets *Hic Mulier* and *Haec Vir*. See Linda Woodbridge, *Women and the English Renaissance: Literature and the Nature of Womankind, 1540–1620* (Urbana: University of Illinois Press, 1984), 139–51.

41 Homi Bhabha, "Of Mimicry and Man: The Ambivalence of Colonial Discourse," *October* 28 (1984): 125–33; and Lacan, "Of the Gaze." See also Luce Irigaray, "Women on the Market," in *This Sex Which Is Not One*, trans. Catherine Porter (Ithaca: Cornell University Press, 1985): "To play with mimesis is thus, for a woman, to try to recover the place of her exploitation by discourse, without allowing herself to be simply reduced to it. It means to resubmit herself—inasmuch as she is on the side of the 'perceptible' of 'matter'—to 'ideas,' in particular to ideas about herself, that are elaborated in/by a masculine logic, but so as to make 'visible,' by an effect of playful repetition, what was supposed to remain invisible: the cover-up of a possible operation of the feminine in language" (76).

42 Irigaray, "Women on the Market," 186.

43 For an excellent overview of these relations among men, see chapter 1 of Margaret King, *Women of the Renaissance* (Chicago: University of Chicago Press, 1991).

44 Cittadella, *Notizie*, 291–97, reproduces in their entirety the proclamations of 1462 and 1496 on prostitution and several other public offenses, as well as several repressive laws against women passed in the 1440s. Bernardo Prosperi's letter to Isabella d'Este Gonzaga of 7 April 1496 (Archivio Gonzaga, Archivio

di stato di Mantova) refers with approval to the "grossi punitione [*sic*]," Ercule's edicts reserved for these offenders. On the expulsion of the prostitutes from Rome, see Larivaille, *La vita quotidiana,* 184–201. For Venice, see Pavan, "Police des moeurs," 241–88; and Ruggiero, *Boundaries.* For historical background on the more general question of moral and sexual tolerance, see Boswell, *Christianity.*

45 Facchini, *Il palio,* 14, cites a 1456 manuscript in which the jurist Ugo Trotti expresses interest in the women's race and speculates on whether a prince has the right to forbid such contests, as Borso had recently done. Trotti's remarks indicate that Borso sought to repress the race on the grounds that it was immoral: "Sic diebus nostris fecit Dux noster illustris et verissimus patriae parens Divus Borsius Estensis ut effraenatam a lascivam adolescentium multitudinem a prodigalitate avertecet et ad virtutes veras et frugem meliores vitae revocaret."

46 Facchini, *Il palio,* 14, cites the ducal edicts of 23 April 1476. Caleffini's *Diario* entry for 24 April 1476 records that "pute insino a 14 anni" ran that race. The editor of Caleffini's diary infers from this entry that all accounts of the races featuring women must be referring to runners who were really young girls. Chronicle and historical evidence suggests to me the contrary: that Caleffini may be remarking an innovation in the format of the *palio.*

47 Archivio Gonzaga Serie F.I.3, busta 2038–39, gride, fasc. 8, 22 giugno 1495, fol. 20v.: "Sua Ex.tia ha deliberato che a questa festa proxima de S.to Petro non corrino come già solevono le meretrice publice et de mala vita: ma in loco suo ha ordinato corrino le contadinelle: si che essendo alcuna che vogli correre vegni a consignarsi al tempo debito che non li serà facto ne dicto despiacere ne ingiuria alcuna."

48 In Ferrara as elsewhere, masks were often the object of early modern legislation because they functioned well beyond their immediate instrumental value in individual crimes: disguises struck at the base of the ruling-class monopoly on visual symbols, permitting political subjects to throw up barriers to a ducal gaze that demanded the transparency of the social whole. See, for general information, Gundersheimer, "Crime and Punishment"; and "Il Palio di San Giorgio nelle norme penali e di polizia degli statuti," *Rivista di Ferrara,* Year 2 (June 1934): XII, no. 6. The Mantuan edicts of the late fifteenth century permit masks at carnivals and other feasts but prohibit the carrying of arms of any kind while in disguise. See, e.g., Francesco Gonzaga's *grida* of 1 January 1492: Archivio Gonzaga Serie F.I.3, busta 2038–39, fol. 7r. Also regular in the years 1488–1527 are Mantuan edicts against the harming of Jews, street brawls and violent games, carrying arms, and disruption of public executions.

49 See Georges Bataille's remarks on heterogeneity and kingly power, which, despite the chronological distance of the period they address, are far from irrelevant in the Ferrarese context: "The Psychological Structure of Fascism," in Bataille, *Visions of Excess: Selected Writings, 1927–1939,* ed. and trans. Allan

Stoekl (Minneapolis: University of Minnesota Press, 1985), 137–60. Also highly suggestive are Bataille's reflections on prostitution in his *Erotism. Death and Sensuality,* trans. Mary Dalwood (San Francisco: City Lights, 1986).

50 Steven Mullaney, "Civic Rites, City Sites: The Place of the Stage," in *Staging the Renaissance: Reinterpretations of Elizabethan and Jacobean Drama,* ed. David Scott Kastan and Peter Stallybrass (New York: Routledge, 1991), 17–26, 23.

51 Two examples are Machiavelli who, throughout *Il principe* refers to models of political failure as feminine (e.g., the Medes in ch. 6, cowardly men in ch. 15, a despised prince and Alexander in ch. 19, disarmed subjects in ch. 20) before exhorting the Medici to seize Fortuna (also a woman) and turn Italy's fate around; and Castiglione's emasculated Duke Guidobaldo, who as a figure for the Italian courts is supplanted by the Duchess, a feminine surrogate, in *Il libro del Cortegiano,* ed. Bruno Maier (Turin: UTET, 1981). On Castiglione, see Joan Kelly, *Women, History, and Theory* (Chicago: University of Chicago Press, 1977); and Carla Freccero, "Politics and Aesthetics in Castiglione's *Il Cortegiano:* Book III and the Discourse on Women," in *Creative Imitation: New Essays on Renaissance Literature in Honor of Thomas M. Greene,* ed. David Quint, Margaret W. Ferguson, G. W. Pigman III, and Wayne A. Rebhorn (Binghamton: Medieval and Renaissance Texts and Studies, 1992), 259–80. On the broader political language of the downtrodden Italy as feminine body, see Margaret Brose, who traces this identification back to Dante and Petrarch: "In . . . poem 128 of the *Rime sparse,* the figuration of Italy as a vilified female body serves both to enable a specifically male poetic language and to justify the call for a rebirth of Italic political consciousness" (1); Brose, "Petrarch's Beloved Body: 'Italia mia,' " in *Feminist Approaches to the Body in Medieval Literature,* ed. Linda Lomperis and Sarah Stanbury (Philadelphia: University of Pennsylvania Press, 1993), 1–20.

52 See Daniela Frigo, "Dal caos all'ordine: sulla questione del 'prender moglie' nella trattatistica del sedicesimo secolo," in *Nel cerchio della luna. Figure di donne in alcuni testi del XVI secolo,* ed. Marina Zancan (Venice: Marsilio, 1983), 57–94; as well as Natalie Zemon Davis, "Women on Top," in her *Society and Culture in Early Modern France* (Stanford: Stanford University Press, 1975).

53 Trexler, "Correre," 870, cites P. Pellini, *Dell'historia di Perugia,* pt. 1 (Venice, 1664), 534.

54 Caterina's taunt is recounted by Machiavelli in his *Discorsi,* 3:6. See John Freccero, "Medusa and the Madonna of Forlì: Political Sexuality in Machiavelli," in *Machiavelli and the Discourse of Literature,* ed. Albert R. Ascoli and Victoria Kahn (Ithaca: Cornell University Press, 1993), 161–78. My thanks to Julia Hairston for discussion of her work in progress on Machiavelli's revisions of this anecdote to emphasize Caterina's reproductive role. On the Freudian reception of this imagery of female genital exposure, see Neil Hertz, "Medusa's Head: Male Hysteria under Political Pressure," in his *The End of the Line: Essays on Psychoanalysis and the Sublime* (New York: Columbia University Press, 1985), 161–216.

55 Manfred Lurker, *Dictionary of Gods, Goddesses, Devils, and Demons,* trans. G. L. Campbell (London: Routledge and Kegan Paul, 1987), 57, 319. On the designation of this gesture as *anasyrmos,* see Helen King, "Agnodike and the Profession of Medicine," *Proceedings of the Cambridge Philological Society* 212 (n.s., 32) (1986): 53–77.

56 On another aspect of political power as reflected through women's performance in public ritual, see Sharon T. Strocchia, "Funerals and the Politics of Gender in Early Renaissance Florence," in *Refiguring Woman: Perspectives on Gender and the Italian Renaissance,* ed. Marilyn Migiel and Juliana Schiesari (Ithaca: Cornell University Press, 1991), 155–68.

57 Giuseppe Pardi, ed., *Diario ferrarese dall'anno 1409 sino al 1502 di autori incerti* (Bologna: Zanichelli, 1928–33), 263.

58 For Florence, see Trexler, "Correre," 884–85.

59 For races on Pentecost and Saint Mary Magdalene's Day (July 22), see Otis, *Prostitution,* 71; and Trexler, "Correre," 884–86. Otis mentions in addition a race in Foligno on Saint Felix's Day. Trexler documents races on the feast of the Virgin's Assumption in Brescia and Padua and similar races for different saints' days in Rome and Pienza.

60 Biographical information about Saint George relies heavily on legendary sources. His cult seems to date from the sixth century, when monasteries and inscriptions appeared in his honor in Jerusalem, Jericho, and Beirut as well as in cities in Ethiopia and Egypt. An officer in the Christian militia, he is thought to have been martyred under either Dacian the Persian emperor or the Roman emperor Diocletian. Many spectacular legends arose recounting miracles he performed while in the custody of his executioners. The celebrated tale of his defeat of the dragon to save a young girl originated during the Crusades, after George was thought to have aided several Christian victories in 1089. See Paolo Toschi, *La leggenda di San Giorgio nei canti popolari italiani* (Florence: Olschki, 1964).

61 H. H. Scullard, *Festivals and Ceremonies of the Roman Republic* (Ithaca: Cornell University Press, 1981), 76–79.

62 Scullard, *Festivals,* 110–11.

63 Hans Peter Duerr, *Nacktheit und Scham: Der Mythos vom Zivilisations-prozess* (Frankfurt a.M.: Suhrkamp Verlag, 1988), 303, n. 39, which refers to Scullard, *Festivals,* 172ff.

64 On Aphrodite's association with city-sponsored prostitution in classical Athens and Corinth, see Halperin, "Atene."

65 Zorzi, "Il sipario," refers to the *palio* as a "contest of humiliation." See also Ranieri Varese, *Il palazzo di Schifanoia* (Bologna, 1980): "Vi partecipavano, o erano costretti, prostitute, scemi di borgata a cavallo di asini, ebrei forzati a correre ignudi, confusi tra loro, obbligate a subire le beffe del popolo e il disprezzo paternalistico dei nobili." Cited in Mazzacurati, *Il Rinascimento dei*

moderni. La crisi culturale del XVI secolo e la negazione delle origini (Bologna: il Mulino, 1985), 304. Insofar as they evoke but do not document the scene of *palio* violence, these scholarly sources require the same scrutiny as the earlier, popularizing monographs.

66 See Georges Dumézil, *Mitra-Varuna: An Essay on Two Indo-European Representations of Sovereignty*, trans. Derek Coltman (New York: Zone Books, 1988): "The flagellation of female passers-by referred to another, more scabrous incident in the Romulus story: having kidnapped the Sabine women for his men, the young leader discovered, to his annoyance, that they were sterile. He consulted an oracle, which replied, 'Let a he-goat penetrate the Roman women!' An augur then rendered a somewhat more decorous interpretation of this robust injunction: the women were struck with goatskin thongs, and they conceived" (28). Dumézil sees the winter and end-of-winter maskers of modern Europe as, in part, a bastardization of this tradition.

67 Catalano, *Vita di Ludovico Ariosto* (Geneva: Olschki, 1930), 106. It perhaps bears noting that in modern Italian, the verb *scopare* means not only "to sweep with a broom," but in its common slang usage denotes the sex act, for either sex.

68 Catalano cites from Bernardo Prosperi's letter to Isabella of 21 September. On "running the town," see the Ferrarese statutes reproduced in Cittadella, *Notizie,* 291–97. Matteo Bandello's novella (IV.16) about the Roman prostitute Isabella de Luna, whose punishment for refusing to pay a debt was "che dal boia su la publica strada le fossero date su il culo ignudo cinquanta buone stafilate," also describes a festive atmosphere in which "concorse mezza Roma a così nobile spettacolo" (Bandello, *Tutte le opere* 2:745). See chapter 5 of this volume. On public tortures more generally, see the fundamental work of Michel Foucault, *Discipline and Punish: The Birth of the Prison,* trans. Alan Sheridan (New York: Vintage, 1979).

69 Trexler, "Correre," 887, citing A. Zanelli, "La festa dell' Assunta in Brescia nel medio evo," *Archivio Storico italiano,* ser. 5, vol. 9 (1892): 17. Renaissance exemplarity for women nearly always involved public punishment for transgressions in the sexual sphere or, in the case of positive exemplars, heroic self-destruction as a preferable alternative to loss of chastity. Among the many literary examples is Ariosto's Isabella, who tricks her would-be seducer Rodomonte into slaughtering her; see *Orlando furioso,* canto XXIX. See Castiglione, *Il Cortegiano,* book 3, for many further examples. On exemplarity for male humanists, see Timothy Hampton, *Writing from History: The Rhetoric of Exemplarity in Renaissance Literature* (Ithaca: Cornell University Press, 1990). On the centrality of violence against women in humanist myths of foundation, see Stephanie H. Jed, *Chaste Thinking: The Rape of Lucretia and the Birth of Humanism* (Bloomington: Indiana University Press, 1989). The 1425 case of Ugo and Paresina in Ferrara provides another instance of this public discourse on women's chastity. After Paresina's betrayal of her husband, Niccolò d'Este, with her stepson

Ugolino, Niccolò not only had his wife and son beheaded (privately) but also ordered the public execution of a number of other noblewomen in the city who were known to be "serving" their husbands as Paresina had served him. To what extent Niccolò's order was carried out is unknown. See A. Solerti, *Ugo e Paresina: Storia e leggende secondo nuovi documenti* (Rome, 1893), *Nuova antologia,* ser. 3, vols. 45–46; and Edmund G. Gardner, *Dukes and Poets of Ferrara* (London: Archibald Constable, 1904), 36–39.

70 King, *Women of the Renaissance,* 23.

71 Again, to take the simplest and most accessible example, see Castiglione, *Il Cortegiano,* book 3 (e.g., ch. 37: "[alle donne] sia lecito mancare in tutte l'altre cose, acciò che possano mettere ogni lor forza per mantenerse in questa sola virtù della castità, senza la quale i figlioli sariano incerti").

72 See Jacqueline Rose, "The Imaginary," in *The Talking Cure: Essays in Psychoanalysis and Language,* ed. Colin MacCabe (New York: St. Martin's Press, 1981), 132–61; as well as Lacan, "The Mirror Stage," in his *Écrits. A Selection,* trans. Alan Sheridan (New York: Norton, 1977). For further description of Lacan's "mirror stage" with reference to a Renaissance text, see chapter 2 of this volume.

73 See Lacan, "What Is a Picture?" in *The Four Fundamental Concepts;* and Mitchell and Rose, *Feminine Sexuality,* introduction II.

74 Turner, *Ritual Process,* vii–viii.

75 See Bargellesi, *Palazzo Schifanoia;* and Warburg, "Arte italiana."

76 It was Aby Warburg who broke with the long tradition of seeking allegorical significance in these enigmatic middle bands of the cycle and in 1912 attributed their meanings to systems explicated by the Arab astrologer Abu Ma'shar (d. 886), themselves based on ancient Indian and Egyptian sources and passed faithfully into medieval European thought. Pellegrino Prisciani, Ferrara's premier humanist in Borso's day, who may have conceived this design for the Sala and who oversaw the painters' progress, was professor of astrology in the Studio di Ferrara. I thank James Sutton for sharing with me his unpublished work on Prisciani. See also Werner L. Gundersheimer, *Ferrara: The Style of a Renaissance Despotism* (Princeton: Princeton University Press, 1973), 234–35.

77 On this sort of extension, which Berger would call *reascriptive reversal,* see his "Body to Cosmos."

78 On perspective, Zorzi, "Il sipario," 11, notes, "La libertà della concezione spaziale consente all'esecutore un rovesciamento prospettico, secondo il quale le dimensioni dei cavalieri in corsa risultano inferiori a quelle dei cavalieri fermi in secondo piano. Le figure del duca a dei cortigiani sovrastano, con intento espressionistico, la fila sgranata dei concorrenti; al di qua di questa il popolo è assente, o meglio, si situa all'esterno del quadro, coincidendo con gli occhi di chi osserva il dipinto."

79 Bakhtin, *Rabelais;* see also Peter Stallybrass, "Patriarchal Territories: The Body

Enclosed," in *Rewriting the Renaissance: The Discourses of Sexual Difference in Early Modern Europe,* ed. Margaret W. Ferguson et al. (Chicago: University of Chicago Press, 1986).

2   That Elusive Object of Desire

1   According to Emilio Bigi, in the geography of Ariosto's time, India was the generic designation for southern Asia, and Media referred to the region south of the Caspian Sea; Tartaria indicated the lands west and north of Cathay, which, for both Ariosto and Boiardo, was identified as a province of India. See Bigi's note to octave 5 of canto I in his edition of the poem.

2   Conventionally speaking, Angelica's fairness is a function of the Petrarchist canon of feminine beauty, a canon so powerful as to subordinate any realist considerations whatsoever of her racial difference. The matter of race in Renaissance heroic poetry and in early modern culture remains largely to be explored. For recent studies, see St. Clair Drake, *Black Folk Here and There* (Los Angeles: UCLA Center for Afro-American Studies, 1990); as well as *Women, "Race" and Writing in the Early Modern Period,* ed. Margo Hendricks and Patricia Parker (New York: Routledge, 1994). On the Petrarchist canon in relation to Ariosto and Tasso, see Fredi Chiappelli, "Ariosto, Tasso, e la bellezza delle donne," *Filologia e critica* 10 (1985): 325–41; and, more recently, Naomi Yavneh, "The Ambiguity of Beauty in Tasso and Petrarch," in *Sexuality and Gender in Early Modern Europe,* ed. James Grantham Turner (Cambridge: Cambridge University Press, 1993). I am indebted also to an unpublished paper on this topic by Judith López, "Why Is Clorinda White?"

3   On errancy in the *Furioso,* see D. S. Carne-Ross, "The One and the Many: A Reading of *Orlando furioso,* Cantos 1 and 8," *Arion* 5.2 (1966): 195–234; and his sequel essay, "The One and the Many: A Reading of the *Orlando furioso,*" *Arion,* n.s., 3.2 (1976): 146–219; Eugenio Donato, " 'Per selve e boscherecci labirinti': Desire and Narrative Structure in Ariosto's *Orlando furioso,*" *Barroco* 4 (1972): 17–34; repr. in *Literary Theory/Renaissance Texts,* ed. Patricia Parker and David Quint (Baltimore: Johns Hopkins University Press, 1986), 33–62. Most influential for my own reading has been Patricia Parker, *Inescapable Romance: Studies in the Poetics of Mode* (Princeton: Princeton University Press, 1979), 3–53. See also Sergio Zatti, *Il "Furioso" fra epos e romanzo* (Lucca: Paccini Fazzi, 1990).

4   Cited in Nardina Fantuzzi Guarrasi, *La donna nella vita e nelle opere dell' Ariosto. Bollettino storico reggiano* 7.26 (1974). These readings perhaps take oblique suggestion from Rajna's observation that Angelica is "the soul" of Boiardo's (but not Ariosto's) poem: "Costei presso il Boiardo è l'anima del poema; tutte le altre sono *donne,* essa sola è *la donna,*" from *Le fonti dell' "Orlando furioso"* (1900; reprint, Florence: Sansoni, 1975), 43. Even Ariosto's near contemporary Rus-

celli, however, saw Angelica as a symbol of womanhood at its best. See his commentary to canto I in his edition of the poem (Venice: Valgrisi, 1556). For Ruscelli's other observations on "le vere donne," see his introductions and annotations to cantos IX, XXI, XXVII, XXVIII, XXIX, XXXVII, and XLIII.

5   Important exceptions to my claim regarding the lack of attention to Angelica include Mario Santoro, "L'Angelica del *Furioso:* fuga dalla storia," in his *L'anello di Angelica* (Naples: Federico & Ardia, 1983), 57–82; repr. in Santoro, *Ariosto e il Rinascimento* (Naples: Liguori, 1989), 111–33; Peter De Sa Wiggins, *Figures in Ariosto's Tapestry: Character and Design in "Orlando furioso"* (Baltimore: Johns Hopkins University Press, 1986); and Valeria Finucci, *The Lady Vanishes: Subjectivity and Representation in Castiglione and Ariosto* (Stanford: Stanford University Press, 1992).

6   Exemplary are the remarks of Castiglione's characters in *The Book of the Courtier;* see Baldessarre Castiglione, *Il libro del Cortegiano,* ed. Bruno Maier (Turin: UTET, 1981), books 1 and 3. See also on women's education: *Prediche di Fra Giordano da Rivalto* (Florence, 1831); Paolo da Certaldo, *Libro di buoni costumi,* ed. A. Schiaffini (Florence: Le Monnier, 1945), 159; Francesco da Barberino, *Reggimento e costumi di donna,* ed. G. E. Sansone (Rome: Zauli, 1995); Leonardo Bruni, "De studis et literis," in *The Humanism of Leonardo Bruni: Selected Texts,* trans. and ed. Gordon Griffiths, James Hankins, and David Thompson (Binghamton: Medieval and Renaissance Texts and Studies, 1987), 235–50; Leon Battista Alberti, *I libri della famiglia,* ed. Ruggiero Romano and Alberto Tenenti (Turin: Einaudi, 1980), 266–67; Maria Ludovico Lenzi, ed., *Donne e madonne. L'educazione femminile nel primo Rinascimento italiano* (Turin: Loescher, 1982); Margaret L. King and Albert Rabil, eds., *Her Immaculate Hand: Selected Works by and about the Women Humanists of Quattrocento Italy* (Binghamton: Medieval and Renaissance Texts and Studies, 1983); W. H. Woodward, ed., *Vittorino da Feltre and Other Humanist Educators* (Cambridge: Cambridge University Press, 1921); Ludovico Dolce, *Dialogo . . . della institutione delle donne* (Venice: Giolito, 1545); Giovanni Michele Bruto, *La institutione di una fanciulla nata nobilmente* (Anvers: Jean Bellere & C. Plaintain, 1555); Juan Luis Vives, "The Education of a Christian Woman," trans. Richard Hyrde, in *Vives and the Renascence Education of Women,* ed. Foster Watson (New York: Longmans, Green; London: Edward Arnold, 1912). Among secondary sources, see Ruth Kelso, *Doctrine for the Lady of the Renaissance* (Urbana: University of Illinois Press, 1956); Phyllis Stock, *Better Than Rubies: A History of Women's Education* (New York: Putnam, 1978); Anthony Grafton and Lisa Jardine, *From Humanism to the Humanities: Education and the Liberal Arts in Fifteenth- and Sixteenth-Century Europe* (London: Duckworth, 1986), 29–57; Pamela Joseph Benson, *The Invention of the Renaissance Woman: The Challenge of Female Independence in the Literature and Thought of Italy and England* (University Park: Pennsylvania State University Press, 1992); Margaret L. King, *Women of the Renaissance* (Chicago: University of Chicago Press, 1991).

7 For representative examples, see Agostino Strozzi, *Defensione delle donne* (Biblioteca Nazionale di Firenze, Cod. Palat. 726 MS); Bartolommeo Goggio, *De laudibus mulierum* (MS, British Library), on which see Werner Gundersheimer, "Bartolommeo Goggio: A Feminist in Renaissance Ferrara," *Renaissance Quarterly* 33.2 (1980): 175–200; Giuseppe Zonta, ed., *Trattati del Cinquecento sulla donna* (Bari: Laterza, 1913); Galeazzo Flavio Capella, *Della eccellenza et dignità delle donne* (1525) (Venice: Gregorio de Gregori, 1526), on which see also Pamela Joseph Benson, "An Unrecognized Defender of Women in the *Orlando Furioso*," *Italica* 57.4 (1980): 268–70; and Cornelius Henricus Agrippa, *The Nobility and Preeminence of the Female Sex,* trans. and ed. Albert Rabil Jr. (Chicago: University of Chicago Press, 1996). See also Conor Fahy, "Three Early Renaissance Treatises on Women," *Italian Studies* 11 (1956): 30–55; Joan Kelly, "Early Feminist Theory and the *Querelle des Femmes,*" in her *Women, History, and Theory* (Chicago: University of Chicago Press, 1984); Constance Jordan, *Renaissance Feminism: Literary Texts and Political Models* (Ithaca: Cornell University Press, 1990); and her more recent "Renaissance Women and the Question of Class," in Turner, ed., *Sexuality and Gender;* Benson, *Invention.* On women's own intervention in these controversies, see chapter 4 of this volume.

8 Deanna Shemek, "Of Women, Knights, Arms, and Love: The *Orlando Furioso* and Ariosto's *Querelle des femmes,*" *MLN* 104.1 (1989): 68–97.

9 See Ian Maclean, *The Renaissance Notion of Woman: A Study in the Fortunes of Scholasticism and Medical Science* (Cambridge: Cambridge University Press, 1980); and G. E. R. Lloyd, *Polarity and Analogy: Two Types of Argumentation in Early Greek Thought* (1966; reprint, Cambridge: Cambridge University Press, 1977).

10 My claims about Angelica's flatness as a character should not be taken to mean, however, that she does not embody an influential literary (and social) model of femininity. Angelica's apparent shallowness as well as her desirability and deceit are alive and well as feminine models, most evidently in the cinema, television, and advertizing. In the title essay of *Il "soggetto" del 'Furioso,'* Eduardo Saccone suggests a reading to which my own is indebted: "Angelica che fugge, perduta, (s)fuggente, e non mai veramente trovata (e semmai trovante), si accampa nel quadro—in primo piano—come l'oggetto stesso del desiderio: 'sempre mancante, sempre *perduto*' di una 'alterità insuperabile'" (*Il "soggetto" del 'Furioso' e altri saggi tra Quattro e Cinquecento* [Naples: Liguori, 1974], 226–27, emphasis in original). For related reflections on Angelica as noncharacter, see Carne-Ross, "The One and the Many" (1966), 197.

11 Attilio Momigliano, *Saggio su "L'Orlando furioso"* (1928; reprint, Bari: Laterza, 1946), 58.

12 See Castiglione, *Il libro del Cortegiano,* 3:52.

13 See Carne-Ross, "The One and the Many" (1966), on "Angelica: the image of flight." Cf. Mario Santoro, *L'anello di Angelica,* which reads Angelica's repeated flights from pursuant knights as a protest and as "il modo di sottrarsi . . . alla

egemonia maschile, ma che, nello stesso tempo, rappresenta anche metaforicamente il ripudio di una realtà segnata dalla violenza e dalla pazzia" (117).

14   This assumption is, of course, regularly upset as early as the romances of Chrétien de Troyes. See Karin Boklund, "On the Spatial and Cultural Characteristics of Courtly Romance," in *Semiotics and Dialectics: Ideology and the Text,* ed. Peter V. Zima (Amsterdam: John Benjamins B.V., 1981), 387–444. Eric Rohmer's film *Perceval* highlights the semiotic heaviness of chivalric culture by directing the camera constantly toward the emblems of knighthood: feet in stirrups, heavy visors, shields, coats of arms.

15   Donato, "Per selve e boscherecci labirinti," draws the theory of mimetic desire from René Girard, *Deceit, Desire, and the Novel: Self and Other in Literary Structure,* trans. Yvonne Freccero (Baltimore: Johns Hopkins University Press, 1965).

16   Donato's framing of desire in the *Orlando furioso* is not unusual, however, for its exclusive attention to Ariosto's male characters; notions of "feminine" desire long existed only as mechanical complements to theories of masculine desire. Recognizing the radically different connotations society assigns to the male and female bodies, more recent gender theorists have explored the contrasting positions of desire into which convention has historically cast the two sexes. Drawing on work in such diverse fields as anthropology, linguistics, philosophy, semiotics, political theory, and psychoanalysis, one aim of such theories is to interrogate representations of desire, both masculine and feminine, in order to understand just how the traditional psychic models of gender take cultural form. Literary texts, because they so often thematize and enact mechanisms of desire, and because they are in some sense articulations of social values, offer particularly suggestive perspectives on these questions. See Teresa de Lauretis, "Desire in Narrative" and "Semiotics and Experience," both in *Alice Doesn't: Feminism, Semiotics, Cinema* (Bloomington: Indiana University Press, 1984), 103–57, 158–86. Substantial contributions in this area have also come recently from studies of lesbian desire and what Judith Butler calls "the materiality of the body"; see her *Gender Trouble* (New York: Routledge, 1990) and *Bodies That Matter: On the Discursive Limits of "Sex"* (New York: Routledge, 1993). See also de Lauretis, *The Practice of Love* (Bloomington: Indiana University Press, 1994).

17   See Jacques Lacan, *The Four Fundamental Concepts of Psychoanalysis,* ed. Jacques-Alain Miller, trans. Alan Sheridan (New York: Norton, 1981). See in particular "The Subject and the Other: Alienation" (203–15) and "Of the Gaze as Objet Petit a" (67–122). Also see Lacan, "The Mirror Stage as Formative of the Function of the I" and "The Signification of the Phallus," both in Lacan, *Écrits* (New York: Norton, 1977); and Juliet Mitchell and Jacqueline Rose, eds., *Feminine Sexuality: Jacques Lacan and the École Freudienne* (New York: Pantheon, 1982); Larysa Mykyta, "Lacan, Literature, and the Look: Woman in the Eye of Psychoanalysis," *Substance* 39.12.2 (1983): 49–57; Ellie Ragland-Sullivan,

"Jacques Lacan: Feminism and the Problem of Gender Identity," *Substance* 36.11.3 (1982): 6–20. See also my discussion in chapter 1 of this volume.

18 Lacan pointed to medieval courtly love (such as that depicted with ironic nostalgia in the *Furioso*) for early examples of the modern mystification of Woman. See Mitchell and Rose, *Feminine Sexuality,* 48, 145, 156.

19 Only in myth is this contradiction reconcilable. Marina Warner illustrates the humanly impossible "whole" being of the Madonna, who is both mother and virgin, in *Alone of All Her Sex: The Myth and the Cult of the Virgin Mary* (New York: Knopf, 1976).

20 See Lacan, "Of the Gaze," 67–104. See also Mykyta, "Lacan, Literature, and the Look": "It is as a result of the illusion of perfect reciprocity between what is looked at and the subject looking, the illusion that since no thing stands between them, then nothing stands between them, that the seeing subject can imagine that it is contemplating itself as an undisturbed consciousness. Since seeing as an illusion of unmediated wholeness is possible only by avoiding . . . the source and possibility of vision . . . the gap that makes it possible, then seeing as part of the scopic drive can be . . . that which . . . eludes the evidence of a certain original disunity or lack" (53).

21 See Mykyta, "Lacan, Literature, and the Look": "It is by seeing the woman as an object that does not speak or look that the man can believe he is approaching her when what he approaches is only the cause of his desire (for her). . . . The sexual triumph of the male passes through the eye, through the contemplation of the woman. Seeing the woman ensures the satisfaction of wanting to be seen, of having one's desire recognized. . . . Woman is repressed as subject and desired as object in order to efface the gaze of the Other, the gaze that would destroy the illusion of reciprocity and one-ness that the process of seeing usually supports" (54).

22 In chapter 5 of book 3, for example, il Magnifico specifies that a woman's most important contribution to courtly life is her ability to entertain men in conversation, always reflecting in her discourse the tastes and culture of her interlocutor: "parmi convenirsi sopra ogni altra cosa una certa affabilità piacevole, per la quale sappia intertenere ogni sorte d'omo con ragionamenti grati ed onesti, ed accommodati al tempo e loco ed alla qualità di quella persona con cui parlerà." In chapter 9 he explains that women should strive for knowledge in many fields, even though activity in most of these is forbidden to them by propriety, "e questo per saper laudare ed apprezzar i cavalieri più e meno, secondo i meriti." Finally in book 3, chapter 52, Cesare Gonzaga offers what appears to him to be the ultimate tribute to women. All of the greatest achievements of culture, he points out, have resulted from a male's desire to please a female spectator: "Non vedete voi che di tutti gli esercizi graziosi e che piaceno al mondo a niun altro s'ha da attribuire la causa, se alle donne no?

Chi studia di danzare e ballar leggiadramente per altro, che per compiacere a donne? Chi intende nella dolcezza della musica per altra causa, che per questa? Chi a compor versi, almen nella lingua vulgare, se non per esprimere quegli affetti che dalle donne sono causate? Pensate di quanti nobilissimi poemi saremmo privi, e nella lingua e nella latina, se le donne fossero state da' poeti poco estimate." Left unanswered—and unasked—in the *Libro del Cortegiano* is why any woman might think to practice these arts herself, save to create the proper atmosphere for men's inspiration and self-display.

23 In the case of the *palio* described in chapter 1, this recognition of alterity and possession, of separation and integration, allows the male spectators to distance themselves from both models of femininity the festival illustrates (the chaste and the unchaste) and yet to posit male control over the sexual economy of the community. See Samuel Weber, *The Legend of Freud* (Minneapolis: University of Minnesota Press, 1982): "If the unconscious means anything whatsoever, it is that the relation of self and others, inner and outer, cannot be grasped in an interval between polar opposites but rather as an irreducible dislocation of the subject in which the other inhabits the self as its condition of possibility" (32).

24 Fredi Chiappelli discusses Ariosto's increased attention to Angelica and Olimpia's inner mental states in the final edition of the *Furioso* in "Sul linguaggio dell'Ariosto," in *Ludovico Ariosto: Convegno Internazionale* (Rome: Accademia Nazionale dei Lincei, 1975), 33–48.

25 Wiggins, *Figures*, 171. Wiggins, in a sensitive reading of the visual motifs in this bower, sees Angelica here as dangerously immersed in self-contemplation and isolation. Although he notes that "being seen regularly imperils [Angelica's] integrity," Wiggins views this detail as relevant to the ultimate dangers of self-exile from society. On Angelica's narcissism, see Finucci, *The Lady Vanishes*, ch. 4: "The Narcissistic Woman: Angelica and the Mystique of Femininity," 107–44.

26 See Emilio Bigi's note in *Orlando furioso*, 115; as well as Momigliano, *Saggio*, 56. Sacripante, of course, exemplifies perfectly the subject of mediated desire to which Donato's reading refers. He also recalls Lacan's description of envy: "Everyone knows that envy is usually aroused by the possession of goods which would be of no use to the person who is envious of them, and about the nature of which he does not have the least idea. Such is true envy—the envy that makes the subject pale before the image of a completeness closed upon itself, before the idea that the *petit a*, the separated *a* [for *autre*—D.S.] from which he is hanging, may be for another the possession that gives satisfaction, *Befriedigung*" (*Four Fundamental Concepts*, 116).

27 The classic study of Ariosto's narrator is, of course, Robert Durling's fifth chapter in *The Figure of the Poet in Renaissance Epic* (Cambridge: Harvard University Press, 1965).

28 Eric Nicholson discusses the theatrical aspects of this scene in his essay, "Ro-

mance as Role Model: Early Female Performances of Ariosto and Tasso," forthcoming in *Renaissance Transactions: Ariosto and Tasso,* ed. Valeria Finucci (Durham: Duke University Press, 1999). See Lacan, *Four Fundamental Concepts,* 105–19, on the mediating function of masks in sexual encounter: "It is no doubt through the mediation of masks that the masculine and the feminine meet in the most acute, most intense way. Only the subject—the human subject, the subject of the desire that is the essence of man—is not, unlike the animal, entirely caught up in this imaginary capture. He maps himself in it. How? In so far as he isolates the function of the screen and plays with it. Man, in effect, knows how to play with the mask as that beyond which there is the gaze" (107).

29 On gender reversal in the *Furioso,* see John McLucas, "Ariosto and the Androgyne: Symmetries of Sex in the *Orlando Furioso*" (Ph.D. diss., Yale University, 1983); on men as mothers, see 172–81. For a psychoanalytic analysis of similar dynamics in Tasso's work, see Lynn Enterline, *The Tears of Narcissus: Melancholia and Masculinity in Early Modern Writing* (Stanford: Stanford University Press, 1995).

30 Saccone, *Il soggetto,* also makes the connection between Angelica and Lacan's notion of the *petit a.*

31 In the *Orlando innamorato,* readers will recall, Angelica had treated Baiardo well while under a spell that made her love Rinaldo. In those days, Rinaldo despised Angelica because they had drunk, respectively, from fountains of hate and love. Now their roles are perfectly reversed, for each has drunk from the contrary fount. On horses as signifiers of intellect and destiny, see A. Bartlett Giamatti, "Headlong Horses, Headless Horsemen: An Essay on the Chivalric Epics of Pulci, Boiardo, and Ariosto," in *Italian Literature: Roots and Branches. Essays in Honor of Thomas Goddard Bergin,* ed. Giose Rimanelli and Kenneth John Atichity (New Haven: Yale University Press, 1976), 265–307.

32 It is also true, as one helpful reader remarked to me, that the *Orlando furioso* appears to have no space for fulfilled desire as such, this being by definition the end of all that moves both romance and epic narratives forward. Yet, other female and male characters are partly defined by desire in the poem (Bradamante, Fiordiligi, Orlando himself), while Angelica has, up to the point of her exit, desired no one. Within a framework that posits this character as an emblem of femininity, it appears important that her falling in love at all (as well as the fulfillment of that love) enrages the narrator.

33 *Orlando furioso,* 139. I borrow freely here from Barbara Reynolds's felicitous translation (New York: Penguin, 1977), 141.

34 Just as interesting is the comparison of the critical treatment of Angelica's lament with those of the laments of Orlando, Isabella, and Bradamante, all of which are usually taken without irony (Bradamante's constituting an occasional exception). Giuseppe Toffanin, in an exemplary refusal to consider the protests of the plaything Angelica, refers with hostile condescension to Angelica's com-

plaint as "questa voce di signorina viziata" [this voice of a spoiled little girl]; see Toffanin, *Il Cinquecento* [*Storia letteraria d'Italia*] (Milan: Vallardi, 1965), 191.

35 Angelica speaks again briefly in canto X, octave 111, under very similar circumstances.

36 See, for parallel instances, Chariton, *Chaereas and Challirhoe,* 37, 76; Xenophon of Ephesus, *An Ephesian Tale,* 162; and other examples in *Collected Ancient Greek Novels,* ed. B. P. Reardon (Berkeley: University of California Press, 1989).

37 See Mitchell and Rose, *Feminine Sexuality,* 149–71.

38 On the flower as *jouissance,* see Saccone, *Il soggetto,* 227–29. See also Jacqueline Rose's introduction to Mitchell and Rose, *Feminine Sexuality:* "As negative to the man, woman becomes a total object of fantasy (or an object of total fantasy), elevated into the place of the Other and made to stand for its truth. Since the place of the Other is also the place of God, this is the ultimate form of mystification" (50).

39 On Ruggiero's and the reader's emblematic frustration in this instance, see Daniel Javitch, "Cantus Interruptus in the *Orlando furioso,*" *MLN* 95 (1980): 66–80.

40 Lacan's extremely complex notion of the Real designates something like the unmediated experience human subjects would encounter, were they able to discard the structures of the Imaginary and the Symbolic—to see "objectively." Since the coalescence of the subject depends, in Lacan's formulation, on precisely those gridlike structures, the Real is significant only as the concept of some basic material of experience posited as "out there" in dialectical relation with Imaginary and Symbolic operations. See Ellie Ragland-Sullivan, *Jacques Lacan and the Philosophy of Psychoanalysis* (Urbana: University of Illinois Press, 1987), ch. 3: "A Lacanian Theory of Cognition," 130–96.

41 Saccone, *Il soggetto,* argues with lucid elegance for a reading of the poem in which reason and fidelity stand opposed to the violent and the irrational as foundations for a society no longer chivalric (and based on free alliances), but rather civil (and based on obligations): "Una volta pronunciata la promessa, nell'universo ariostesco la libertà è finita, s'entra nel regno della necessità: la rottura di quel supremo contratto comporta il decadere del nome stesso di uomo" (200). The pact, the promise, *la fede,* thus constitute the "soggetto" of the *Furioso.* See Saccone's "*Cloridano e Medoro,* con alcuni argomenti per una lettura del primo *Furioso*" (161–200), as well as the title essay (201–47).

42 See Lacan, *Four Fundamental Concepts,* 67–78.

43 On Angelica's act of writing as an active transformation of the written tradition that produced her, and on her carved love knots as a "grapheme for copulation," see Millicent Marcus, "Angelica's Loveknots: The Poetics of Requited Desire in *Orlando furioso* 19 and 23," *Philological Quarterly* 72 (1993): 33–51. Marcus is right in noting that Angelica revolutionizes this tradition "to

dominate the writing and to have it speak of present, consummated, female-initiated love" (36). I would add that Ariosto still does not transmit her words and gives us instead Medoro's poetic description of the couple's joys.

44 For a perceptive reading of this misrecognition in a poststructuralist key, see Albert Ascoli, *Ariosto's Bitter Harmony: Crisis and Evasion in the Italian Renaissance* (Princeton: Princeton University Press, 1987), 323–24.

45 See Sigmund Freud, "Mourning and Melancholia" (1917) [1915], in *The Standard Edition of the Complete Psychological Works,* ed. James Strachey (London: Hogarth Press and the Institute of Psychoanalysis, 1953–74), 14:237–58. The classic poetic example of successful mourning is Pan, who accepts the reeds he embraces as a substitute for his lost love, Syrinx, and becomes a lyric poet. See Peter Sacks, *The English Elegy: Studies in the Genre from Spenser to Yeats* (Baltimore: Johns Hopkins University Press, 1985). For two contrasting views of mourning and melancholia in early modern literature, see Juliana Schiesari, *The Gendering of Melancholia: Feminism, Psychoanalysis, and the Symbolics of Loss in Renaissance Literature* (Ithaca: Cornell University Press, 1992); and Enterline, *Tears of Narcissus.* Orlando's response is somewhat sketchier than the instances described by these two authors, as his character is less developed. Schiesari focuses on the undervaluation of feminine mourning in a culture that celebrates male melancholia as a creative force; while Enterline argues for a more ambiguous notion of gendered subjectivity than Schiesari's reading suggests. Closer to my treatment here is Enterline: "The representation of suffering in these texts points, variously, to a loss of sense of personal agency in language, a loss of 'voice,' a loss of reference, a loss of the capacity to distinguish between literal and figurative senses, and, overall, a loss of a sense of authority over one's own discourse" (6).

46 On stripping naked as a sign of madness in the medieval tradition of lunacy, see Paolo Valesio, "The Language of Madness in the Renaissance," *Yearbook of Italian Studies* 1 (1971): 199–234.

47 See Carne-Ross, "The One and the Many" (1966 and 1976).

3   Gender, Duality, and the Sacrifices of History

1 For a rapid survey of the many significances attributed to Ariosto's motto, see Emilio Bigi's note accompanying the line in his edition of the *Furioso* (Milan: Rusconi, 1982), 1948–49. Saccone argues eloquently that the motto refers to the painful compromise exacted of all the major characters in the poem; see Eduardo Saccone, "Prospettive sull'ultimo Ariosto," *MLN* 98 (1983): 55–69; as well as his *Il soggetto del "Furioso" e altri saggi fra quattro e cinquecento* (Naples: Liguori, 1974), 161–247.

2 David Quint has shown how the *Furioso* divides into two equal parts and moves deliberately out of Boiardo's romance form into that of epic in order to inject

the telos of time and history into the poem's conception of human experience; see Quint, "The Figure of Atlante: Ariosto and Boiardo's Poem," *MLN* 94 (1979): 77–91. Quint's more recent *Epic and Empire* (Princeton: Princeton University Press, 1993) offers a major theorization of these two genres, with particular attention to "the politicization of epic poetry." Quint argues that throughout the history of the two forms in the West, "to the victors belongs epic, with its linear teleology; to the losers belongs romance, with its random or circular wandering. Put another way, the victors experience history as a coherent, end-directed story told by their own power; the losers experience a contingency that they are powerless to shape to their own ends" (9). See also Riccardo Bruscagli, " 'Ventura' e 'Inchiesta' fra Boiardo e Ariosto," in his *Stagioni della civiltà estense* (Pisa: Nistri-Lischi, 1983), 87–126; Saccone, *Il soggetto,* 101; Patricia Parker, *Inescapable Romance: Studies in the Poetics of a Mode* (Princeton: Princeton University Press, 1979); and Peter V. Marinelli, *Ariosto and Boiardo: The Origins of the "Orlando Furioso"* (Columbia: University of Missouri Press, 1987): "The truth is that the *Innamorato* resists, as a matter of principle and in a manner extraordinary in Renaissance fiction, the closing off of any action" (76). Sergio Zatti, in *Il "Furioso" fra epos e romanzo* (Lucca: Maria Pacini Fazzi, 1990), characterizes the relation between epic and romance in the *Furioso* as one of reciprocal implication.

3   Alberti's patriarch character, Giannozzo, recounts how he taught his young wife to defer to him in all things. Employing the ancient analogy of household to state, he taught her also to protect the domestic sphere like a city against invaders: "Sa' tu quel che noi faremo? Come chi fa la guardia la notte, in sulle mura per la patria sua"; from *I libri della famiglia,* ed. Ruggiero Romano and Alberto Tenenti (Turin: Einaudi, 1980), 270.

4   Giacomo Lanteri, *Della economica* (Venice: Valgrisi, 1560), 109. Cited in Daniela Frigo, "Dal caos all'ordine: Sulla questione del 'prender moglie' nella trattatistica del sedicesimo secolo," in *Nel cerchio della luna: Figure di donna in alcuni testi del XVI secolo,* ed. Marina Zancan (Venice: Marsilio, 1983), 57–93; see 86–87. See also Guido Ruggiero, "Marriage, Love, Sex, and Renaissance Civic Morality," in *Sexuality and Gender in Early Modern Europe,* ed. James Grantham Turner (Cambridge: Cambridge University Press, 1993), 10–30; and in the same volume, Constance Jordan, "Renaissance Women and the Question of Class" (90–106); and Margaret F. Rosenthal, "Venetian Women Writers and Their Discontents" (107–32).

5   On textual repression in the service of narrative resolution, see Fredric Jameson, *The Political Unconscious: Narrative as a Socially Symbolic Act* (Ithaca: Cornell University Press, 1981), 49.

6   Among the many narrative segments whose resolutions readers have found unsettling over the centuries, we include Olimpia's vindication and marriage (XI), Angelica's marriage to Medoro (XIX), the death of Isabella (XXIX),

and Marfisa's laws imposed on Marganorre's former state (XXXVII). Saccone ("Prospettive sull'ultimo Ariosto") writes of Ariosto's lack of idealism:

> Già nel primo *Furioso* si doveva a questa lucida visione (il "lucido inter-vallo" di xxiv, 3) la rappresentazione di un Orlando che riacquistava il senno, ma perdeva Angelica; di un Rinaldo che conservava, restandone contento, la moglie, ma rinunciando alla verità sul di lei conto; di una Isabella che serbava la fede al suo Zerbino, ma al prezzo della vita; di un Ruggiero che portava a compimento la sua educazione, superando con successo tutti i bivi posti sul percorso della sua maturazione umana a cristiana: poteva così sposare Bradamante e dare origine alla famosa casa d'Este, ma al prezzo, cui vanamente aveva cercato di sottrarlo il paterno Atlante, di una morte precoce dopo sette anni. (68)

My aim here is to consider the parallel compromise demanded of Bradamante.

7   Susanne Lindgren Wofford, *The Choice of Achilles: The Ideology of Figure in the Epic* (Stanford: Stanford University Press, 1992), 12. I am indebted to Wofford's study of the martial epics of Homer, Virgil, Spenser, Milton, and Cervantes for my understanding of epic ideology and poetic closure. Viewing textual closure and narrative resolution as moments of "reduction necessary for the fulfillment of literary pattern" (12), moments that should not necessarily be privileged in the task of interpretation, Wofford offers a reading that stresses the rhetori-cal interplay between epic's professed ideology and the various fictional and poetic registers that undercut or question that ideology. In Wofford's perspec-tive, poetic devices—ranging from traditional tropes and figures (epic simile, apostrophe, metalepsis, prosopopoeia, etc.) to generic conventions and meta-narrative gestures—engage in "critical interplay" with epic's narrative action (9). A residue of this interplay remains in the conflicting values readers assign to the "message" of a work's closure:

> The open-endedness of the form—in the face of an asserted ideological closure—helps explain why so much epic poetry has provoked contro-versy about the extent of its programmatic or even propagandistic effect. It can be shown, for instance, to generate the terms of the debates about the *Aeneid,* in which one side argues for the centrality of the poem's celebration of Augustus and Augustan values (the extreme position labelling the poem propaganda), while the other argues that the poem criticizes the Augustan military ethos and laments the costs of conquest (the extreme view transforming the poem into an anti-Augustan work). I argue that the poem celebrates and criticizes at once, but in different ways and in different fictional and poetic registers. (12)

Similar controversy appears in critical readings of the *Orlando furioso,* most re-cently regarding its politics of gender. On closure, see also Jameson, *The Political*

Unconscious; and Frank Kermode, *The Sense of an Ending: Studies in the Theory of Fiction* (Oxford: Oxford University Press, 1966).

8   I thank Albert R. Ascoli for sharing with me his essay "Ariosto's 'Fier Pastor': Structure and Historical Meaning in *Orlando Furioso,*" forthcoming in *Ariosto: Contemporary Perspectives,* ed. Massimo Ciavollella and Roberto Fedi (Toronto: University of Toronto Press), and for permission to quote the following passage:

> In [the] ceaseless play between one piece of writing and another, the text/context distinction, along with the literature/history opposition, lose much of their clarity. Within the *Furioso* pieces of poem take turns as text and context for one another, while the numerous "contexts" evoked by Ariosto's text, literary and historical alike, both determine its meaning and are recontextualized and reinterpreted by it. . . . I have suggested instead splitting the difference (verbally as well as conceptually) between "text" and "context" to designate the incessant dynamic of reciprocal appropriation and ironization within the *Furioso* and between the *Furioso* and its external interlocutors and circumstances as "cotextuality" [Ascoli 1987:45].

9   Wofford, *Choice of Achilles,* 6. Also suggestive are Quint's remarks on the "bad conscience" of Tasso's *Gerusalemme liberata* in its more severe closure of the narrative involving its female warrior, Clorinda; see his *Epic and Empire,* 246.

10 Pamela Benson's reading takes Bradamante as "the ideal lady of the [humanist] controversy about women"; see her *Invention of the Renaissance Woman: The Challenge of Female Independence in the Literature and Thought of Italy and England* (University Park: Pennsylvania State University Press, 1992), 148–55.

11 Daniel Javitch's *Proclaiming a Classic: The Canonization of "Orlando Furioso"* (Princeton: Princeton University Press, 1991) takes this literary quarrel and the Renaissance publishing history of the *Furioso* as its topic. The different redactions of the *Furioso* have been the subject of meticulous editorial study, for details of which I refer readers to the critical edition of Debenedetti and Segre (Bologna: Commissione per i testi di lingua, 1960). See also Alberto Casadei, *Il percorso del "Furioso": Ricerche intorno alle redazioni del 1516 e del 1521* (Bologna: Il Mulino, 1993); and Robert Davey Henderson, "The First *Orlando Furioso:* Compositional Seasons and Political Strategies" (Ph.D. diss., University of California, Berkeley, 1995).

12 On this trend, see Daniel Javitch, "La politica dei generi letterari nel tardo Cinquecento," *Studi italiani* 3.2 (1991): 5–22. Three general studies treat the critical reception of the *Orlando furioso:* Giuseppina Fumagalli, *La Fortuna dell' "Orlando furioso" in Italia nel secolo XVI* (Ferrara: Zuffi, 1910); Walter Binni, *Storia della critica ariostesca* (Lucca: Lucentia, 1951); and Rafaello Ramat, *La critica ariostesca dal secolo XVI ad oggi* (Florence: La Nuova Italia, 1954). In addition there exist

two major bibliographies of Ariosto criticism: Giuseppe Fatini, *Bibliografia della critica ariostea 1510–1956* (Florence: Le Monnier, 1958); and Robert Rodini and Salvatore Di Maria, *Ludovico Ariosto: An Annotated Bibliography of Criticism, 1956–1980* (Columbia: University of Missouri Press, 1984). See also Caterina Badini, "Rassegna ariostesca (1976–1985)," *Lettere italiane* 38 (1986): 104–24. Revisions to Rodini and Di Maria appear in Robert Rodini, "Selected Bibliography of Ariosto Criticism, 1980–87," *MLN* 103 (1988): 187–203; and a further update in *Annali d'Italianistica* 12 (1994): 299–317.

13   See Bernard Weinberg, *A History of Literary Criticism in the Italian Renaissance* (Chicago: University of Chicago Press, 1961), chs. 9, 10; Joel Spingarn, *Literary Criticism in the Renaissance* (1899; reprint, New York: Harbinger, 1963), ch. 4, 67–77; Robert L. Montgomery, *The Reader's Eye: Studies in Didactic Literary Theory from Dante to Tasso* (Berkeley: University of California Press, 1979), chs. 1, 4; Baxter Hathaway, *Marvels and Commonplaces: Renaissance Literary Criticism* (New York: Random House, 1968). See also the important revisions of Weinberg in Javitch, *Proclaiming a Classic* and "Politica dei generi"; as well as two recent essays by Dennis Looney: "Ariosto the Ferrarese Rhapsode: A Compromise in the Critical Terminology for Narrative in the Mid-Cinquecento," in *Interpreting the Italian Renaissance: Literary Perspectives,* ed. Antonio Toscano (Stony Brook: Forum Italicum, 1991), 139–50; and "The Misshapen Beast: The *Furioso*'s Serpentine Narrative," in *Counter Currents: The Primacy of the Text in Literary Criticism,* ed. Raymond Prier (Albany: SUNY Press, 1992), 73–97. Looney's essays reappear in expanded form in his *Compromising the Classics: Romance Epic Narrative in the Italian Renaissance* (Detroit: Wayne State University Press, 1996).

14   I place the term *national* in quotes because Italy clearly did not form a national state until the nineteenth century. Italians discussed their common *natione* and its weakness in relation to politically unified peoples, however, throughout the cultural debates of the Cinquecento.

15   Quint's *Epic and Empire* supplies a cogent reading of the political stakes in such linear narratives as these critics seek. On narrative frustration in the *Furioso,* see Daniel Javitch, "Cantus Interruptus in the *Orlando Furioso,*" *MLN* 95 (1980): 66–80; Parker, *Inescapable Romance,* 16–53; and D. S. Carne-Ross, "The One and the Many: A Reading of the *Orlando Furioso,* Cantos 1 and 8," *Arion* 5.2 (1966): 195–234, followed by its sequel, "The One and the Many: A Reading of the *Orlando Furioso,*" *Arion,* n.s., 3.2 (1976): 146–219.

16   Bakhtin, "Toward a Methodology for the Human Sciences," in *Speech Genres and Other Late Essays,* ed. Caryl Emerson and Michael Holquist, trans. Vern W. McGee (Austin: University of Texas Press, 1986), 159–72; and in the same volume, "The Problem of Speech Genres" (60–102). See also Gary Saul Morson and Caryl Emerson, *Mikhail Bakhtin: Creation of a Prosaics* (Stanford: Stanford University Press, 1990), 271–305; and Katerina Clark and Michael Holquist, *Mikhail Bakhtin* (Cambridge: Harvard University Press, 1984), 275–94.

17   Juan Luis Vives, "The Instruction of a Christian Woman" [1523], trans. in *Vives and the Renascence Education of Women,* ed. Foster Watson (New York: Longmans, Green, 1912). The Spanish humanist wrote this work for Catherine of Aragon, wife of Henry VIII and mother of Mary Tudor. Appearing first in Latin and translated into English in 1529, it was published in forty editions (including Spanish, English, French, Dutch, German, and Italian translations) and became the leading work of the century on women's education. On Vives, see also Benson, *Invention,* 157–82.

18   I have consulted the trilingual edition of this text (London: Adam Islip, 1598). Ruth Kelso cites as the first edition that of Jean Bellere and C. Plaintain published in Anvers in 1555; see her *Doctrine for the Lady of the Renaissance* (Urbana: University of Illinois Press, 1956).

19   Literary genres have been associated with social distinctions from their very earliest formulations. On Greek and Roman genre theory, see Daniel L. Selden, "Genre of Genre," in *The Search for the Ancient Novel,* ed. James Tatum (Baltimore: Johns Hopkins University Press, 1994), 39–64: "All ancient genres originated in important and recurrent real-life situations, and their institutionalization as patterns of regular response supplied some of the fundamental architecture for the social order. It comes as no surprise, then, that a formal theory of literary genres first emerges as a part of political philosophy" (39).

20   See Plato, *Laws* 700–701c.

21   See Weinberg, *History of Literary Criticism,* chs. 9, 10; and Hathaway, *Marvels and Commonplaces,* "The Rise of Literary Criticism," 3–42.

22   *Discorso di M. Giovambattista Giraldi Cinthio Nobile Ferrarese, Et Segretario dell' Eccellentiss. Duca di Ferrara, Intorno al Comporre de i Romanzi A M. Giovambattista Pigna con molte considerationi intorno ad altre sorti di Poesia* (Venice: Gabriel Giolito de Ferrari et Fratelli, 1554). Subsequent references to this treatise will appear in the body of the text. A partial translation of the *Discorso* appears in Allen H. Gilbert, *Literary Criticism, Plato to Dryden* (Detroit: Wayne State University Press, 1962), 262–73. This translation of the section on the non-Aristotelian epic bears page indications to the 1554 Venetian edition cited above. I have used my own translations. For reflections on the pluralism of medieval Europe that was sacrificed in these general programs of national standardization, see María Rosa Menocal, "Life Itself: Storytelling as the Tradition of Openness in the *Conde Lucanor,*" in *Oral Tradition and Hispanic Literature: Essays in Honor of Samuel G. Armistead,* ed. Mishael M. Caspi (New York: Garland, 1995), 469–95.

23   On the political resonance of this common insistence, see Giancarlo Mazzacurati, "Dai balli nel sole al bucato di Nausica: l'eclisse dei linguaggi 'naturali,'" in *Il Rinascimento dei moderni* (Bologna: Il Mulino, 1980), 297–324.

24   Giraldi (*Discorso,* 11) praises Boiardo and Ariosto for staging conflicts in their poems that allow Christians to take satisfaction in the victories of their fellows over pagan enemies.

25 *I Romanzi di Giovambattista Pigna al S. Donno Luigi da Este Vescovo di Ferrara. Divisi in tre libri. Ne quali della poesia e della vita dell'Ariosto con un nuovo modo si tratta* (Venice: [Erasmo] Vincenzo Valgrisi, 1554): "Romanzi secondo la commune opinione in Francese detti erano gli annali e perciò le guerre di parte in parte notate sotto questo nome uscivano. Poscia alcuni dalla verità partendosi, quantunque, favolegiassero, così appunto chiamarono li scritti loro" (11–12). Subsequent references to this edition will appear in the body of the text.

26 *The Basic Works of Aristotle,* ed. Richard McKeon (Chicago: University of Chicago Press, 1973), 689. Cf. Horace, *Ars Poetica* 119ff., on character consistency. My thanks to Daniel Javitch for our very useful discussions of these theories.

27 For a concise overview of this tradition, along with its humanist revisions, see Ian Maclean, *The Renaissance Notion of Woman: A Study in the Fortunes of Scholasticism and Medical Science* (Cambridge: Cambridge University Press, 1980). See also Thomas Laqueur, *Making Sex: Body and Gender from the Greeks to Freud* (Cambridge: Harvard University Press, 1990).

28 Pigna seems to mistake Maria for her daughter, Margaret.

29 As was discovered later, Ariosto had a direct source for his description of the moon's topography. See Cesare Segre, "Leon Battista Alberti e Ludovico Ariosto," in his *Esperienze ariostesche* (Pisa: Nistri-Lischi, 1966), 85–96.

30 Filippo Sassetti, *Il discorso contro l'Ariosto,* edito per la prima volta su l'originale Magliabechiano .CI.IX, cod.125, pp. 189–213. Nota di Giuseppe Castaldi (Rome: Tipografia della R. Accademia dei Lincei, 1914). Subsequent references to this edition will appear in the body of the text. Sassetti was elected a member of the Accademia Fiorentina on 17 January 1573, and in 1574 he entered the Accademia degli Alterati (see Castaldi's *Nota,* p. 477 [9]). The *Discorso*'s year of composition is unknown. On Sassetti, see Daniel Javitch, "Narrative Discontinuity in the *Orlando Furioso* and Its Sixteenth Century Critics," *MLN* 103.1 (1988): 50–74; as well as his earlier "Cantus Interruptus."

31 In vol. 5 of Tasso, *Opere,* ed. Bruno Maier (Milan: Rizzoli, 1965). Tasso mistakenly addressed his *Apologia della Gerusalemme liberata* to the Accademia Fiorentina, not realizing his detractors had been the members of the younger Accademia della Crusca. See Looney, "Misshapen Beast" and "Ferrarese Rhapsode." For a not entirely persuasive discussion of the psychological and political underpinnings of Tasso's defense of his poem, see Margaret W. Ferguson, *Trials of Desire: Renaissance Defenses of Poetry* (New Haven: Yale University Press, 1983), 54–136. Ferguson argues that Tasso's "Apologia" arises from his relations to the Neapolitan rebellions of 1547 and 1585.

32 See Torquato Tasso's *Discorso della virtù femminile* (Venice: Bernardo Giunti, 1582); *Discorso in lode del matrimonio e un dialogo d'amore* (Milan: Tini, 1586); and *Il padre di famiglia,* in *Delle rime, et prose* (Ferrara: Simon Vasalini, 1585).

33 On Tasso's treatment of femininity and female characters, see Lynn Enterline, *The Tears of Narcissus: Melancholia and Masculinity in Early Modern Writing* (Stan-

ford: Stanford University Press, 1995), 84–145; Juliana Schiesari, *The Gendering of Melancholia: Feminism, Psychoanalysis, and the Symbolics of Loss in Renaissance Literature* (Ithaca: Cornell University Press, 1992); Marilyn Migiel, "Secrets of the Sorceress: Tasso's Armida," *Quaderni d'Italianistica* 8.2 (1987): 149–66; and idem, "Tasso's Erminia: Telling an Alternate Story," *Italica* 64.1 (1987): 62–75. Walter Stephens writes aptly of the "uncomfortable 'feminism' of Tasso's poem" (189) and of the *Liberata*'s "attempts to turn Christian misogyny, of which Paul was essentially the founder, into a kind of feminism" (185) in his "Saint Paul among the Amazons: Gender and Authority in *Gerusalemme Liberata*," in *Discourses of Authority in Medieval and Renaissance Literature,* ed. Kevin Brownlee and Walter Stephens (Hanover: University Press of New England, 1989), 169–202.

34   Tommaso Campanella, *La Città del sole,* in *Opere di Bruno e di Campanella* (Milan: Ricciardi, 1956), 1114–15. For some explication of this passage, see the translation and notes by Daniel J. Donno in *"La Città del sole": Dialogo poetico / "The City of the Sun": A Poetical Dialogue* (Berkeley: University of California Press, 1981). I have departed from Donno's translation in order to retain more of the literal sense of Campanella's text. See also Lina Bolzoni, "Campanella e le donne: fascino e negazione della differenza," *Annali d'Italianistica* 7 (1989): 193–216. My thanks to Sherry Roush for sharing with me her knowledge of Campanella.

35   Bradamante later, in a gesture that accords with the advice of Ariosto's narrator, will request that the names of the Estensi *women* be added to this narrative of future history (XIII.55–73). On this canto's references to contemporary Estense history, see Henderson, *The First "Orlando Furioso."*

36   See Valeria Finucci's lively and provocative chapter, "Undressing the Warrior/ Re-dressing the Woman: The Education of Bradamante," in *The Lady Vanishes: Subjectivity and Representation in Castiglione and Ariosto* (Stanford: Stanford University Press, 1992), 227–54; Maggie Günsberg, *"Donna Liberata?* The Portrayal of Women in the Italian Renaissance Epic," in *Women and Italy: Essays on Gender, Culture and History,* ed. Z. G. Baranski and S. W. Vinal (London: Macmillan, 1991), 173–208; Judith Bryce, "Gender and Myth in the *Orlando Furioso,*" *Italian Studies* 47 (1992): 41–50; and Juliana Schiesari, "The Domestication of Woman in *Orlando Furioso* 42 and 43, or A Snake Is Being Beaten," *Stanford Italian Review* 10.1 (1991): 123–43; as well as the more idiosyncratic reading of Wiley Feinstein, "Bradamante in Love: Some Post-feminist Reflections on Ariosto," *Forum Italicum* 22.1 (1988): 48–59.

37   On Marfisa's rejection of femininity, see Peter De Sa Wiggins, *Figures in Ariosto's Tapestry: Character and Design in the "Orlando Furioso"* (Baltimore: Johns Hopkins University Press, 1986), 182–92. Benson, *Invention,* sees Marfisa as "part of the past" while Bradamante represents a possible future for women of Ariosto's day (124–31).

38   Both of these features, surplus and supplanting, correspond to the characteristics of the supplement as described by Jacques Derrida. See Derrida, *Of Gram-*

matology, trans. Gayatry Chakravorty Spivak (Baltimore: Johns Hopkins University Press, 1976); and idem, "The Law of Genre," *Glyph* 7 (Baltimore: Johns Hopkins University Press, 1980), 202–32. See also Barbara Johnson's introduction to her English translation of Derrida's *Dissemination* (Chicago: University of Chicago Press, 1981), vii–xxxiii.

39   Elizabeth J. Bellamy's discussion of armor in the *Orlando furioso* as symbolic of "both protection against bodily fragmentation and also a proleptic symbol of wholeness" is especially well formulated for Bradamante's case. See her *Translations of Power: Narcissism and the Unconscious in Epic History* (Ithaca: Cornell University Press, 1992), 94.

40   The 1516 edition in place of "e senza far parola" bore the phrase "E senza altra contesa." Ariosto thus accentuated the issue of speech in the second and third editions.

41   On the sources for the women's contest, see Pio Rajna, *Le fonti dell' "Orlando furioso"* (1876; reprint, Florence: Sansoni, 1975), 502–5.

42   I discuss this episode in "Of Women, Knights, Arms, and Love: The *Orlando Furioso* and Ariosto's *Querelle des Femmes,*" *MLN* 104.1 (1989): 68–97. On the function of hair in Renaissance poetry, see Naomi Yavneh, "The Ambiguity of Beauty in Tasso and Petrarch," in Turner, ed., *Sexuality and Gender,* 133–57.

43   Guido Waldman's inexact translation of lines 102.5–6 obscures Bradamante's remarkably rigorous foregrounding of categories *as such* in this speech; see *Orlando furioso* (Oxford: Oxford University Press, 1974): "But who will say, unless I take off all my clothes, / whether or not I am *of the same sex as she.*" Cf. the more accurate Barbara Reynolds translation (Middlesex: Penguin, 1977): "Unless I strip quite naked, who can say / *If what she is I can be shown to be?*" (emphasis mine).

44   On the ontological dimension of Renaissance conceptions of womanhood, see Jordan, "Question of Class."

45   Here I register a difference with numerous readers of this speech, among them John McLucas, "Amazon, Sorceress, and Queen: Women and War in the Aristocratic Literature of Sixteenth-Century Italy," *Italianist* 8 (1988): "First, she says she came as a *man* and thus should not be judged as a lady" (39, emphasis added). Bellamy, *Translations of Power,* revises the story in several details: "*Entering as a woman,* Bradamante is then told by her cruel host that only the fairest woman will be allowed to spend the night. Ullania is on the verge of being thrown out of the castle, when Bradamante 'reverts' to *her male identity,* stepping forward and *demanding to be considered a male knight* and thus Ullania's 'proper' escort. . . . Though she handily defeats three knights, it is only through the arbitrariness of her own speech act (*her own self-declaration that she is 'male'*) that her competition with Ullania as a female can be circumvented and 'resolved' " (118, n. 52, emphasis added). Finucci's observations in *The Lady Vanishes* are contradictory: "On the surface, Bradamante seems to suffer from

penis envy since she dresses like a man, behaves like a man, and *claims that she is a man* even when everybody is convinced otherwise, as in the Rocca di Tristano episode" (210, emphasis added); and "Bradamante argues that her gender is whatever she claims it is at any particular moment. . . . Bradamante, in short, grounds gender difference in biology, which makes it too difficult to verify" (247). My point is quite different: that Bradamante's speech systematically defers the assignment of gender and rigorously questions the content of that category. Since Bradamante at no point in the episode declares she is male, the critical tendency to read "cavallier" as masculine suggests we still unwittingly share some of the same biases that Bradamante's speech questions.

46 Charles Ross, in "Ariosto's Fable of Power: Bradamante at the Rocca di Tristano," *Italica* 68 (1991): 155–75, also emphasizes Bradamante's juridical language in this episode. Ross argues against several recent feminist readings of the Rocca di Tristano episode, asserting that it "is about more than the limitations of gender" and insisting instead that its subject is "the justice of custom itself, which has hardened into a social order" (157). My point is that gender functions at the Rocca and in the *Furioso* as a prime example of custom as Ross describes it.

47 On Ariosto's more comprehensive relation to Machiavelli, see Giuseppe Mazzotta, "Power and Play: Machiavelli and Ariosto," in *The Western Pennsylvania Symposium on World Literatures Selected Proceedings: 1974–1991,* ed. Carla E. Lucente (Greensburg, Pa.: Eadmer Press, 1992), 151–70; reprinted in *The Play of the Self,* ed. Ronald Bogue and Mihai I. Spariosu (Albany: SUNY Press, 1994), 183–202. Mazzotta contrasts Machiavelli's tragic *"real-politik"* with what he describes as an Ariostan Stoic politics, a visionary "ethics of play" (168) wherein "play and art embody the mentality that both radically opposes and contains (in every sense of the word) the principles and practices of power" (165). We might see Bradamante in this instance as willing to "play" her game in either field of state power, the diplomatic forum or the field of martial combat. Ross, "Ariosto's Fable of Power," sees Bradamante's intimation of potential violence as a parody of justice: "Her terms make her a winner only if she is a warrior" (165). This, however, is precisely the insight of Machiavelli's *Il Principe.*

48 This self-possession extends, in my view, to Bradamante's weeping over Ruggiero's presumed betrayal of her only after leaving the company and waking from dreams in the privacy of her room. Her relatively controlled behavior here directly contrasts with the public madness exhibited by Orlando and Rodomonte in the face of parallel circumstances. Elissa Weaver's "Lettura dell'intreccio del *Orlando furioso:* il caso delle tre pazzie d'amore," *Strumenti critici* 11.34, fasc. 3 (1977): 384–406, minimizes this difference but illustrates persuasively the strong parallels that encourage comparison of the three characters' melancholy. In contrast, Finucci, in *The Lady Vanishes,* sees Bradamante at this point as a hysteric: "Later that night, while still at the Rocca, Bradamante is demasculinized a second time with a narrative follow-up: she is portrayed as

desperately crying over Ruggiero. The scene confirms that she is just a hysteric, despite her earlier public bragging about her manly valor" (249).

49   The comic and parodic dimensions of this scene of botched suicide have not been lost on readers, among whom see Bellamy, *Translations of Power,* 95.

50   On moral interlace, see C. P. Brand, "L'entrelacement nell'*Orlando furioso*," *Giornale storico della letteratura italiana* 154 (1977): 509–32. On interlace more generally, see Eugène Vinaver, *The Rise of Romance* (New York: Oxford University Press, 1971), 68–98; see also Weaver, "Lettura dell'intreccio."

51   On Bradamante and Brandimarte as doubles, see Wiggins, *Figures,* 193–94, 199–200.

52   Bradamante's jousts between cantos XXXII and XXXVI are all aided by the magic lance. Many of the poem's principal characters benefit from such favors (e.g., Orlando's impenetrable skin, Ruggiero's use of the magic shield of Atlante, Astolfo's horn and lance, Rodomonte's dragon-skin armor). Giovanni Sinicropi notes that of all the enchanted aids in the *Furioso,* only this lance (which changes hands a number of times) falls into its users' possession by chance and operates, as a rule, without the possessor's awareness. Sinicropi sees Bradamante's lance as a primary element in the construction of parody in the contests where she employs it. See his "La struttura della parodia; ovvero: Bradamante in Arlì," *Strumenti critici* 45 (1981): 232–51. For Finucci, *The Lady Vanishes* (236), the lance devoids Bradamante's martial tasks of seriousness. Cf. Daniela Delcorno Branca, *"L'Orlando furioso" e il romanzo cavalleresco medievale* (Florence: Olschki, 1973), 81–103, which argues that enchanted weapons furnish keys to the paladins' destinies and notes that as a rule in Ariosto, "Armi 'affatate' e invulnerabilità non sono tuttavia elementi che diminuiscono la lealtà e la prodezza dei cavalieri" (83). In general concurrence with Branca regarding the lance as a sign of providential protection is Julia M. Kisacky, "Magic and Enchanted Armaments: Moral Considerations in Boiardo and Ariosto," *Forum Italicum* 30.2 (1996): 253–73.

53   See Peter V. Marinelli's perceptive and elegant reading of this "fulcrum" moment between the two poems: "Con atto umano," in *Ariosto and Boiardo,* 52–82.

54   Boiardo's unfinished poem breaks off in the midst of the episode Ariosto is about to continue, the poet claiming to be unable to continue writing while the French invade Italy. The proximity of the two themes of Bradamante's hybrid gender and Italy's need for a new leader is suggestive. Finucci reads Bradamante's wounds as the "retelling of her castration" (*The Lady Vanishes,* 240–45), but in my view this "castration" underscores her potential masculinity.

55   See *Orlando innamorato,* III.viii.61, for Boiardo's version of this story.

56   Here too I differ with Finucci: "When she reads Bradamante according to cultural stereotypes, Fiordispina comes up with a man and wants the woman to be in actuality what she seems to be in appearance. When she listens to her, however, she discovers an androgynous female, and for this person she has no desire"

(*The Lady Vanishes,* 214). C. P. Brand, *A Preface to the "Orlando Furioso"* (Edinburgh: Edinburgh University Press, 1974), 59, sees Fiordispina as "wanton."

57   For her sharp reading of this episode (with which I maintain a number of differences), see Finucci's chapter "Transvestite Love: Gender Troubles in the Fiordispina Story," 198–225, in *The Lady Vanishes.* Finucci sees Fiordispina's desire in terms of penis envy, and her reading of the episode revolves around the themes of masquerade and castration: "Why is the desire for a penis so central to the structure of longing and satisfaction in this narrative? . . . Why indeed does Fiordispina show to such an extent what Freud considers essential to female development—penis envy [*Penisneid*]?" John McLucas, citing Paolo Valesio, notes that the frustrated passion of Fiordispina marks the truncation of the *Orlando innamorato* and suggests a congruence between these two women's lack of a man to consummate the sex act and Italy's lack of a leader to rescue the peninsula from invasion ("Amazon, Sorceress, and Queen," 34). Most suggestive is Bellamy, who focuses on the episode's "lesbian, transvestitic, and incestuous undercurrents" and on Fiordispina's "initial responsiveness to a suit of armor that hides the truth (or lie) of gender difference" (*Translations of Power,* 116).

58   In Lacan's terms, we might see Fiordispina as constrained by the obligation to fulfill desire within the realm of the Symbolic. On Lacan's Symbolic, see chapter 2 of this volume.

59   Here we might contrast the other twins, Ruggiero and Marfisa, who participate to a lesser degree in the illustration of fluid gender categories. Marfisa's insistence on the island of murderous women that she can joust on the field and then in the sexual tournament in the women's beds—her sword compensating for her anatomy—ambiguously suggests her readiness to sleep with women. Ruggiero's interface with these thematics appears in his mistaking Ricciardetto for Bradamante in the first place and the subsequent remapping of his desire back onto the sister through the brother.

60   The figure of Sappho was recognized in humanist culture as an instance of *donna con donna* love, and stories of women's sexual encounters in convents circulated widely and nervously. In the *Dialogo delle bellezze delle donne* (1541), ed. Adriano Seroni (Florence: Sansoni, 1993), Agnolo Firenzuola's character Celso recounts the Platonic myth of origins, explaining that those dual beings who were feminine in both their halves before being split apart—as well as all women descended from such beings—"amano la bellezza l'una dell'altra, chi puramente e santamente, come la elegante Laudomia Forteguerra la illustrissima Margherita d'Austria; chi lascivamente, come Saffo la Lesbia anticamente, e a'tempi nostri a Roma la gran meretrice Cicilia Vineziana: e queste così fatte per natura schifano il lor marito, e fuggono la intrinseca conversazione di noi altri; e queste dobbiamo credere che si fanno monache volentieri, e volentieri vi stanno, che sono poche; perchiocché ne' munisteri le più vi stanno per forza, e vivonvi disperate" (542–43). For further reference to lesbian erotics in

the Cinquecento, see Pierre Brantôme, *Les Dames galantes* (1566; reprint, Paris: Garniere Frères, 1960), 120; trans. Alec Brown as *The Lives of Gallant Ladies* (London: Elek Books, 1961), 128. See also Judith Brown, *Immodest Acts: The Life of a Lesbian Nun in Renaissance Italy* (New York: Oxford University Press, 1986); Carla-Chiara Perrone, " 'So che donna amo donna . . .': 'La Calisa' di Maddalena Campiglia," in *Les Femmes écrivains en Italie au Moyen Age et à la Renaissance* (Aix-en-Provence: Publications de l'Université de Provence, 1994), 293–314; and Patricia Simons, "Lesbian (In)Visibility in Italian Renaissance Culture: Diana and Other Cases of *Donna con Donna*," *Journal of Homosexuality* 27.1–2 (1994): 81–122. See also the final chapter of this volume. For related discussion, see Janel Mueller, "Troping Utopia: Donne's Brief for Lesbianism," in Turner, ed., *Sexuality and Gender,* 182–207. John McLucas explores the *Orlando furioso*'s sustained interest in androgyny in "Ariosto and the Androgyne: Symmetries of Sex in the *Orlando furioso*" (Ph.D. diss., Yale University, 1983).

61   See canto XXVI, octave 77, in which Ricciardetto is unequal to the task of fighting Mandricardo and falls from his horse. On the other hand, Bradamante also has her betters. In XXVI.23 we learn that Marfisa is superior to her as a fighter.

62   On narrative repression, see Jameson, *Political Unconscious.*

63   Among them, Rajna and Momigliano. For a discussion of this dissatisfaction among Ariosto's critical readers, see Benson, *Invention,* 148–55.

64   Ariosto's privileging of a woman in this way was innovative. Sixteenth-century readers such as Sassetti and Tasso (discussed earlier in this chapter) recognized and objected vehemently to Bradamante's exemplary status in the poem. They tied it, accordingly, to their opinions about women's proper place in the family and society. Lillian Robinson, *Monstrous Regiment: The Lady Knight in Sixteenth-Century Epic* (New York: Garland, 1985), argues that the popularity of the women knights in Renaissance literature reflects the contemporary development of the theory and practice of "statesmanship" and "statecraft." The imperatives of the early modern state, writes Robinson, "imply a transcendence of absolutes. They connote manipulation, flexibility, compromise, balance, control. . . . [T]he new character of the state no longer harmonized with the absoluteness of the masculine stereotype. It was not *woman* the Renaissance state required, but a principle that the culture defined as female" (105). Robinson's characterization of these new values in political interactions is legitimate, and she offers an important insight in seeing Bradamante as a possible model for the head of state. I find no evidence, however, that the qualities she names were ever characterized as feminine in this period. Machiavelli specifically identifies these positive traits as masculine, and contemporary *querelle* writings commonly portray women as simple, small-minded, fickle, stubborn, and lustful in contrast with the practical traits required for good government. Ariosto irritated conservative readers by assigning these qualities to a female character,

but he depicts such skills as not feminine but hybrid in their gender association. Weaver, in a different vein, sees Bradamante here as a metonymic figure for state politics, arguing that the interlace of events surrounding Bradamante's actions in cantos XXX–XXXIV constitute "la concreta espressione nel poema delle delusioni storiche del poeta" regarding Italy's political misfortunes ("Lettura dell'intreccio," 401). See also Patricia Parker, "Virile Style," in *Premodern Sexualities,* ed. Louise Fradenburg and Carla Freccero (New York: Routledge, 1996), 199–222.

65   I discuss this episode in "Of Women, Knights, Arms, and Love." For a fuller treatment, see Albert R. Ascoli, "Il segreto di Erittonio: poetica e politica sessuale nel canto trentasettesimo dell'*Orlando furioso,*" forthcoming in *La Rappresentazione dell'Altro nei testi del Rinascimento,* ed. Sergio Zatti (Lucca: Pacini Fazzi, 1998).

66   The episode of Leone's betrothal to Bradamante and all its ensuing problems appears for the first time in the 1532 edition of the poem. Among its many commentators, see Attilio Momigliano, *Saggio sull' "Orlando furioso"* (Bari: Laterza, 1973), 140; Walter Moretti, *L'ultimo Ariosto* (Bologna: Patròn, 1977), 96; and Finucci, *The Lady Vanishes,* 227–54.

67   I am not, of course, arguing that Ariosto was explicitly heeding Aristotelian standards of verisimilitude, which came into critical play only after his death, but that he probably desired some minimum of coherence with contemporary Italian mores for his dynastic couple of Estensi ancestors. Here I am in general agreement with Benson, *Invention:* "To think of Bradamante as entirely independent is to misapprehend Ariosto's characterization of her: she is always portrayed as an accomplished woman with domestic goals" (152). Similarly Finucci, *The Lady Vanishes:* "It is entirely inaccurate to complain that Bradamante is too conventional at the end of this romance epic, for her final actions are consistent with her characterization throughout" (240). I perceive more ambivalence in the poem's representation of this model than either of these critics does, however; and in my view Bradamante's obligations reflect on much more than the issues of gender hierarchy and domesticity.

68   On the crucial importance of the pact in Ariosto's poem and more generally in Renaissance political culture, see Saccone, *Il soggetto,* 161–247.

69   Amone, in fact, recognizes his own subordination and defers to Carlo Magno: "Amon, che contrastar con la Corona / non può né vuole, al fin sforzato cede" (XLV.24.5–6) [Amon, who neither can nor will defy the Crown, at last is forced to yield]. See also Julia L. Hairston, "Enclosing the Maternal Body: Motherhood in Alberti, Machiavelli, and Ariosto" (Ph.D. diss., Johns Hopkins University, 1998). Finucci entertains the possibility that Beatrice is the only really powerful woman in the *Furioso;* see *The Lady Vanishes,* 298, n. 19.

70   The implication may be that Ruggiero *is* the stronger of the two, since Bradamante did her best to defeat the opponent she did not know was her beloved,

while Ruggiero sought not to injure his desired wife. The couple's joust contributes in this sense to Bradamante's relative diminishment in stature as the poem moves toward closure. On the other hand, the poem reiterates several times the *parity* of these two contestants, despite their difference of defensive and offensive strategies; see, e.g., XLV.81:

> Carlo e molt'altri seco, che Leone
> esser costui credeansi, e non Ruggiero,
> veduto come in arme, *al paragone*
> di Bradamante, forte era e leggiero;
> e, senza offender lei, con che ragione
> difender si sapea; mutan pensiero,
> e dicon:—Ben convengono amendui;
> * *ch'egli è di lei ben degno, ella di lui*— (Emphasis added.)

71 Albert R. Ascoli, *Ariosto's Bitter Harmony: Crisis and Evasion in the Italian Renaissance* (Princeton: Princeton University Press, 1987), 329–31.

72 Ariosto's use of the subjunctive form *abbia,* which is not entirely necessary in this grammatical context, heightens the ambiguity of Marfisa's claim.

73 Bellamy, *Translations of Power,* 109, 113.

74 On Cassandra's veil, see Ascoli's splendid, lengthy discussion (*Ariosto's Bitter Harmony,* 258–393). I fully accept the possibility Ascoli raises, that the focus in the image of Bradamante as reader of the wedding tent may be precisely her *inability* to recognize future history among the Estensi for the violent experience it will be, as the fate of Cassandra was to prophesy the truth but never be believed. Bradamante remains, nonetheless, the only character in the wedding episode who recognizes the veil's images as an Estense genealogy. We might even see this moment in the text as one of ironic self-reflexivity, for Bradamante reads Estense future history as romance—that is, as a narrative containing no real violence.

75 On the *"furore* of aggression" in the *Furioso,* see Bellamy, *Translations of Power,* 86–87.

76 On the pre-Ariostan versions of Bradamante, see Marinelli, *Ariosto and Boiardo;* and Benson, *Invention,* 125–26; as well as the classic Rajna, *Le fonti,* 45–55, 593–97.

77 On the ekphrastic mode in the *Orlando furioso,* see the final chapter in Marianne Shapiro, *The Poetics of Ariosto* (Detroit: Wayne State University Press, 1988), 192–239; and Katherine Hoffman, "The Court in the Work of Art: Patronage and Poetic Autonomy in *Orlando furioso,* Canto 42," *Quaderni d'Italianistica* 13.1 (1992): 113–24.

78 Rodomonte wears the dragon-skin armor of his ancestor Nimrod (XIV.118) up until his vow in canto XXXV after being defeated by Bradamante. When he appears at the wedding (XLVI.103), Ariosto explicitly recalls this pledge: "poi

che tutto l'anno e tutto 'l mese / vede finito, e tutto 'l giorno appresso, / con nuove arme e cavallo e spada e lancia / alla corte or ne vien quivi di Francia."

79 Cf. as feminine revenge Dido's curse on the parting Aeneas, in which she predicts war between Carthage and Rome in similar language (*Aeneid* 4.526–28, 860–65). See also Laura Terracina's evocation of this vengeance, as discussed in chapter 4 of this volume.

80 Eugène Vinaver, *The Rise of Romance* (Oxford: Clarendon, 1971), 92.

4   Getting a Word in Edgewise

1 Neapolitan nobles since 1275, the Terracina family appears to have hailed from Brescia. See Lina Maroi, *Laura Terracina: poetessa napoletana del secolo XVI* (Naples: Francesco Perella, 1913); and Angelo Borzelli, *Laura Terracina: poetessa del Cinquecento* (Naples: M. Marzano, 1924). Although both monographs stand in need of revision, they provide the fullest available discussions of Terracina and her work to date. See also Benedetto Croce, "La casa di una poetesa" (1901), in his *Storie e leggende napoletane* (Bari: Laterza, 1948), 275–89. Croce claims the Terracina family died out altogether in the eighteenth century. Of more recent vintage is a *tesi di laurea* by Rossanna di Stefano, "Ricerche su Laura Terracina, petrarchista napoletana" (Università degli studi di Roma, Facoltà di lettere e filosofia, 1974–75). My thanks to Amedeo Quondam for directing me to di Stefano's work.

2 I have consulted *Rime della signora Laura Terracina e in fine una Diceria del Doni* (Venice: Giolito, 1553). Following di Stefano's information, this edition would fall between the princeps (1548) and Giolito's sixth edition (1556). The 1547 edition is presumed by Bongi to be lost. See S. Bongi, *Annali di Gabriel Giolito de' Ferrari* (Rome, 1890–93), 227. Like the surviving previous editions described by others, this one bears a dedication to Vincenzo Belprato, conte d'Aversa, signed by Lodovico Domenichi, who edited the collection. The volume also features an index of first lines in its final pages.

3 The quoted phrase is taken from Borzelli, *Laura Terracina,* 11.

4 See Maroi, *Laura Terracina,* 104.

5 Published only in one edition, by Giunti of Florence, copies of the *Seconde rime* are reported by di Stefano to be held in the Biblioteca Corsiniana (Col. 130 D 1) and the Angelica (Coll. RR 2 3). The Angelica was unable to locate its copy for me; I rely on secondary sources for its description.

6 The *Discorso's* title varied slightly in its different editions. Also common was the variant, *Discorso sopra il principio di tutti i canti d' "Orlando furioso."* My discussion is based on comparison of the 1550 and 1559 editions published in Venice by Gabriel Giolito de Ferrari. Canto XXXVII is here reproduced from *La prima parte de'discorsi sopra le prime stanze de'canti d' "Orlando furioso"* (Venice: Luigi Valvassori & Giovan Domenico Micheli, 1584). My further consultations of Gio-

lito's 1551, 1557, and 1565 editions and the 1567 Venetian edition published by Domenico Farri reveal abundant differences in punctuation among all of the above, and several bear the marks of lexical revision by author or editors. I must leave to others the philological tasks of sorting out these differences. My sincerest thanks to Elissa Weaver, who, in a gesture of dazzling *sprezzatura,* shared with me a large personal file containing bibliography and notations regarding the collocations of Terracina's works in European and American libraries.

7 *Settime rime. Sovra tutte le donne vedove di questa nostra città di Napoli titolate e non titolate fatte per la Signora Laura Terracina* (Naples: Mattia Cancer, 1561). I have consulted the only known, intact copy of this work, which is held in the Biblioteca dell'Oratorio dei Gerolamini, Naples. I am grateful to Gordon Poole for facilitating my access to that library. The only other copy known to survive is a damaged one held by the University Library of Naples. Terracina was apparently slow in publishing this very formulaic collection; she apologizes in her prefatory remarks for the incongruent fact that by the time of its issue many of the women praised in its rhymes were either remarried or deceased. The great number of women she set out to praise nonetheless suggests the high incidence of widowhood among sixteenth-century women. On this precious volume, see Giovanni Bresciano, "Ricerche bibliografiche: Di tre rarissime edizioni napoletane del sec. XVI sconosciute ai bibliografi," *Revue des bibliotèques* 9 (1899): 21–27. On widowhood generally in early modern Europe, see Margaret King, *Women of the Renaissance* (Chicago: University of Chicago Press, 1991), 56–62.

8 *La seconda parte de' discorsi sopra le seconde stanze de' canti d' "Orlando furioso." Della Sig. Laura Terracina detta nell'Academia de gl'Incogniti, Febea* (Venice: Luigi Valvassori & Giovan Domenico Micheli, 1584). The copy of this edition to which I refer is held in the collection of the Folger Shakespeare Library.

9 This volume in manuscript is catalogued in Florence's Biblioteca Nazionale as codice CCXXIX [553—E—5—19—321].

10 Terracina appears also in a few Cinquecento poetic anthologies, but never with the frequency of Vittoria Colonna and Veronica Gambara, who are clear favorites in the editions I have consulted. Typical for the ratio of male poets to female poets in these anthologies is the *Rime di diversi nobili huomini et eccellenti poeti nella lingua toscana* (Venice: Giolito, 1547), which features sixty-nine male poets (some represented by numerous compositions) and one poem by a woman, Veronica Gambara. For volumes that include Terracina, see *Rime diverse di molti eccellentissimi autori nuovamente raccolte. Libro primo* (Venice: Giolito, 1549); and *Rime di diversi signori napoletani e d'altri* (Venice: Giolito, 1556). Di Stefano also cites *Del tempio alla divina signora donna Giovanna D'Aragona, fabricato da tutti i più gentili spiriti e in tutte le lingue principali del mondo. Prima parte* (Venice: Plinio Pietrasanta, 1554); and *Rime di diversi nobilissimi et eccellentissimi autori in morte della Signora Irene delle Signore di Spilimbergo . . .* (Venice: Domenico e Gio. Battista Guerra, 1561).

11 See note 1 above; see also Natalia Costa-Zalessow, "Su due sonetti del Cinque-

cento attribuiti a L. Terracina," *Forum Italicum* 15.1 (1981): 22–30, which, how-ever, persuasively argues against this attribution. Recent notice of Terracina in collections and encyclopedic works brings her into the discussion of literary history but, unfortunately, features confusing errors. An anthology of Italian feminist poetry mistranslates the *Discorso*'s title as *The Discourse on the Principle in All the Cantos of "Orlando Furioso."* See *The Defiant Muse: Italian Feminist Poems from the Middle Ages to the Present,* ed. Beverly Allen, Muriel Kittel, and Keala Jane Jewell (New York: Feminist Press, 1986), 9. In *An Encyclopedia of Continental Women Writers,* ed. Katharina M. Wilson (New York: Garland, 1991), 3:1127–28, Rinaldina Russell in an otherwise informative entry refers to the *Discorso* as a "Summary," mistakenly adding that the *Seconda parte* (1567) deals with Ariosto's *Cinque canti.* Nancy Dersofi's longer entry in *Italian Women Writers: A Bio Biblio-graphical Sourcebook,* ed. Rinaldina Russell (Westport, Conn.: Greenwood Press, 1994), 422–30, provides useful biographical and bibliographical descriptions but repeats Russell's error regarding the second *Discorso* and attributes a quoted passage from the first *Discorso*'s canto XXXVII to canto XXX. Apropos of the *Cinque canti,* Terracina appears to have doubted that Ariosto was their author. In any case, she preferred not to write on them at all, as she considered them inferior to the *Orlando furioso.* An octave following the *Discorso* declares:

> Havria seguito anchor, i cinque canti,
> Che l'habbia fatti, dicon l'Ariosto,
> I quai son gionti al fin de gl'altri canti;
> Come si vede, da ingegnosi, tosto,
> Non parlarò di questi nuovi canti,
> Cosi ho determinato, e ho proposto
> Non che lo stil non sia dotto ingegnoso;
> Ma non mi parno uguali al Furioso.

12   See Luciana Borsetto, "Narciso ed Eco: Figura e scrittura nella lirica femminile del Cinquecento," in *Nel cerchio della luna: Figure di donna in alcuni testi del XVI secolo,* ed. Marina Zancan (Venice: Marsilio, 1983), 192–94. On Stampa's use of echo, see Ann Rosalind Jones's essay in *Refiguring Woman: Perspectives on Gender in the Italian Renaissance* (Ithaca: Cornell University Press, 1991), as well as her brief remarks in *The Currency of Eros: Women's Love Lyric in Europe, 1540–1620* (Bloomington: Indiana University Press, 1990), 28.

13   See my chapters 1 and 2 for further discussion of Lacan's "gaze."

14   I cite from John Hollander, *The Figure of Echo: A Mode of Allusion in Milton and After* (Berkeley: University of California Press, 1981), 8. For Ovid's myth, see *Metamorphoses* 3 (365–510); for Longus, see *Daphnis and Chloe,* trans. Christopher Gill, in *Collected Ancient Greek Novels,* ed. B. P. Reardon (Berkeley: University of California Press, 1989), 327.

15 By famous contrast, Terracina's "source" author, Ariosto, intervened directly in the printing of the *Orlando furioso,* actually entering revisions in his text as it was being typeset. Olga Silvana Casale discusses the relations between editorial practices, book distribution, and cataloguing in Italian libraries, and the critical understanding of "minor" and "minimal" texts (with illustrations from Croce's edition of Veronica Franco's letters) in "Le scritture femminili tra strumenti di ricerca e edizioni," in *Les Femmes écrivains en Italie au Moyen Age et à la Renaissance* (Aix-en-Provence: Publications de l'Université de Provence, 1994), 33–49.

16 Jones, *Currency of Eros,* 36.

17 My figures for the number of these editions remain deliberately general because several editions I have consulted do not appear in Maroi's chronology of Terracina's publications. This suggests that their number may be considerably higher than previously estimated.

18 Octave 1 of each canto ends in Ariosto's line 1 from the corresponding *Furioso* canto; octave 2 ends with line 2, etc. Ariosto's rhymed couplet appears unbroken at the end of octave 7.

19 On the *Orlando furioso* as Europe's first best-seller, see Daniel Javitch, *Proclaiming a Classic: The Canonization of "Orlando Furioso"* (Princeton: Princeton University Press, 1991).

20 Terracina was not the only poet to draw on the *Furioso* for feminist aims. The Venetian defender of women, Moderata Fonte, wrote a romance modeled on the *Orlando furioso* in which the principal characters are feminine. Fonte's canto IV illustrates her own mode of citation from Ariosto, which might best be described as *imitatio,* when compared with the opening octaves of Ariosto's canto XX:

> Le donne in ogni età fur da Natura
> Di gran giudicio e d'animo dotate,
> Nè men atte a mostrar con studio e cura
> Senno e valor degli uomini son nate.
> E perchè, se comune è la figura,
> Se non son le sostanze variate,
> S'hanno simile un cibo e un parlar, denno
> Differente aver poi l'ardire e il senno? (*I Tredici canti del Floridoro* [Venice:
> Rampazzetti, 1581])

> [Women of every era have been endowed with
> spirit and good judgment,
> nor are they born less apt than men to display
> wisdom and valor. So why, if their forms are
> like, if their substance differs not, if their
> food and speech be in common with men, should
> they differ from men in good sense and courage?]

Now available in a modern edition by Valeria Finucci (Modena: Mucchi, 1995). Fonte's more explicitly feminist writing appears in *Il merito delle donne* (Venice: Domenico Imberti, 1600), now also republished in a modern edition, ed. Adriana Chemello (Venice: Eidos, 1988), and in a translation by Virginia Cox from University of Chicago Press (1997). On Fonte (b. Modesta del Pozzo, 1555), see Beatrice Collina, "Moderata Fonte e *Il merito delle donne*," 142–64; and Paola Malpezzi Price, "A Woman's Discourse in the Italian Renaissance: Moderata Fonte's *Il Merito Delle Donne*," 165–81, both in *Annali d'Italianistica* 7 (1989), special issue: *Women's Voices in Italian Literature,* ed. Rebecca West and Dino S. Cervigni.

21   Whether due to flaws in the editorial and printing processes or to a lack of clarity in the text itself, many of Terracina's stanzas defy efforts to perceive their coherence. My thanks to Eduardo Saccone and David Quint, two careful readers of translations and specialists of the Cinquecento (the latter an accomplished translator himself), for their generous assistance in deciphering some of Terracina's vexingly difficult lines. I hasten to add that neither they nor the other colleagues I called on in moments of perplexity are responsible for the final product, which is mine alone and which readers of Italian will recognize as a compromise. I eagerly await emendations by subsequent readers.

22   This feature of the *Furioso* marked its lack of generic coherence for Ariosto's detractors in the latter sixteenth-century debates; see chapter 3 of this volume.

23   Maroi, *Laura Terracina,* 49.

24   See Joseph Octave Delepierre, *Centoniana, ou Encyclopédie du centon* (London: Miscellanies of the Philobiblon Society, 1866–68), vols. 9, 10.

25   Jeffrey Schnapp, "Reading Lessons: Augustine, Proba, and the Christian Detournement of Antiquity," *Stanford Literature Review* 9.2 (1992): 99–123.

26   On the *centoni* of Vittoria Colonna and Chiara Matraini, see Borsetto, "Narciso ed Eco."

27   Also relevant may have been the popularity of Ovid's *Heroides* throughout Europe. On the emergence of the Ovidian lament as a Renaissance genre, see Jones, *Currency of Eros,* 36–78.

28   Alfred Einstein cites Tromboncino's "Queste non son più lagrime che fuora" (1517) as the first musical composition of record to draw its libretto from the *Furioso;* see his *The Italian Madrigal,* 3 vols., trans. H. Krappe et al. (Princeton: Princeton University Press, 1971), 206. For a list of Ariosto's stanzas set to music, see Maria Antonella Bolsano and James Haar, "L'Ariosto in musica," in *Ariosto, la musica, i musicisti: Quattro studi e sette madrigali ariosteschi,* ed. A. Bolsano (Florence: Olschki, 1981), 47–88. See also James Haar, "Arie per cantar stanze ariostesche," 31–46 (especially 32–33), in the same volume.

29   Terracina's contacts with the madrigal tradition may also explain the apparent poverty of some of her rhyme patterns. Alessandro Martini, in "Ritratto del

madrigale poetico fra Cinque e Seicento," *Lettere italiane* 33 (1981): 528–48, as-
cribes to the tradition itself a deliberate predilection for uninventive rhymes
and avoidable repetitions of rhymed words. Discussing verses by Marino he
observes, "Basta un'occhiata agli altri madrigali per convincersi che le rime
facili e prevedibili e le parole in rima internamente ripercosse dominano
ovunque" (539).

30 Haar asserts, "Non soltanto si prendevano a prestito i versi dell'Ariosto, ma li si
alterava e riaddattava in nuove serie di stanze, magari pubblicate in libriccini
economici come mescolanza di parafrasi volgarizzate frammiste in citazioni
testuali; tali libercoli erano numerosissimi negli anni '20, '30 e '40 (ne sono
esempio le *Stanze trasmutate dell'Ariosto* di Leonardo detto il Furlano, stampate
nel 1545)" ("Arie per cantar," 34).

31 G. B. Pigna, *Scontri de' luoghi, i quali M. Lodovico Ariosto mutò doppo la prima im-
pressione del suo "Furioso." Et la cagione perche lo facesse di luogo in luogo* (1554),
Osservazione 52. I cite from the 1568 Valgrisi edition of the *Furioso,* which
includes the *Scontri.* Pigna comments on the revision of the line "E gran con-
trasto in giovenil pensiero":

> Che gl'ignoranti à caso possano ritrovar quello, che gli scienziati non
> hanno saputo con istudio ritrovare, più volte se n'è veduto la prova, et
> hora il medesimo si vede. Percioche citandosi i versi del Furioso per
> le strade, i fanciulli apparano molti cominciamenti di Canti, come che
> egli siane à ciò più comodi. Tra gli altri s'è cantato questo, al quale per
> dar'aria, posero la Ò che è esclamante, in vece della E, che non facea
> quell'effetto; et dissero, Ò gran contrasto in giovenil pensiero. Alla cui
> mutatione s'accostò l'Ariosto. Di qui ci penseremo, che non sia mal fatto
> il por mente à i versi che vanno per la bocca di gente del volgo; che se
> bene per lo più li stroppiano, possono ancora dicendogli al riverso dar
> loro per disgratia miglior forma e suono migliore." (596–97)

Also cited in Giuseppina Fumagalli, *La fortuna dell' "Orlando furioso" in Italia nel
sec. XVI* (Ferrara, 1912), 397; and in Haar, "Arie per cantar," 34. On the inter-
penetrations between oral poetry and music in Ariosto's day, see also James
Haar, *Italian Poetry and Music in the Renaissance, 1350–1600* (Berkeley: University
of California Press, 1986), especially ch. 4; as well as Einstein, *Italian Madrigal,*
166–211.

32 All historical evidence regarding Terracina's education points to the barest of
instruction, typical for most noble and middle-class girls of the day. Maroi
remarks, "Ella crebbe senza quella perfetta e profonda istruzione classica, in-
dispensabile requisito alla cultura della dama della Rinascenza; crebbe vergine
di ogni vernice storica e filosofica, ma in compenso ebbe ingegno acuto e vi-
vido" (*Laura Terracina,* 33). Borzelli corroborates Maroi's view. Both authors

imply that Terracina's editors performed grammatical corrections as well as poetic revisions on her texts. While Borzelli's palpable sexist bias allows him to omit that many male poets, too, availed themselves of editorial ameliorations, Terracina's disadvantages in this regard are more than plausible. On another female poet tied to the tradition of the *cantari,* see Mario Martelli, "Lucrezia Tornabuoni," in *Les Femmes écrivains,* 51–86.

33   Terracina's Sacripante poem features the lines "Amor, tu causi tutto il penar mio, / tu mi fai torto," cited in a villanella by Ghinolfo Dattari (1535–1617). I am indebted to Mary Di Quinzio for this citation, for many bibliographical references, and for her rapid and generous introduction to the Ariostan madrigal tradition. At a later stage the interest and expertise of Ellen Rosand and Linda Austern were also invaluable. For Dattari's libretto, see Ghinolfo Dattari, *Le villanelle,* ed. Giuseppe Vecchi (Bologna: Palmaverde, 1955), 9–10. See also the entries by Emil Vogel, *Biblioteca della musica vocale italiana di genere profano stampata dal 1500 al 1700. Con aggiunti da Alfred Einstein* (Hildesheim: Georg Olms, 1962), 199–200; Stanley Sadie, ed., *New Grove Dictionary of Music and Musicians,* vol. 5 (London: Macmillan, 1980), 252; and Carlo Schmidl, *Dizionario universale dei musicisti,* vol. 1 (Milan: Sonzogno, 1926), 411.

34   Einstein, *Italian Madrigal,* 206.

35   Javitch, *Proclaiming a Classic,* 173, n. 13.

36   Paul Grendler, *Schooling in Renaissance Italy: Literacy and Learning, 1300–1600* (Baltimore: Johns Hopkins University Press, 1989), 299.

37   I cite from Rinaldina Russell in Wilson, ed., *An Encyclopedia,* 1228.

38   The bibliography on women's education in early modernity is extensive and growing. Representative studies include Ruth Kelso, *Doctrine for the Lady of the Renaissance* (Urbana: University of Illinois Press, 1956); Patricia H. Labalme, ed., *Beyond Their Sex: Learned Women of the European Past* (New York: New York University Press, 1980); Maria Ludovico Lenzi, *Donne e madonne. L'educazione femminile nel primo Rinascimento italiano* (Turin: Loescher, 1982); Anthony Grafton and Lisa Jardine, "Women Humanists: Education for What?" in their *From Humanism to the Humanities: Education and the Liberal Arts in Fifteenth- and Sixteenth-Century Europe* (London: Duckworth, 1986); and relevant chapters in Margaret L. King, *Women of the Renaissance;* and in Pamela Joseph Benson, *The Invention of the Renaissance Woman: The Challenge of Female Independence in the Literature and Thought of Italy and England* (University Park: Pennsylvania State University Press, 1992).

39   On displacement, see Jacques Derrida, *Of Grammatology,* trans. Gayatry Chakravorty Spivak (Baltimore: Johns Hopkins University Press, 1976); and "The Law of Genre," in *Glyph* 7 (Baltimore: Johns Hopkins University Press, 1980), 202–32. See also Spivak, "Displacement and the Discourse of Woman," in *Displacement: Derrida and After,* ed. Mark Krupknik (Bloomington: Indiana University Press, 1983), 169–95.

40 These include Elionora Sanseverina (2), Costanza D'Avalo (10), the contessa of Calisano (12), Isabella of Toledo (16), Isabella Colonna (20), Vittoria and Hieronima Colonna of Aragon (26), Isabella of Molfete (32), Giovanna Aragona Colonna (35), Veronica Gambara (37), Maria Aragona (38), and Clarice Drusina (43).

41 These laudatory and defensive gestures toward women extend, moreover, into the poems that follow the *Discorso* in the Giolito edition, as well as into Terracina's other works. Particularly noteworthy among these is Terracina's collection of lyrics dedicated to the widows of Naples (*Settime rime*), a group of women numbering no fewer than 202.

42 I discuss this episode briefly in the context of Ariosto's larger treatment of the woman question in "Of Women, Knights, Arms, and Love: The *Querelle des Femmes* in Ariosto's Poem," *MLN* 104. 1 (1989): 68–97. See, for a major reading of this canto, Albert R. Ascoli, "Il segreto di Erittonio: poetica e politica sessuale nel canto trentasettesimo dell'*Orlando furioso*," forthcoming in *La Rappresentazione dell'Altro nei testi del Rinascimento,* ed. Sergio Zatti (Lucca: Pacini Fazzi, 1998). See also Benson, *Invention,* 131–48; and John McLucas, "Ariosto and the Androgyne: Symmetries of Sex in the *Orlando Furioso*" (Ph.D. diss., Yale University, 1983), 233–46. For another feminine appropriation of Ariosto's canto XXXVII, see Eric Nicholson's fascinating discussion of the actress Flaminia Romana's dramatization and revision of the Drusilla episode, in his forthcoming essay, "Romance as Role Model: Early Female Performances of Ariosto and Tasso," in *Renaissance Transactions: Ariosto and Tasso,* ed. Valeria Finucci (Durham: Duke University Press, 1999).

43 The 1559 edition reads *mondo* [world] rather than *modo* [manner]. Such variations are also indicated for some stanzas I transcribe below.

44 Giolito's 1550 edition substitutes for *Afri* in this line the word *Arabbi:* "Anzi più mal, che fer l'Arabbi a Roma." Arabs and Africans were not always distinguished by sixteenth-century Italians, as both fell into the category of dreaded infidel. Terracina's reference to the Africans alludes presumably to the Carthaginians, who fought three Punic Wars against the Romans between 264 and 146 B.C. Virgil speaks of Arabs (*Aeneid* 7.793ff., 8.918ff.) as the enemies of Rome; and of course a range of Africans and Arabs figure as the mostly undifferentiated foes of Charlemagne in the *Orlando furioso,* where the scene of conflict, however, is Paris. Terracina may have revised her reference to avoid obvious allusion to the Punic Wars, which were won by Rome; but she may also have wished to evoke a more contemporary threat. It was, after all, the Arab and the Turk who haunted the imaginations of early modern Europeans, and the city of Buda had fallen to the Ottomans in 1541. The oscillations of this term as it appears in the *Discorso* deserve further study, but such study exceeds the scope of the present work.

45 For discussion of the tradition of Dido before and after Virgil, see Marilynn

Desmond, *Reading Dido: Gender, Textuality, and the Medieval "Aeneid"* (Minneapolis: University of Minnesota Press, 1994).

46 The 1550 Giolito edition bears here the rather inscrutable line "Ogn'un va lieto gia tiene e discorso."

47 This theme of women's perilous proximity to prostitution reemerges in nineteenth-century feminist *verista* and melodrama narratives; see, e.g., Emilia Ferretti Viola (pseud. Emma, b. 1844), *Una fra tante* (Rome: Lucarini, 1988).

48 Naples had passed to Spanish rule in 1504.

49 Also of interest in this spirit are poems in Terracina's other collections. The *Seste rime* features two political "prophecies" written by Terracina in 1552 and 1553.

50 In octave 6 she evokes the dangers for both soldiers and civilians at the hands of the Saracens. As she recalls Ariosto's narrative, she probably ponders as well the fears her contemporaries harbored before the threat of the Turk. Terracina's evocation of the *Furioso*'s storming of Paris thus overlaps with the concerns of her dedicatory octave, as she sings the horrors of war shared by medieval and early modern cities alike.

> Hor state attenti a le muraglie, e avezzi
> O paladin di Francia, o di Parigi,
> Che' saracin vi voglion tutti a pezzi
> A fil di spada porvi, e in fier litigi,
> Et in vergogna, danno, e in disprezzi
> di se lasciando horribili vestigi. (XIV.6.1–6)
>
> [Now beware of the city walls, as practiced
> oh paladin(s) of France, or of Paris;
> for the Saracens want to cut you all to pieces,
> and put you to the sword's blade and set you in fierce conflict
> and in shame, ruin, and contempt,
> leaving behind horrible vestiges of themselves.]

The 1559 version of the octave given here, though clearer in many respects, eliminates entirely a variant verse appearing in the 1550 edition at line 6: "Le vostre donne; e far le strade bigi" [to cast your women, turning your streets to ash].

51 The 1550 edition here reads "Qual pensier, qual desir la mente indonne."

52 Men, too, of course, have questioned the morality of war. Terracina's immediate inspiration for her reflections here takes its cue in part from Ariosto's stanzas (XIV.2–9) on the battle of Ravenna, one of the century's bloodiest.

53 Thus Terracina's opening canto in the *Seconda parte* begins with a dedicatory octave to Pope Pius V, followed by this stanza:

> Le donne, i cavalier, l'arme, gl'amori,
> Le cortesie, l'audaci imprese io canto,

> Che furo al tempo, che passaro i Mori
> D'Africa il mare, in in Francia nocquer tanto
> Seguendo l'ira, e i giovenil furori
> D'Agramante il Re, che si diè vanto
> **D'arder Parigi; e poi c'havrò ciò fatto,**
> *Dirò d'Orlando in un medesmo tratto."*

The line in boldface type is Terracina's; the italicized verse is the first line of octave 2 in Ariosto's opening canto.

54 An exception are Ariosto's final couplets for each octave 1, which for reasons of this work's structure must be eliminated.

55 She makes these excuses again in the final canto of the work:

> S'io nel principio havessi avuto ingegno
> Incominciata non avrei tal opra:
> Ma perché mi pregò, chi anzi era degno
> Di commandarmi, e n'ha dominio sopra,
> Sforzata fui star del suo imperio al segno. (XLVI.6.i–v).

56 Terracina was married at the age of forty to a relative named Polidoro Terracina. Her complaints in contemporary poems suggest the union was not a happy one, as her husband was apparently of a jealous nature and sought to restrict her activities. Traiano Boccalini's report in his 1612 *Ragguagli di Parnaso* (seconda centuria, 35) that Terracina was killed by her husband, Francesco Mauro, out of jealousy over a garter she claimed to have received from Edward VI of England appears to be the product of its author's fantasy.

57 On Ariosto's linguistic revisions to conform with Tuscan standardization, see Cesare Segre, *Esperienze ariostesche* (Pisa: Nistri-Lischi, 1966), 29–44.

58 Terracina's use of the article here leaves open the question of whether she refers to *man,* or to *the* man, i.e., Ariosto.

59 Schnapp, "Reading Lessons."

60 Schnapp, "Reading Lessons," 119. Terracina's self-denigrations are frequent from the beginning of her poetic production to the final canto of the second *Discorso*.

5   From Insult to Injury

1 Subsequent references to the will refer to Archivio Urbano (Rome) Sez. I, 856, ff.172ss. My sincere thanks to Julia Hairston for obtaining this document for me in microfilm, and to Giorgina Dopico-Black for her invaluable assistance in deciphering its Spanish hand.

2 On the "cult of remembrance" as reflected in such testamentary directives, see Samuel K. Cohn Jr., *The Cult of Remembrance and the Black Death: Six Renaissance Cities in Central Italy* (Baltimore: Johns Hopkins University Press, 1992);

and chapter 2 of his *Women in the Streets: Essays on Sex and Power in Renaissance Italy* (Baltimore: Johns Hopkins University Press, 1996).

3 See, among others, E. Rodocanachi, *Courtisanes et bouffons* (Paris, 1894); Pio Pecchiai, *Donne del Rinascimento in Roma* (Padua: CEDAM, 1958); Paul Larivaille, *La Vie quotidienne des courtisanes en Italie au temps de la Renaissance* (Paris: Hachette, 1975); Lynne Lawner, *Lives of the Courtesans: Portraits of the Renaissance* (New York: Rizzoli, 1987); Georgina Masson, *Courtesans of the Italian Renaissance* (London: Secker and Warburg, 1975); Margaret F. Rosenthal, *The Honest Courtesan: Veronica Franco, Citizen and Writer in Sixteenth-Century Venice* (Chicago: University of Chicago Press, 1992); Marcella Diberti Leigh, *Veronica Franco: Donna, poetessa, e cortigiana del Rinascimento* (Ivrea: Priuli & Verlucca, 1988).

4 See letter 51 from Beatrice da Ferrara to the duke of Urbino, in *Lettere di cortigiane del Rinascimento*, ed. A. Romano (Rome: Salerno, 1990), 142–47. Beatrice tells the duke that she went to confess herself to the priest at the church of Sant'Agostino, along with several other women of her profession, whereupon the priest "vedendose sì notabile audienza, ad altro non attendea se non in volerne convertirne tutte. Oh, oh, oh, dura impresa! Per me aria potuto cicalare cento anni!" See also Leah Otis, *Prostitution in Medieval Society* (Chicago: University of Chicago Press, 1985), 71; Richard Trexler, "Correre la Terra: Collective Insults in the Late Middle Ages," *Mélanges de l'École française de Rome* 96 (1984): 845–902, esp. 884–86, rev. and repr. in Trexler, *Dependence in Context in Renaissance Florence* (Binghamton: Center for Medieval and Renaissance Studies, 1994), 113–70.

5 For extensive discussion of another example of such charitable contributions, see Rosenthal, *Honest Courtesan*, 58–115.

6 Pio Pecchiai, *Roma nel Cinquecento* (Bologna: Licinio, 1948), 37, 315–17. Explaining one aspect of Isabella's will, Pecchiai also notes that the law "dichiarava irriti e nulli i testamenti delle cortigiane dove non fosse espresso il lascito d'un quinto delle sostanze delle testatrici a favore delle Convertite" (316).

7 Pierre Brantôme, *Les Dames galantes* (Paris: Garnier Frères, 1960), 120. A certain "Laura madre dela Pandora" is also named in Isabella's will, in which she is left "cien escudos de monedas." My thanks to Elizabeth Cohen and Thomas Cohen, who shared with me two other appearances of Isabella de Luna from the Roman archives. An *avviso* in the Vatican Library's series Urb. lat. 1038, ff. 111v–112r, reports for 25 December 1555 that in recent days the mother of "una bella puta detta Pandore" has complained of Isabella de Luna's taking the girl and holding her in her house. Isabella was ordered to prison, but she fled her house and indeed the city along with the girl. Caught in Rimini on her way to Venice, she was conducted back to Rome's Castello for trial. Isabella also makes a brief archival appearance on 6 September 1557 in the trial of Pompeo Giustini, a Roman nobleman (ASR Governatore, Tribunale Criminale, Processi, busta 31 [xvi century], caso 1, f. 54r). In this case she is reported to have

spoken with the defendant from her window as he passed on his horse, asking him why he did not heed the call to arms and rush to defend the pope against the arrival of Spanish troops. Here, Isabella's Spanish identity functions to project her as a signifier of the Spanish threat to Rome.

8 Pierre Brantôme, *The Lives of Gallant Ladies,* trans. Alec Brown (London: Elek Books, 1961), 128.

9 On *donna con donna* relations in this period, see Patricia Simons, "Lesbian (In)Visibility in Italian Renaissance Culture: Diana and Other Cases of *Donna con Donna," Journal of Homosexuality* 27.1–2 (1994): 81–122; Carla-Chiara Perrone, " 'So che donna amo donna . . .': *La Calisa* di Maddalena Campiglia," in *Les Femmes écrivains en Italie au Moyen Age et à la Renaissance* (Aix-en-Provence: Publications de l'Université de Provence, 1994); as well as Judith Brown, *Immodest Acts: The Life of a Lesbian Nun in Renaissance Italy* (New York: Oxford University Press, 1986).

10 Pecchiai, *Roma,* 316. I am unable to confirm Pecchiai's claims of full archival documentation for the Bandello tales.

11 Here I mark my agreement with Cohn, who throughout his *Women in the Streets* warns against the uncritical use of literary evidence in discussions of social history. On the other hand, I would add that literary sources—and especially favorite narratives and characters—always reveal to us the fantasies entertained by a given culture. The correspondence between those fantasies and reality is as questionable for historical periods as for the present. On courtesans, see Larivaille, *La Vie quotidienne,* ch. 6: "Le Revers de la médaille": "à distance de plusieurs siècles surtout, les conditions réelles de la prostitution à l'époque de la Renaissance italienne risquent-elles d'être en grande partie déformées et occultées sous l'image flattée qu'en donnent la littérature et les arts de l'époque. La triomphe de la courtisane honnête, en particulier, risque, si on n'y prend garde, d'être l'arbre qui masque la forêt: une forêt où il s'en faut que toutes les plantes atteignent à la même luxuriance" (126). See also Otis, *Prostitution;* Jacques Rossiaud, *Medieval Prostitution* (Oxford: Oxford University Press, 1988); Romano Canossa and Isabella Colonello, *Storia della prostituzione in Italia dal Quattrocento alla fine del Settecento* (Rome: Sapere 2000, 1989); Richard Trexler, "La Prostitution florentine au XV siècle: Patronage et clientèles," *Annales: Economies, Sociétés, Civilisations* 36 (1982): 983–1015, trans. and rev. in Trexler, *Dependence in Context,* 373–414; Elizabeth Pavan, "Police des moeurs, société et politique à la fin du Moyen Age," *Revue historique* 536 (1980): 240–88.

12 On the location of the municipal brothels, see Rossiaud, *Medieval Prostitution,* 59; Trexler, "La Prostitution"; and chapter 1 of this volume.

13 See Pietro Aretino, *Le sei giornate* (Bari: Laterza, 1969); and his *Lettere,* 2 vols. (Milan: Mondadori, 1960); Francisco Delicado, *La Lozana Andalusa* (Madrid: Porrua, 1975); and Thomas Coryat, *Coryat's Crudities* (Glasgow: University of Glasgow Press, 1905). All references to Bandello refer to the edition of Fran-

cesco Flora, *Tutte le opere di Matteo Bandello* (Verona: Mondadori, 1952). Isabella appears in II.51 and IV.16.

14   Bandello's tales are also sources for Massinger's *The Picture*, Webster's *The Duchess of Malfi*, and Beaumont and Fletcher's *Maid of the Mill* and *Triumph of Death*. See Donatella Riposio, "Il Bandello e la sua fortuna inglese: dalle novelle 'Out of Bandell' al palcoscenico scespiriano," in *Matteo Bandello novelliere europeo. Atti del convegno internazionale di studi 7–9 novembre 1980,* ed. Ugo Rozzo (Tortona: Cassa di Risparmio di Tortona, 1982), 559–82.

15   I know of no complete translation of Bandello's stories into English. *The Novels of Matteo Bandello Englished by John Payne,* 6 vols. (London: Villon Society, 1890) includes one of the tales of Isabella (II, 51)—renumbered by Payne as II, 39 in his volume 5—but not the other. To the best of my knowledge Bandello's IV.16, is translated into English for the first time in appendix 2 of this book.

16   On this point, see Riccardo Bruscagli, "Mediazioni narrative nel novelliere del Bandello," in Rozzo, ed., *Matteo Bandello,* 61–94.

17   Bandello, *Tutte le opere,* "Ai candidi ed umani lettori": "E se bene io non ho stile, ché il confesso, mi sono assicurato a scriver esse novelle, dandomi a credere che l'istoria e cotesta sorte di novelle possa dilettare in qualunque lingua ella sia scritta" (4).

18   ". . . come io parlo così ho scritto, non per insegnar altrui, né accrescer ornamento alla lingua volgare, ma solo per tener memoria de le cose che degne mi sono parse d'essere scritte" (Bandello, *Tutte le opere,* 8). For an account of the controversy early in our century over Bandello's status as chronicler, plagiarizer, or inventor of his own tales, see T. G. Griffith, *Bandello's Fiction: An Examination of the "Novelle"* (Oxford: Basil Blackwell, 1955). See also Mario Pozzi, "La novella come 'cronaca': struttura e linguaggio delle novelle bandelliane," in Rozzo, ed., *Matteo Bandello,* 103–26.

19   See D. Maestri, "La tradizione delle cornici e l'ordine' delle novelle bandelliane," in Rozzo, ed., *Matteo Bandello,* 95–102.

20   From the *Arabian Nights* to the *Decameron* and the *Canterbury Tales* we find the framing motif that staves off death (or some symbolic equivalent) with narrative. See Giuseppe Mazzotta, *The World at Play: A Study of Boccaccio's "Decameron"* (Princeton: Princeton University Press, 1986). This function of storytelling is visible as well in such testimonial works as Primo Levi, *Se quest'è un uomo* (Turin: Einaudi, 1967). See also Ursula Le Guin, "It Was a Dark and Stormy Night; or, Why Are We Huddling about the Campfire?" in *On Narrative,* ed. W. J. T. Mitchell (Chicago: University of Chicago Press, 1981), 187–96. For highly suggestive remarks on the question of framing and openness, see María Rosa Menocal, "Life Itself: Storytelling as the Tradition of Openness in the *Conde Lucanor,*" in *Oral Tradition and Hispanic Literature: Essays in Honor of Samuel G. Armistead,* ed. Mishael Caspi (New York: Garland, 1995), 469–95. Menocal's reading of literary history is perhaps compromised by a concep-

tion of "the medieval" that appears to be wherever there is textual openness or an embrace of uncertainty (e.g., in Cervantes, Paz, and Borges). Her contrasts between this orientation—whatever we may finally call it—and the clearly "modern" one that privileges originality, authorial control, interpretability, and linguistic purity are nonetheless valid; and they might fruitfully be brought to bear on the Cinquecento drive toward standardization that has formed the backdrop of the present study of gender and other categories. Bandello too might well appear among the "medievals" of Menocal's tradition, for the aspects of his collection I describe here.

21 As Mario Pozzi observes of this "mimesi della cronaca": "[A Bandello] la cronaca appare come una fonte impareggiabile e inesauribile di materiale letterario. . . . Pertanto con una palese polemica contro il culto della forma, egli vede negli 'accidenti' il *proprium* della prosa: che serve fingere il meraviglioso o ricercarlo nei grandi miti classici dal momento che la cronaca ci offre quotidianamente avvenimenti che paiono 'fole di romanzi, o de favole che si fingono su le mani'?" ("La novella come 'cronaca,'" 106–7). See also Giorgio Patrizi, "La retorica della realtà nelle *Novelle*," in *Matteo Bandello*, ed. Rozzo, 183–98. More generally, see Benedetto Croce, "Novelle," in his *Poesia popolare e poesia d'arte. Studi sulla poesia italiana dal Tre al Cinquecento* (Bari: Laterza, 1946), 487–502.

22 See, e.g., Sergio Blazina, "Novelle di supplizio e di tortura: Bandello e Boccaccio," in Rozzo, ed., *Matteo Bandello*, 261–74.

23 Hayden White has shown how historical writing is shaped according to narrative patterns of plot and necessity in his *Tropics of Discourse: Essays in Cultural Criticism* (Baltimore: Johns Hopkins University Press, 1978); and in his essay "The Value of Narrativity in the Representation of Reality," in Mitchell, ed., *On Narrative*, 1–24.

24 Rocco's insistence that she not tear up his papers anticipates Isabella's irreverence for documents in Novelle IV.16.

25 Larivaille, "Le Revers," cites this tale as an illustration of the "risks of the trade" (128–29). See also the discussion of IV.16, by A. C. Fiorato in "L'image et la condition de la femme dans les *Nouvelles* de Bandello," in *Images de la femme dans la littérature italienne de la Renaissance. Préjugés misogynes et aspirations nouvelles,* ed. A. Rochon (Paris: Université de la Sorbonne Nouvelle, 1980), 169–286, esp. 275–82.

26 On the other hand, my assumption in this regard may also be a function of the honest courtesans' successful portrayal of themselves as refined. Isabella's will stipulates that a musical instrument she had lent to a Neapolitan musician be returned to her.

27 Flora translates in n. 3: "Che vuol mai questo vigliacco ubriacone?"

28 On prostitutes before the courts, see Elizabeth Cohen, "Camilla la Magra, prostituta romana," in *Rinascimento al femminile,* ed. Ottavia Niccoli (Bari: Laterza, 1991), 163–96. Cohen's essay is also an excellent overview of the prostitute's

life in Renaissance Rome. See also Thomas Cohen and Elizabeth Cohen, *Words and Deeds in Renaissance Rome. Trials before the Papal Magistrates* (Toronto: University of Toronto Press, 1993). On women's access to the courts more generally, see also Cohn, *Women in the Streets*, 16–38, which focuses on Florence.

29 As Trexler, "Correre," notes, these games were also the early versions of what later became the various civic *palios*.

30 *I diarii di Marino Sanuto* (Venice: Visentini, 1897), tomo 49, col. 429. Fiorato, "L'image et la condition" (279), also notes the nexus between Bandello's and Sanuto's Margaritonas.

31 On homoerotic relations in early modernity, see Michael Rocke, *Forbidden Friendships: Homosexuality and Male Culture in Renaissance Florence* (Oxford: Oxford University Press, 1996); Trexler, "La Prostitution" and "Correre"; and Guido Ruggiero, "Marriage, Love, Sex, and Renaissance Civic Morality," in *Sexuality and Gender in Early Modern Europe*, ed. James Grantham Turner (Cambridge: Cambridge University Press, 1993), 10–30; as well as Ruggiero's earlier *The Boundaries of Eros: Sex Crime and Sexuality in Renaissance Venice* (New York: Oxford University Press, 1985).

32 This is not to say, as some critics of this position have understood such statements to mean, that history is only text, that there is no historical reality. It is rather to assert that whatever our idea of history, we can never "go there" except through (often contradictory) documents that are interpreted differently by individual researchers and through (inevitably subjective) narrative accounts. My thinking here is indebted to Fredric Jameson's suggestion that "history is *not* a text, not a narrative, master or otherwise, but that, as an absent cause, it is inaccessible to us except in textual form, and that our approach to it and to the Real itself necessarily passes through its prior textualization, its narrativization in the political unconscious"; from *The Political Unconscious: Narrative as a Socially Symbolic Act* (Chicago: University of Chicago Press, 1981), 35, emphasis in original. See also White, *Tropics of Discourse* and "The Value of Narrativity."

33 Fiorato, too ("L'image et la condition," 278), presents IV.16 as a conclusion to the narrative of II.51: "L'arrogance de cette femme de mauvaise vie, qui se moque de manière provocante des lois de la société et de l'autorité établie, trouve d'ailleurs sa sanction dans une autre nouvelle où son amour propre est mis à rude épreuve." The preface to II. 51 reinforces its focus on women, as Bandello dedicates it to his nephew, in a gesture of avuncular instruction regarding the ways of women: "Sogliono ordinariamente le donne, còlte a l'improviso, aver secondo i casi le risposte pronte. . . . Ma qual donne praticano più diversità di cervelli de le cortegiane de la corte di Roma?"

34 See my note in appendix 2 regarding this pair of expressions.

35 The phrase in quotes recalls Eve Kosofsky Sedgwick, *Between Men: English Literature and Male Homosocial Desire* (New York: Columbia University Press, 1985).

36 Unlikely as it may seem, prostitutes often served as general examples to women in early modern ritual and literature, probably because they were available for public display in a way that married or marriageable women were not. On prostitutes as symbols of female fertility in springtime festivals and on their roles "ad bonarum mulierum exemplum," see chapter 1 of this volume. See the *Lamento d'una cortigiana ferrarese* for the image of a courtesan paraded on a cart through the city to illustrate the dangers of syphilis; printed in Giovanni Aquilecchia, "Per l'attribuzione del *Lamento d'una cortigiana ferrarese*," in *Tra latino e volgare. Per Carlo Dionisotti* (Medioevo e umanesimo 17) (Padua: Antenore, 1974), 3–25. On the different question of exemplary punishments as actual practice in early Renaissance Florence, see Cohn, *Women in the Streets,* esp. ch. 6.

37 Stephanie H. Jed, *Chaste Thinking: The Rape of Lucretia and the Birth of Humanism* (Bloomington: Indiana University Press, 1989). Jed's account is concerned both with the recurrence of the Lucretia story (and others like it) in narratives of cultural foundation and with the Florentine humanism that redoubled Livy's theme of purity in its association of Florentine republicanism with textual "castigation." Here it may be appropriate to acknowledge that Jed's last, very nuanced point has prompted several skeptical commentators to object that the associative link between textual and personal/social castigation is not explicit in the writings of Florentine humanists and therefore cannot be associated with their political tradition. This refutation based on omission is hardly persuasive, but it is symptomatic of the enduring scholarly investment in an idealized vision of the Renaissance and of the republican tradition. Considering the enormity of the cultural and political questions Jed illuminates and—it must be said—the figurative, careful, and tentative fashion in which she sets out her inquiry, these objections appear to me as strenuous efforts not to see the forest for the trees. See, e.g., the review of Jed's book by Ronald Witt in *Renaissance Quarterly* 43.3 (1990): 604–6, which opens: "This book endeavors to show that Italian Renaissance humanism was motivated by acceptance of violence to women, and to offer women an acceptable means of approaching humanist writings without humiliation." See also Annabel Patterson's comments in *Reading between the Lines* (Madison: University of Wisconsin Press, 1993), 297–98. Patterson remarks the "unfortunate tendency of feminist *literary* criticism to ally itself with arguments ultimately pernicious to the traditions of sociopolitical idealism, which are feminism's best hope of broadening its mandate" (emphasis in original). As for Bandello, his *novelle* include both a retelling of the Lucretia story itself (II.21) and his own variation, perhaps his best known tale, in the story of Giulia da Gazuolo (I.8).

38 Susanne Wofford, "The Social Aesthetics of Rape: Closural Violence in Boccaccio and Botticelli," in *Creative Imitation: New Essays on Renaissance Literature in Honor of Thomas M. Greene,* ed. David Quint, Margaret W. Ferguson, G. W. Pigman III, and Wayne Rebhorn (Binghamton: Medieval and Renaissance Texts

and Studies, 1992), 189–238. Wofford cites Paul Schubring, *Cassoni: Truhen und Truhenbilder der italienischen Frührenaissance* (Leipzig: Verlag Hiersemann, 1923), finding thirteen *cassone* examples of the rape of Lucretia, six of the rape of the Sabine women, and several depicting Susannah and the elders. Other popular subjects for these panels were the adventures of Aeneas and Dido, scenes of Paris and Helen, allegorical scenes of "triumphs" of love, and several stories from Boccaccio, including the story of Griselda and that of Nastagio discussed here.

39 Giovanni Boccaccio, *Decameron* (reprint, Florence: Accademia della Crusca, 1976).

40 Wofford, "Social Aesthetics," 202. On the *cassoni* more generally, see Cristelle L. Baskins, "Typology, Sexuality, and the Renaissance Esther," in Turner, ed., *Sexuality and Gender*, 31–54. An irresistible note on Hollywood: The link examined by Wofford survives in such apparently wholesome reincarnations as Stanley Donan's 1954 musical, *Seven Brides for Seven Brothers*, itself the basis of a later television series. In this musical western, Livy inspires the kidnapping of six women and their imprisonment through the winter in an avalanche-blocked household as a form of courtship for six brothers who are otherwise unschooled in the arts of wooing. Said brothers are, of course, civilized by their contact with these feminine models of good grooming and manners, while the women overcome their initial terror and are won over to love these rustic but decent men. The brothers' initial encounter with Livy's story of the rape of the Sabine women (as read to them by bride number one) results in both their idea to imitate the kidnapping strategy and their lyric outburst in a song inspired by the rape of the Sabine women, "Oh the women was sobbin', sobbin', sobbin'!"

41 Wofford, "Social Aesthetics," 222. She continues more broadly in this vein on 227: "The Boccaccian novella, then (and, I would argue, the novella after Boccaccio), is characterized by an ideological conflict between the claims made in its ending (the interpretation it itself presents) and the supplemental questions raised by the narrative excess of that closure, especially as that supplement comes to be identified with a suppressed female challenge to the misogynistic wit and narrative direction of the novella."

42 See my chapter 1.

43 Wofford, "Social Aesthetics," 204.

44 Michel Foucault, *Discipline and Punish. The Birth of the Prison,* trans. Alan Sheridan (New York: Vintage, 1979), 8, 16.

45 Niccolò Machiavelli, *Il Principe,* Chapter 18 in *Tutte le opere* (Florence: Sansoni, 1971), 283.

46 See Friedrich Nietzsche, "Genealogy of Morals," in *Basic Writings of Nietzsche,* essay 2, sec. 3, trans. and ed. Walter Kaufmann (New York: Modern Library, 1968).

47 On this logic, see the pages dedicated to "Women on the Market" in Luce Irigaray's *This Sex Which Is Not One* (Ithaca: Cornell University Press, 1985).

Among sixteenth-century writers we find this contradiction stated explicitly as well. See the remarks of the character Ludovico in Francisco Delicado's dialogue attacking courtesans, *Il ragionamento del Zoppino* (Milan: Longanesi, 1969): "Che ordin trovi tu dunque, poiché è di necessità far quel fatto? Bisogna pur aver pratica di puttane, poiché dalle oneste donne aver non si può mai quel che l'uom vuole, e da' monasteri peggio. Che vuo'tu, che si buggeri?" (38).

48   I take the phrase in quotes from Francis Barker, *The Tremulous Private Body. Essays on Subjection* (London: Methuen, 1984), 25.

Index

Accademia degli Incogniti, 127

Achilles, 108

Aeneas, 143

Africa, 85; North, 143

Agrippa, Cornelius Henricus, 209 n.7

Alberti, Leon Battista, 17, 78; *I libri della famiglia,* 78, 208 n.6, 216 n.3

Aquilecchia, Giovanni, 245 n.36

Arabian Nights, 163

Arabs, 64, 85, 237 n.44

Aretino, Pietro, 162, 201 n.39, 241 n.13

Ariosto, Ludovico, 6–14, 36, 45–70 passim, 76–81, 86–92, 96, 98, 109–119, 123–156 passim; *Orlando furioso,* 6, 8–14, 45–53, 60, 69, 73–81, 86–93, 98, 110, 114–117, 121–143, 149–150, 155–156

Aristotle, 46, 83; *Poetics,* 80–83

Ascoli, Albert R., 79, 120, 215 n.44, 218 n.8, 228 n.65, 229 nn.71 and 74, 237 n.42

Audience, 6, 9–10, 18, 23, 31, 35–38, 44, 83, 88, 130–134, 175, 178, 212 n.23; female, 13–14, 38, 42, 81, 98, 122, 137, 156

Badini, Caterina, 219 n.12

Bakhtin, Mikhail, 7–8, 19, 31, 43, 81, 192 nn.8 and 10, 195 n.8, 219 n.16

Baldini, Antonio, 45

Bandello, Matteo, 8, 15, 158–181 passim, 187; as source for Fenton, 163; as source for Painter, 163; as source for Shakespeare, 162; *Novelle,* 159, 162–163

Barberino, Francesco da, 208 n.6

Bargellesi, Giacomo, 195 n.5, 206 n.75

Barker, Francis, 247 n.48

Baskins, Cristelle L., 246 n.40

Bataille, Georges, 202 n.49

Baubo (hag), 32

Beer, Marina, 193 n.12

Bellamy, Elizabeth, 121, 223 n.39, 225 n.49, 226 n.57, 229 nn.73 and 75

Bembo, Pietro, 140, 151; *Prose della volga lingua,* 151

Benson, Pamela Joseph, 191 n.3, 208 n.6, 209 n.7, 218 n.10, 222 n.37, 227 n.63, 228 n.67, 229 n.76, 236 n.38, 237 n.42

Berger, Harry Jr., 194 n.3, 196 n.12, 206 n.77

Bhabha, Homi, 29, 201 n.41

Bigi, Emilio, 58, 192 n.11, 207 n.1, 215 n.1

Binni, Walter, 218 n.12

Blazina, Sergio, 243 n.22

Boccaccio, 9, 82, 134, 163, 174, 176; *Decameron,* 163, 174; *De mulieribus claris,* 134

Deanna Shemek is Associate Professor of Literature at the
University of California, Santa Cruz.

Library of Congress Cataloging-in-Publication Data
Shemek, Deanna.
Ladies errant : wayward women and social order in early
modern Italy / Deanna Shemek.
   p.   cm.
Includes index.
ISBN 0-8223-2155-6 (alk. paper). — ISBN 0-8223-2167-X
(pbk. : alk. paper)
   1. Italian literature—History and criticism.   2. Women in
literature.   3. Social structure in literature.   I. Title.
PQ4053.W6S53   1998
850.9′352042′0902—dc21   97-32552